In the Jingle Jangle Jungle

In the Jingle Jangle Jungle

Keeping Time with the Brian Jonestown Massacre

Joel Gion

RARE BIRD
LOS ANGELES, CALIF.

RARE BIRD

THIS IS A GENUINE RARE BIRD BOOK

Rare Bird Books
6044 North Figueroa Street
Los Angeles, California 90042
rarebirdbooks.com

First published in Great Britain in 2024 by White Rabbit,
an imprint of The Orion Publishing Group Ltd
Carmelite House, 50 Victoria Embankment
London EC4Y 0DZ
Hachette UK

whiterabbitbooks.co.uk
orionbooks.co.uk

For more information, address:
Rare Bird Books Subsidiary Rights Department
6044 North Figueroa Street
Los Angeles, California 90042

Set in Meridien LT
Printed in the United States

In the interest of time and authenticity,
British style has been retained
throughout intentionally.

10 9 8 7 6 5 4 3 2 1

Library of Congress Cataloging-in-Publication Data available upon request

Contents

List of Illustrations   vii

Prologue   ix

PART I

J.O.B.	3
Try Me	14
I Wanna Get Paranoid	22
Cymbal	29
Tambourine Person	36
The System	42
High Tide and Green Hair	49
Countdown	59
Toppermost of the Poppermost	68
Walk the Earth	75
Arrival	82
Reappearing	88
Animal Pants	98
Cookie Jar	104
Armed with Shovels and Dangerous	110
The Life	114
Timothy Leary's Bed	121
The Johnny Depp Viper Room Massacre	130
The Rinky Dink Doublethink	135
Final Destination	140
Bande à part	150
The Last Hitchhiker on Earth	159
Reel World for Real	165

PART II

If You're Going to San Francisco, Be Sure to Wear Some
  Horseshoes   173
Dog Day at the Salvation Army   182
Manic Digression   188
Take It or Give It   193
Electric Kool-Aid Puke Fest   203
The Marlboro Man vs the Man   212
BANG!   217
Go Directly to Jail Do Not Pass Go Do Not Collect $200   222
Butts County to the Bottom of the Hill   228
Blackballed from Berserkeley   234
Fails of the City   242
Heaven Can Wait   250
The Burning Bug   257
Thumping Bible Thumpers Bible Thumping, or Something   264
Pow! Wham! Zap!   268

PART III

He Blew It   277
Zen Bobbyism   285
Riders on the Norm   289
Strung Out in Sunset Ralphs   296
Canadian Club   300
The Sunny-Side Up Eggs vs Both Kinds of Bacon   306
The Final Blow It   313
Gordon's Heavy Foot   318
Beach Town Massacre   325
Hey Joel, Where You Gonna Go?   333
Digging to the Roots   339

Acknowledgements   351
References and Credits   353

List of Illustrations

p.43 Busking on Haight Street, 1994 (courtesy of Jean-Paul Ligon)

p.78 Couchsurfing, 1995 (courtesy of Joel Gion)

p.81 Days before my first "disappearance," 1995 (courtesy of Joel Gion)

p.96 The Brian Jonestown Massacre with Mara Keagle, Bimbos, 1996 (courtesy of Desirée Pfeiffer)

p.96 Dean and me, Bimbos, 1996 (courtesy of Desirée Pfeiffer)

p.96 Dave D, our manager, and me, Bimbos, 1996 (courtesy of Desirée Pfeiffer)

p.97 Anton and me, Bimbos, 1996 (courtesy of Desirée Pfeiffer)

p.97 Anton and me, Bimbos, 1996 (courtesy of Desirée Pfeiffer)

p.138 Peter from The Dandy Warhols and me, 1996 (courtesy of Joel Gion)

p.148 Arriving in Portland, 1996 (courtesy of Ondi Timoner)

p.196 Monterey Pop Festival, 1997 (courtesy of Lindsay Ljungkull)

p.196 Jeff Davies and Peter Hayes at Monterey Pop Festival, 1997 (courtesy of Lindsay Ljungkull)

p.197 Monterey Pop Festival, 1997 (courtesy of Lindsay Ljungkull)

p.197 Monterey Pop Festival, 1997 (courtesy of Lindsay Ljungkull)

p.240 My fake ID card, 1997 (courtesy of Joel Gion)

p.262 Official promo shot by Mick Rock (courtesy of the estate of Mick Rock)

p.265 Myself, Anton and Miranda at home (courtesy of Bob Berg/Getty Images)

p.272 Charles, Dean and Anton in San Francisco, 1998 (courtesy of Lindsay Ljungkull)

p.278 Strung Out in Heaven tour, 1998 (courtesy of Joel Gion)

p.291 Chinatown (courtesy of Jonathan Kochan)

p.302 Canadian cabin, 1998 (courtesy of Joel Gion)

p.311 Dean, Charles and Adam (courtesy of Lindsay Ljungkull)

p.336 Night of the Bloody Tambourine (courtesy of Joel Gion)

p.342 *Dig!* at the Sundance Film Festival (courtesy of Joel Gion)

Jacket: author headshot (courtesy of Andreas Turau)

Prologue

I lumber up onto the packed Greyhound bus and all eyes worriedly fix on me, as I knew they would, being that the entire front of my body from the waist up is splattered with dried blood. My powder-blue corduroy Levi's trucker jacket helps to accentuate the bloody visual by two-toning the blood dried within and over the fuzzy perforated fabric lines. I look down to see what they are seeing and I am indeed the body-count movie slasher Manson Family man with exploding hair and face framed by werewolf facial fur. What few empty seats there are suddenly start filling with pushed-over bags and extending legs. Now midway down the unwelcoming aisle of frightened-looking people, I glance over my shoulder toward the front again to make sure I haven't passed anything open just as the automated announcement instructs "Please give priority for front seats to seniors and people with disabilities". Hmm, nothing about riders who look like axe murderers, so I continue on down the aisle and sit toward the back next to a young girl buried in a book. She stops reading, looks me over and then the book comes back up higher than before.

I wouldn't even be wearing this bloody thing if it wasn't so damn cold in San Francisco today, and I'm way too hungover to add freezing-my-ass-off to the mix. Anyway, the weird part of me was curious as to how it would feel to just own it, being covered in blood while walking through the crowded San Francisco Transbay Bus Terminal. I guess nobody wanted to spend a quarter on reporting the guy who looked to have just stepped out of *The Shining*'s elevator shower now walking around the giant station in a daze, which I suppose actually isn't the strangest thing in the world for this place. The old man at the ticket counter hadn't even bothered to look at me. When I think about it, I'd have had much more to worry about if I'd been sporting this look the last time I was in this dilapidated 1930s art-moderne-plausible terminus, back when life at the drug warehouse

In the Jingle Jangle Jungle

I was living in had gotten too hot and I was skipping town just days before it was raided by the DEA.

That whole situation had started out optimistically in the days of being a giant living space for artistic whimsy through music, photography and painting, as well as a place to deal in mass quantities of ecstasy and LSD, and while I hadn't been involved in the business side, I had been tasked with painting sheets of blotter paper with the liquid acid, and this covered my monthly rent and utilities. Beyond that I was like the in-house musician mascot and charter member of the twenty-four-hour party people.

Over time too much business had crept through the cracks and tipped the scales in the wrong direction, and like the business of business does, it turned everything into something else, something darker with new underground entrepreneurial avenues and I could only watch in dismay as it all morphed away from its early 90s innocence of E's, acid and artists.

My singer Anton Newcombe saved me that time by inviting me up to Portland to restart The Brian Jonestown Massacre with him. Right before that we'd been riding a high with three albums released in the space of a year and enough industry hype built up to do a big record label showcase in Los Angeles, where it all went rapidly south. Down, down into the ground and down, down, further down to the center of the earth where it continued through and out the other side off the coast of Madagascar and up, up and away into outer space ten thousand light years from now until finally being swallowed by the biggest black hole the universe has to offer. We were dysfunctional. Anton started over up in Portland to join the local music scene led by our friends The Dandy Warhols. That didn't work out for some reason, and not long after I got the call. With or without musical allies we were out to spark a musical movement, a "revolution" if you will.

Anyway, if somebody did bother to go find a payphone and call the cops on me, would the situation be any more believable if I just told them the truth? "This blood? The human blood completely covering the front of my jacket? My tambourine did that..."

x

Part I

J.O.B.

I was born in 1970, the year that because of math killed "the 60s". For the entire nine months of my mother's pregnancy, she told everyone I was going to be a girl. She and my father already had my brother the previous year, so in preparation for the upcoming me she'd channeled all her psychic reproductive energy into having a girl. I'm not sure to what extent, if any, her Mother Nature manipulation powers willed it into effect—but I do seem to be fine-tuned-in with my feminine side.

During her final weeks of pregnancy she took me along inside her to my first-ever live concert which was Ike & Tina Turner during the height of their soul-funk heyday. Just a few weeks later I broke my collarbone being born, which I'd like to think was from trying to do a Tina Turner-style strut-shimmy into the world.

I was seven years old the second time my parents took me to visit San Francisco. We spent the day doing all the usual touristy things—Pier 39, Alcatraz Island, Chinatown and the cable car to Union Square. It was as we rolled up and down the steep slopes of Nob Hill that I realized this place was as magical as any place could be. It was dreamlike and timeless and so full of new sensations both wonderful and repulsive, often at the same time.

In the cable car sitting on the wooden bench directly opposite us, leaning into the corner, was the dirtiest man I had ever seen. He was asleep and seemed to be the only person on board not affected by the constant jerking and vibrating rattle of the antiquated wood and iron transport. Maybe more vivid than anything else I experienced that day, I remember the look and smell of that man on our deep descent down Powell Street. His tan suit and large bushy silver beard were covered in multiple shades of different grime coatings. He was caked over in multi-layers of browns and grays like city alleyway camouflage.

So pungent was the smell that it seemed to have actual physical properties in its thick intake. It was hard to breathe in, yet its sheer authority over the senses made it curiously fascinating. I'd never physically felt an odor before. They didn't have those where I was growing up in nearby San Jose, but here it seemed anything could happen. If a cow were to be suddenly seen floating in circles around the top of Coit Tower, I would have accepted it as is.

In reality, what that smell was, I would find out years later was actually not this man's own private brimstone, but the antiquated wooden braking pads of the cable car smoldering as they gripped the moving underground cables. This was only the first of many tricks San Francisco had waiting to play on me.

And so the very week I turned the legal age of eighteen, I raced excitedly through the black darkness like a new-born baby turtle toward the blazing eternal flame of freedom lit by the beats and the hippies. Along with my friend Michael, another escapee from juvenile-age jail, we made the joint official adult transformation into a circa 1930s San Francisco apartment at 2220 Taylor Street in North Beach.

Still, despite my built-in obsession with the city, in all my years daydreaming of a life here the one detail that was never really factored into the fantasy was the reality of needing steady employment. So after failing to pay my share of the rent for the first two months, my new little old Italian landlord paid me a personal visit and in a mere matter of moments advanced my thinking from the *I don't want to do anything* stage to the *I'm willing to do anything* stage.

Michael, who unlike me was fresh with new inheritance money and didn't need to find work, was in the middle of a nonstop coming out-of-the-closet party in the middle of the most closet-less city in the world. My having no bread made it hard to go out and meet people while he seemed to have more and more new friends every day, both gay and straight.

4

Despite not needing to find a job, Michael found himself looking for employment anyway—for me. Realizing he was much better at getting motivated for me to find employment than I was, he quickly found me a job connection through his self-proclaimed "fag hag" friend's boyfriend Eric. He worked as a DJ announcer and part-time security at the Mitchell Brothers O'Farrell Theater, one of the most famous strip clubs in San Francisco.

After meeting and hanging out, with Eric the following afternoon, it was obvious to him that my performing the same required job tasks would likely be an ill-fit. Still, we were in a jam and he wanted to help. "Just come by the club tomorrow and meet the boss," he sighed.

The "boss", it turned out, was one of the Mitchell brothers himself, Jim, who thanks to Eric was hiring me sight unseen. We were in the casino-like lobby of the strip club while Jim Mitchell, in a white shirt and black bow tie gave me the rundown of the joint in what was not only my first job interview of any kind, but also my first time inside of a strip club. I was a freshly minted eighteen-year-old and didn't even know shit about not knowing shit let alone how this was all going to work.

My folded-arms over puffed-out-chest routine seemed to be sort of successfully hiding my overwhelming desire to just run away as he chomped on a cigar and rattled off my duties one by one, each with its own finger point to my chest like a physical exclamation point.

"Don't let anyone jerk off in the seats." Finger recoils back into fist, then he reshoots.

"There's no liquor allowed in the building so make sure nobody is sneaking booze into the bathroom."

He reloads his finger and fires again: "You wear a white shirt and black tie every day, no excuses." I had neither of those.

He then pulls free the slobbery cigar from his mouth which now becomes the new pointer. "Now go in there," pointing the cigar at the showroom double doors, "and watch the girls dance for a while."

I go into the dark theater and take a seat in the back row. It smells like five kinds of dirty and one kind of air freshener that liked to be a loner. There were only four or five strip-club patrons sprinkled throughout the vintage theater seating. One of them began slow clapping as the naked lady dancer onstage gathered her tiny garments from the floor while bowing and prancing backwards off and out of view.

Then suddenly from above like the voice of God running a bingo game I heard Eric:

"AAND NOWW...fasten your jaws and put your hands together for the sultry SAAB-REENAA!"

My stomach knotted. Oh god how was I gonna do that with any confidence let alone at all? I sat there and watched Sabrina move into the spotlight and start doing all her sultry things while the reality of this situation began to push me down lower and lower into the dark depths of the creaking leather movie chair that kept on creaking until it ran out of creaks and this whole idea croaked.

Now almost on the floor, I crawled back out of the sunken chair and crouch-creeped into the aisle and up to the swinging double doors. I peeked through one of the two small portal windows. I saw Jim Mitchell was now on the other side of the lobby with his back toward me, deep in cigar-pointing.

With the tips of my fingers doing barely more than blowing the door a kiss, I quickly skip-toed across the casino carpet and flung open one of the front gold doors and broke into a jog that didn't end until I rounded the corner of the next block.

A few months later I was standing on a corner waiting for a crosswalk light when I happened to glance into a *San Francisco Chronicle* newspaper vending machine: "MITCHELL BROTHERS O'FARRELL THEATER MURDER!" exclaimed the headline.

"Artie Mitchell was shot and killed by brother and business partner Jim Mitchell during a drug-fueled..."

My next employment assignment was set up for me just a few days after the botched Mitchell brothers' job at the Benetton sweater shop in the very touristy waterfront Cannery Shopping Center.

My first day began with learning how to fold a pile of sweaters in such a way as to make a giant version of the individual sweater pattern. Then they had me pick out 250 dollars' worth of store merchandise to be worn during my minimum-wage paying shifts (the cost to be deducted from my first paychecks), followed by a five-minute smoke break from which I never returned.

The next day I took over my own controls and, armed with an empty résumé, walked into Blondie's Pizza at the Powell Street cable car turnaround and was hired on the spot due to the manager wondering by my look if I also liked The Stone Roses. By happy coincidence in 1989, my two favorite things were The Stone Roses and pizza.

Blondie's Pizza was a small slice counter literally in the center of everything. Just behind was the Tenderloin, from where the low-income old schoolers would emerge and the skid row down-and-outers would stumble to cash their change cups into pizza. A few blocks in the other direction was the financial district and its massive hive of business-suited worker bees. Being right where the Union Square–Powell Street cable-car line began, it was ground zero for the masses of tourists converging from every corner of the world.

On a typical day behind the counter back in the large open-kitchen area, you'd see maybe a stoner metal dude covered from hair to toe in white flour rolling away at large slabs of dough, two punk-rock lesbian girlfriends having a jealous argument while flinging cured meats over pies and playing The Pixies' *Surfer Rosa*, bouncing puffs of flour from the white-covered hanging speakers. Flour was everywhere, and the dough station was like an alpine snow cap that dwindled away along the length of the kitchen like the side of a mountain. Last in this pizza factory assembly line and closest to the front counter stood me, sweating in front of giant dual ovens while spinning pizza pies around with a gigantic stop-sign sized spatula on a shovel handle.

The small standing-room-only front area was guarded by Tyrone, a huge muscular statuesque black twenty-one-year-old who also worked weekend nights as a bouncer at a hip hop club. He was tough as hell on the outside but a real kidder and gentle if he liked you. Sometimes in passing he'd move directly into my path, stare me down hard and wait for my eyebrows to rise like a drawbridge, then laugh heartily while giving me a friendly elbow bump that would almost knock me over.

One day he mentioned his latest nightclub job run-in with some thugs in the pursuit of "legit" points in the new gangsta rap world. This was the dawn of one of the most artistically important periods in rap history, but with it came a lifestyle that had droves of twenty-somethings heading out to the clubs on a Saturday night wanting to prove who had the least fucks to give. He knew as security staff he was a target for people wanting to show how hard they were.

Something went down last night and he confessed it had all become too dangerous a situation. Resting his chin atop the broom handle he was holding, he slowly shook his head, eyes full of internal replay. Then this somber trail-off was suddenly self-disrupted with a great burst of laughter, at which point he danced away high-stepping while his upper body acted like he was operating a small rowboat. Not even the heaviest shit was gonna bring him down.

The weekend came and went and when he didn't show up to work Monday or the next day, there was a small worried group of us down in the multipurpose basement discussing what to do when suddenly out of nowhere it hit. The entire room jerked hard and then started shaking rapidly. The walls and ceiling swayed together like an empty refrigerator box blowing in a wind gust. Tables, chairs, everything in the room was vibrating hard and fast—all the metal kitchenware utensils shivered and jingled together in holders atop steel food prep surfaces or came falling to the floor where they continued to rattle and flop around like silver Jesus fish. We were all in frozen shock as everything continued to rattle and rumble, shake, jerk and push and pull, crumble and give as the seconds went from zero to eternity. There is no all-encompassing fear like helplessly waiting for an entire city building to cave in on top of you.

As our manager ordered us all to crowd in together under a door-way, all I could think was *I don't want to die down here*, but there was a fate worse than that on the menu. Surviving down here trapped in the rubble would leave you to the thousands of cockroaches and hundreds of rats we saw giant representatives of each and every day. Eventually the city would close this place down permanently because they were beyond controlling.

Then the ceiling lights exploded and as everything went pitch black and people started screaming suddenly...nothing.

We shared a group single beat pause before we all realized the next move was to get out of there as fast as we could. We ran up the dark stairs, through the kitchen, past the cash registers, through the small eating area and right out into the mass confusion of downtown San Francisco thirty seconds after a 6.9 magnitude earthquake. There are no fallen buildings, but glass is everywhere. Already a man runs past screaming, "The Bay Bridge has collapsed! The Bay Bridge collapsed!"

There was no water and no power, and everyone was going to be walking home today. The false information continued to blow in the wind as I marched home along with the rest of the dazed crowds moving like slow-motion blood streams through the grid systems at the heart of the city.

When I finally got to my North Beach apartment, there was a new crack running the entire length of my bedroom wall. Another nut was running down the street outside, "That was just the pre-shock! They say the real one is coming! The real one is still coming!"

"Fuck this."

I marched over to nearby Washington Square Park and sat cross-legged in the direct dead center of the grass where I was finally and for the first time out of reach of any potentially toppling structures. Soon night fell, and the only lights in the entire city came from the many circling overhead helicopter spotlights. With the city-wide power outage, you could actually see a full sky of stars shining brightly, further adding to the oddity of the entire situation.

I hunkered down on my newly claimed chunk of park property until finally dozing off late into the night still sitting up but with my head down in my lap. Nevertheless, I was restfully comfortable in the knowledge I was safely in one of the few places I knew this whole city couldn't just fall on top of me.

Working at Blondie's I met the girl I'd become engaged to. Her name was Christine, and if Shirley MacLaine's character in *Irma la Douce* were a goth from the streets, that's about what she looked like. I mean the velvet and lace kind of goth that listened to Bauhaus and Nick Cave, not the Marilyn Manson kind that came later, which should have been labeled something else. Her wardrobe only consisted of a few crushed-velvet dresses that she'd handmade herself. They were so close-fitting that because she'd hand-sewn them, she'd always be needing to make little uniform tracks of safety pins along various sections of splitting hemlines, almost like surgical staples. This unconscious added goth-ness was symbolic of her entire make-up, her barely being held together and constantly needing to mend new areas with quick fixes. Her neck and hands bloomed from frilled white lace cuffs and collars with skirt bottoms cut to mini specs over different colored hosiery with jagged runs patterned like bullet holes in boutique-shop glass that ran down into simple strap patent-leather shoes.

Words like hard and rough don't make the cut in describing how Christine's life started out. She was only an infant standing in her crib when she watched her father stab her mother to death with a kitchen knife. From there she was passed from foster home to foster home around the Bay Area. Some of the parents were OK, some were not. When she finally reached the legal adult age and the cops were no longer required to drag her back to guardians who could've gone either way, she moved to San Francisco and wound up in an abandoned building in the Tenderloin with a group of methamphetamine-shooting squatters.

When the two of us met, she'd just recently cleaned up from all the drugs and was looking for something "normal". She had an air about her like she needed rescuing, and being young and romantic, gallantly rescuing a young gorgeous damsel was at the top of my new experiences to-do list. Her seeking a place to live progressed things along fast and after a handful of dates we moved into a tiny studio apartment together on the corner of Haight and Webster. For a period of many months it was more than sufficiently "normal", and we were very much in love.

The problems started when normal became very normal and she eventually began to miss the drug high. Rather than letting her go out and do it elsewhere, as in finding her old crowd, I decided it would be better if I scored some for her so she could do it at home. This also meant, of course, that we both did it together. It was my first time and while I liked the euphoric high I got after we snorted the stuff (luckily, she could forgo the needle), it required long hours. Our little stretch of the Lower Haight in those days was kind of like a war zone at night and I'd already been mugged three times since moving in.

From there a weekly string of inside all-nighter nights followed, and around that time she got pregnant. We became engaged, but then just before the safe cut-off time for an abortion we chickened out and decided not to have it. While for me it was mostly a matter of wanting to wait until we were more financially secure, our co-commitment cop-out unknowingly began to erode her original vision of a normal life and it didn't take long for old insecurities to resurface and new misunderstandings to take root and wind their way around us like dark vines.

If one were to agree that romantic love is a combination of equal portions reality and fantasy, I would have to say our mutual mixture was too heavy on the fantasy. Looking back, we may have not been the greatest fit, but we actually were, in that we were two young people both searching for something completely different from the direction we were currently traveling. A roulette detour that just might by the spin of the wheel landed us on what we didn't even know we were looking for. It worked for a while, and to say I could see all this then would be a lie. I would've clung hard given the chance. Knowing this, she didn't give me one, and one night after work I came home to a note on the bed informing me she'd left for New Orleans.

A few heartbroken weeks later I saw a band flyer taped around a telephone pole saying: "TAKE ACID NOW and come see The Brian Jonestown Massacre". Beneath these instructions was a logo featuring The Rolling Stones' Brian Jones's head. The show date was next week and just a block and a half away at The Peacock Lounge. Even if I was going to follow the flyer's user directions, I would wait until the show got a little closer.

The night of the show I walked alone from my apartment on the corner of Haight and Webster, past the reggae dance club, past the trio of neon-rainbow graffitied roller metal shop shutters, past the Chinese butcher shop, through the Fillmore Street intersection, past Café International, the futon shop where I'd bought the silk sheets that were then used the next day as a Santa Claus sack for my belongings when my apartment was robbed, past the laundromat, past The Horseshoe Cafe and right to the door of The Peacock Lounge & Gold Room.

There was a big line outside and a young guy who would turn out to be one of the band's guitar players was excitedly holding court. Ricky will not long from now be my first friend and introduction into the new local shoegaze/60s/garage/indie/alternative scene, but for now is someone I just see at most all the shows I go to. I sneak glances at him animatedly exciting his friends with positive energy in his Greek fisherman's cap over cherry-red curls, and it's here and now that I see people gravitating to his glow.

The Peacock Lounge had originally been a simple downstairs lounge area for the neighborhood black Freemason meetings that were held on the floor above. In the late 1960s, they remodeled it into a private rental bar and walking inside today was like a time portal straight into a classic Blaxploitation film. Low-lit in red, purple and blues, gold-vein mirror tiles backed booze bottles resting on glass over circular mahogany, white Christmas lights streamed from overhead, leather booths lined a wall, while across the main floor the growing crowd of people stood or sat at round bar tables leading to the small stage.

Then the band came on. I'd never seen Americans, let alone young Americans my own age, playing what was at the time a specifically UK kind of music. I mostly watched Anton as he handled a large hollow-body guitar, its bulbous wooden frame making it look like he was strumming the guitar version of a cello. It was hard to see properly in the low-lit purple and green glitter reflections, but still, I could watch up close for the first time how all those lush noises could be made. The foot effects pedals, the precision and extra technique it seemed to take to hold down the fret notes on those large vintage guitars.

Finally, there was a band to get into that was not only from the USA, but lived in the same neighborhood as me.

Try Me

I turn the corner at Waller Street for the final block before I reach my scribbled destination at 734 Shrader Street, the rehearsal room for The Brian Jonestown Massacre.

"It's the side door," guitarist Ricky had instructed me over a joint in a bathroom stall at the I-Beam, right before the English shoegaze band The Pale Saints went on. I eye the number over the door and verify that this is the building, then walk to the adjacent anonymous-looking narrow door between it and its neighboring Victorian building, both case-study models of the type that sound-staged the original "San Francisco Sound" of the 60s.

Before I enter I adjust my case-less sunburst 360 Rickenbacker electric guitar that I've got strapped on my back, holding the upside-down neck close to my leg so to not bump the headstock against the wall as I navigate the small dark corridor. I'm heading toward what looks to be the backyard, but then here is a side door into the building. This must be it.

Knock knock knock...

The door flies open as I hear "Hey man!" before I have time to visually register that it's Ricky. "C'mon, we were just about to start. I've got an amp all set up for you right here."

I duck my head through the doorway and the lighting is even lower than in the outside corridor. They are setting up and tuning guitars, plugging in effects and tatta-tat-tatting drums so the introductions are the simple acknowledgments of smiles and fast hellos.

I go over to the amp and set my naked guitar against it, then scan around the room to get my bearings amid the individual activity. The walls are partially covered with seemingly random homemade egg carton and foam pad soundproofing, and the decor beyond that is sparse: flyers from the handful of shows The Brian Jonestown Massacre have played so far, including the one I was at after spotting a street flyer, a Telescopes album poster and a few random local band stickers. Despite this originally being a subterranean-like living space, there's no furniture and the carpet is thin. The guitar amps are topped with full-up cigarette ashtrays and repurposed drinking receptacles overfilled with more butts.

I've never been in a DIY-style rehearsal space before, and the dishevelment theme continues throughout. Seemingly random strips of peeling duct tape sparsely zag and zig in random spots on the carpet. Guitar and mic cords messily cover the floor like black licorice-ropes, all taking the most complicated way possible to the plug-in jacks of the big heavy amps and small effects pedals with flashing power lights.

I eye the Fender Twin Reverb guitar amplifier that has been provided for me close up. It's red "on" light looks back at me and the plug-in jack is ready to be connected with my guitar, but I hesitate for a moment, not because I've only been playing the guitar for about six months, but because I can't afford to own an amp of my own and in fact I've never even played through one.

I plug my guitar into the amp and turn the volume on. Everyone is starting to look and sound ready so I strum an E minor chord out slowly, really slow actually, so as to prolong the sound, like maybe that adds something more to it by doing so.

Normally someone would take this setting-up opportunity to squibiddy-doo some random "tasty licks" as a preview to the imminent sonic goods about to be rendered, but I can only play basic chords and don't have any of those. I then strum an open G chord while dragging the strings even slower than before, just to remind everyone that I came here to do business or something and I feel the falseness of my bluff that is about to be exposed at maximum volume.

It had taken me months to spring for my 360 Rickenbacker guitar, one exactly like Ride played at their own I-Beam show almost a year ago now, but I didn't have enough for the case, which I hadn't bothered to get because I'd never pictured myself in a situation like this so soon. Ricky had spotted me while smoking a joint in the bathroom stall and I had the right look, I suppose, in what was a typical-day-for-me attire, armored under a tousled and sprayed Beatles-type haircut with round-toe Chelsea boots, faded jeans and plain black jumper top under café-racer-style leather jacket.

My clothes signified which music subculture I held allegiance to and so here I was. I'd seen and liked his band, was very attentive and seemingly the perfect mate to be pontificated to as I didn't have anything musically going myself except untapped high-grade enthusiasm.

It had been an unspoken celebratory all-day event when the Ride and Lush tour came to town in April of 1991. It was the first big shoegaze show in SF, an event that would help ignite the local scene. Everyone who was about to become the local shoegaze scene was at Rough Trade Records that afternoon for the in-store record signing appearance of both bands. Fittingly on Haight Street, everyone all together now and in daylight for the first time, a new society of reverb and weed, shoegazer baggy babylings that would grow into Britpoppers in just a few short years.

The local chapter of a new worldwide music subculture was born, manifested out of our private record collections and into the streets of San Francisco, and this was the new scene I wanted to be in. All of us bedroom nomads now for the first time had places to be, with our own bands to see, and the more we gathered together the more we built in numbers, turning it all into a music clique of familiar faces repeatedly showing up to listen and see and be seen on the scene. With its 4AD record label aesthetic, shoegaze was a new music style with a sound that had never existed before, and BJM were already the most interesting of our local pack.

Greg sits at the kit in the corner of the room wearing John Lennon glasses. His shortish brown hair and plain white T-shirt give him a more straight-ahead look than the other three, as is often the way with drummers. Travis has longer bright cherry-red hair that frames his all-American boy-goes-geisha face au naturel. His green parka purposely comes off both of the shoulders and he's riding a disjointed line between Kurt Cobain and a frayed teddy bear in that way girls really like. Ricky laughs a lot and when he does he somehow reminds me of Bugs Bunny in drag, but having just taken the make-up off except for the fake eyelashes, if that makes any sense. His hair is back to its dark blond now in its naturally curly frizz. Anton has long brown hair tucked behind his ears, which is probably for shoegaze guitar functional purposes but doubles as providing a "smart" look, rather than long hair for long hair's sake. He'd shown up in San Francisco two years ago already armed with his sound, one that evoked The Chameleons, Spaceman 3, and what was going on at Creation Records in England. He took his influences and turned them into something else, his own new thing.

There's no audition vibe in the room, more like they were just rehearsing anyway. Travis helps me make sure I'm still in tune since my five-block walk over here and we begin.

"What chords do you know?" Travis asks.

"I can play all the major chords and most of the minors."

"OK. Cool."

"Let's strum on E and A," Anton decides while absentmindedly biting on the tip of a guitar pick. We play the chords together for a while and once the drone has been spun long enough for trance inducement, Anton begins to play a slinky-chime guitar lead over it which inspires the others and soon enough they've switched to weird chords that I don't know. I fall off the boat and after a little while the jam ends without me.

Feeling the hit, I play my one "weird" bar chord variation which sparks some promise and we jam on that for a few minutes, but then I can only take it so far because I've never "jammed" with anyone before in my life. Still, there is a glimmer of hope and they pick another song to show me. "Let's do 'Swallowtail'," Ricky enthusiastically suggests.

Anton takes over: "OK, it gets weird but basically you play Em, G, D, C and A," he instructs as he simultaneously begins strumming the chord pattern. I watch his hands and start playing along. I'm comfortable with these chords and as we play I feel like I'm keeping up fine, but then Anton stops us and suggests a three-finger C configuration to me. "It will be easier," he assures, but I already know that finger positioning and I don't really like it. More to the point, it's a sign that he thinks I'm struggling.

In the Jingle Jangle Jungle

We run through the song again until the end, then Travis is the first to speak. "Do you mind if we just run through our whole set first? We've got a show in a few days," he asks in a sort of, "We'll get back to playing with you" way, but everyone inwardly knows we won't be and I'm in fact relieved to have made it through this part of the day. My probably not-all-that-well-hidden embarrassment comes mixed with undeniable bravery for even trying to do this, and they not only recognize this, but it will be further revealed, respect me for not being afraid to try, despite my meager accomplishments.

Regardless of how far out of reach something is, even too far can still pay off in some way and the one part of today's mission that I knew I could pull off before even going in had been accomplished— we were all friends now.

The band continues with their rehearsal while I sit against a wall and watch. The next song is called "Short Wave", sung by Travis. He looks less comfortable singing than Anton, but more than I would, and as they play Anton's looking at me, or more like through me as he strums. It's a glassy-eyed look and hypnotizing in its steadiness, almost as if I'm being scanned while he is "in the zone" of the music.

Being in the room with the sheer immensity of the sound being made by these young boys with freshly inked passports into man-hood who are creating the most ethereal otherworldly sounds, it was all so chill-inducing. The delay, tremolo, distortion and the almighty reverb guitar effects used for this kind of music was just so huge, the room felt like it was expanding, having to try harder to contain all that sound. I sat in wondrous awe that this all could even be, watching Anton mostly and his large hollow-body guitar.

When practice is over the others are immediately ready to hit the streets to find what they could run into for excitement along the Haight, but more likely it was what was going to run into them. There was a whole new thing going on out there and they had a buzz to be the ones that could go next level from the get-go.

Anton offers to show me a few guitar tricks and I hang back while he demonstrates a simple fingering that can move up and down the fretboard in a mostly open-string, sitar-like drone.

I follow along, but I'm also tracking his sedate state and manner. There is an indescribable natural aura about him, a drugless zen of

18

the kind that is up to the observer to find, because he himself seems to be unconscious of it. Like a cool vibe that comes with a house, it just is. He doesn't have to impress you with furniture choices. He would make a good teacher, I recognize, not yet being able to realize a guru-and-student relationship of sorts has just been sown, despite it not being ready to flower overground for another year, after my impending detour into the heydays of the illegal all-night party scene as one of the twenty-four hour party people.

He gives me the secret heads-up that their upcoming show was actually to play on the roof of the Spaghetti Western restaurant on Lower Haight Street. A friend of theirs had access to it from her bedroom window next door, and so they were going to just set up the gear and play without permits or permission.

I watched it that night from a nearby window as they "Let It Be" from the rooftop after the restaurant had closed. At night this section of Haight Street is alive with young excitement seekers and it was prime-time with four popular bars on the block all churning out plenty of curious crowd material. Within the first song the street was filled with people and cars would have to detour around the block, meaning that the cops would soon be coming to shut it all down and hence providing one of the best time-tested and true rock 'n' roll rebel performance narratives.

It was not lost on me that under different circumstances this could have been my first gig with the band, and in a rooftop-style of performance like The Beatles, the band who were the original spark during childhood that had since consumed me totally. This truly would have been a magical way to begin my adventure with the band, but my magic day was still some way in the future.

As the months passed I fell into a whole new circle of friends and was now meeting all kinds of new music people, and although it had felt like forever, I'd finally fully gotten over the breakup. That's when one night as if on cue the doorbell rang and there was Christine out of nowhere standing in my doorway and beaming, "I just got back into town!"

New Orleans had started out well enough, but quickly went further south. With no friends or even contacts, she was lucky enough to find a job working as a cigarette girl on her first day in town, but from there she was connected with a well-paying high-end bachelors' club as an escort girl. Not realizing she was to be a "full service" type of escort girl, in her words she "just had to go with it" for a couple weeks before having to quit because "It got weird". As my thoughts mingled in the possibilities of what "weird" could entail, we suddenly heard "Christine!" from the street below. It was a sort of shout-whisper blend that made me uncertain that I'd even heard it. But then there it was again. She froze up at attention with eyes wide, mouth slightly agape. Her reaction to this was so curious that I just sat there in the silent moment, and then again it was shout-whispered, but louder this time and in an abbreviated grunt manner, almost skipping over some of the letters. "CRsTine!"

She still didn't budge. I went to the window and slightly pulled the curtain back. Down below in the low-lit street I saw a twenty-foot moving truck with a logo all along the side that read "One Big Man & One Big Truck" with an animated flexing muscle-man arm. A big guy stood in front of the open driver's door. He looked like a dirty-blond young Elvis, but his upper mouth did this raised scuba diving mask thing and his nose was flat, while his eyes were a little extra spread apart, like he had a pickle jar stuck over his head. From the neck down this Elvis-head-in-a-pickle jar was all big and all nasty. "In the ghetto" for real.

I turned my head back around while letting the curtain go. She didn't answer my questioning look. Her eyes were wide, with mind wheels turning but couldn't seem to get any traction. Then we heard the big truck engine rumbling up to life.

"Is he leaving?" she asked. I looked back out again and he was still there, now sitting in the driver's seat and gazing up straight into my eyes. He kept them there, then very slowly pulled away while not averting his gaze until his face entered the shadows.

It was then she spilt the rest of her beans. She hadn't just arrived. She'd been back for a couple weeks and was living with this mover ex-con guy. That was until earlier today when they'd had a big blowup and he'd scared the shit out of her.

The problem now was he'd followed her over here. Or maybe that was the intention. I had no way of knowing which way was up in this story now. Then she broke down crying. I went to her, but she suddenly darted up and ran down the stairs and out the door. She wasn't trying to run very fast so I caught up to her before she made it down to the Reckless Records corner. "Hey!" I called. She stopped, then leaned up against the brick wall.

"I'm sorry..." she said sobbing, then wiped the tears with her palm while trying unsuccessfully to not smear her eye make-up. She looked up at me with the mask off for the first time tonight and a smile broke through the sadness. I moved in to hug her when suddenly her eyes flashed wide, fixated on something over my shoulder. Out of nowhere she just started punching me in the chest. I unconsciously grabbed her flying wrists in an effort to stop the punching and that's when two very large hands slapped onto my shoulders and flung me around hard. I only saw a flash of his face as he laid me out flat out on the sidewalk. From the ground I looked up and saw him with his arm wrapped around her shoulders as she cried into his chest. She gave no resistance as they walked away.

I'd heard around the scene about a guy who supposedly sold, among other things, speed. I walked back to my apartment and tracked down his number. In my mind at the time it was to be a symbolic gesture to myself that I would now switch my fortunes from being one of the world's played to one who plays in life. What I did not see coming was that from that night forward I'd begun the bonkers, out-of-my-head journey that would eventually lead me to the mental state where playing the tambourine as a life-identity role made perfect sense.

I Wanna Get Paranoid

The eternal camera in the sky of my mind's eye cuts through the just-starting-to-fade morning fog cover over San Francisco, then zooms into an extreme close-up of a typical Haight-Ashbury Victorian apartment, and on through the bay windows that protrude out of the building in a semicircle, where I lie between black curtains on my black-sheeted floor mattress in black long underwear, not because it's cold, but because to me they are like post-punk pajamas or something.

I rise up on an elbow, then squint out at the corners of Waller and Masonic, and yawn. Instead of getting out of bed, I roll over and into an elbow-walking ballet to the mattress's outer edge and pick up my bedside mirror, careful to balance the tiny plastic pregnant head-shop zip bag, a two-inch length of striped straw with the edge cut slanted and an industrial-size razor blade. I tap out a tiny crystal, then crush it into powder under a dollar bill using my Zippo. I will go out to find adventure, the randomness of the city will provide my winning or losing numbers.

I know speed has a reputation for being a horrible drug that does horrid things to the formal normal now turned into horrific people, and it is in fact all of those things, but by now in the 1993 San Francisco chapter of where proto-Britpop meets illegal all-night underground rave culture, it was a euphoria-inducing, inhibitions-demolishing super-cocaine. This being before toothless trailer park hillbillies became the poster children for the drug, it even felt somewhat cosmopolitan. At least in the club scene of San Francisco anyway. Like Andy Warhol's Factory and amphetamine pills, it was the latest or at least resurgent up-all-night accessory for the swingin' till the sun comes up sect. From flappers' cocaine to the jazz club pep pills, to the mods' Black Beauties and back to cocaine for disco. For most it wasn't about destructive self-abuse, there was a worldwide party going on, and we wanted to go the distance.

The best part of my newly found spirit chemical was its transformative powers to enable an introvert to go artificial-energy super-extrovert and suddenly I was finding every previous private theory, analogy and critique on music that I'd ever squirreled away or thought I'd forgotten about now on deck to be rattled off in rapid-fire in a journey into the unknown of ever-flowing mental alertness constantly finding newly undiscovered territory that was not previously on my map.

As I got further into the drug, the ampheti-piphanies flowed even freer. I could hear myself going while simultaneously hanging outside of my own head like an out-of while still in-body experience. Like circular breathing, I was now chain-thinking and able to add to my own conversation in an uninterrupted constant sequence of thought all the while flowered up in a jazz lingo solo routine. With all of my power breakers now flipped on, I could transcribe in righteous and romantic detail how we, this generation, were fully and legitimately authorized to join in and carry on the grand traditions of all the beautiful Bay Area outsider history that had come before us. What became even more attractive than the feeling of the drug itself was that people listened and suddenly I was being invited out to some social or music-related gathering almost every night.

What I didn't know is that the positive effects have an expiration date which won't reveal itself until one has already passed it. I'm twenty-three years old and I cannot stress enough the amount of naïveté that is involved right now, which is also a rudderless recklessness that I would not wish to trade, but despite my extreme fondness for the feeling, my ol' trusty lack of ambition keeps me from having the necessary finances for a habit, so I came up with a plan.

I have a friend who sells me friend-priced weighed grams of speed for eighty dollars. I then sell off three-quarter baggies at the usual going rate of twenty-five a piece, then I get the remainder of the drugs, which usually weighs out to be about another quarter and now only costs me a fiver.

My enterprise infrastructure consists of a tiny little scale that I'd bought at Pipe Dreams, the last remaining Haight Street head shop where there had once been so many in those morning glory days during the "Summer of Love". It was the smallest model they sold and made of cheap plastic, almost like something you'd find in a cereal box as a kid, which also kind of represents my commitment level to being a drug dealer. Still, it was fun to behave like one for a few hours a week, running my few rounds up and down the Haight, and I'd usually find some action along the way.

Each week's business was pre-dialed and I'd already have the few buyers required on the line waiting for my re-up.

On work days like these I usually get dressed to the tune of the mods' ode to speed dealers, "Here Come the Nice" by The Small Faces, so as to dispel any lingering feelings of dealer's guilt, which always worked. If I still needed to weigh it all out and package the bindles, a lengthier go-to is Primal Scream's modern classic *Screamadelica*, where the Creation Records sound candy-flipped with electronica.

I head out where just around the corner from me is Holey Bagel, a close enough to real-deal bagel counter where I should probably make myself pick up something to eat, but if I go in there for even a single bread disc, fellow music scene anglophile freak Felicity will fill me up with an entire bag, and the whole idea of dealing with all that right now just puts me off. Better to wait until a to-be-determined later date when it will rightfully be a wonderful thing.

The sun is out and the clouds are puffy and parted, thickening in the distance to the west on the far side of Golden Gate Park and also to the east over where the docks and piers give way to the Bay. Queen Anne's extra efforts abound in exuberant color combinations accentuating fine Victorian detailing, replete with fairy-tale-style turret roofs and elf-barrack-like multi-mini A-frames along Masonic and on down to Panhandle Park, where my first stop is Carol's one-bedroom apartment on the other side. I cross through it in a zag, under its canopy of trees that keep the air quality in here cool and breezy and shady and easy. Then it's a hop off its grassy border-curb and into a jaywalk over the busy Fell Street thoroughfare and from there I stride up the stone steps that lead to more classically built Frisco in this especially benevolent morning-glow fresco.

I ring her first-floor apartment and wait in the moving stillness.

Carol answers the door wearing enormous 1970s translucent orange Diane von Furstenberg sunglasses and a faux-fur leopard-print overcoat thing, which I guess on closer inspection could be a robe, as those two things are often kinda one and the same as far as two things go, depending, and once having made the observation I let the possible difference lie as it's becoming a mirror reflecting a mirror to infinity vortex-situation for me.

Last week, the heres and theres of the circumstantial ballet of what-have-yous had her coming by mine for her weekly upping, and she'd brought along a record for me that I *had* to have by Sergio Mendes and Brasil '66, which is also playing today as I enter, as if she was trying to set every scene she resides in with this as its soundtrack. Suddenly I realize that I haven't finished my homework yet. "Isn't this just *greeaat*?" She'd like to have verified again now on home turf. Overall, it's a sweet gesture by her knowing that I'm really into the 60s, but truthfully this record sounds a little high-strung to me now, which is an odd complaint considering, but it will in fact eventually serve to be (like so many Americans back in the 60s) my gateway album into the magical world of 60s Brazilian bossa nova and tropicalia music, so, thanks Carole, wherever you are.

Carole also has a thing for *The Graduate*, self-stylistically speaking. She is a little older than most others these days as a forty-ish person and has taken on the "Mrs. Robinson" image, the leopard-skin coat robe coat robe coat ro—

She also has the same grey streak on the top of her hair and wears her giant sunglasses indoors while waiting for her mother's little helper to produce the help. Despite outward appearances, she seems a bit melancholy under the surface, but of the kind that's hard to solve, like a melancholic onion, to start to peel away the problems would take a very long time, only to discover it's all peel all the way down to the center and even that's peel too, so you find that it was all peel and you've helped in no way, unless you want to start all over again and peel from the top to perform the whole process again, which is probably something helpful in itself, but I highly suspect this is a process for wired older people to be troubled by in the first place and so I'm going to leave peeling alone until down the road when it's my turn to need a-peeling.

So, I don't want to hang and while away the hours behind the bars in her street-level apartment and her self-stylized San Francisco thrift store version of the 1930s movie socialite society Manhattan high-rise apartment. She needs someone more like William Powell in a frayed denim and striped Kurt Cobain get-up.

My Kennedy assassination moment of Nirvana's "Smells Like Teen Spirit" song happened when Christine and I took a San Francisco ferry boat across the Bay to Sausalito and back just for fun. After we docked the two of us just stayed on the boat, taking a prime spot at the rear outside under the puffy clouds and blue sunshine. Then we watched as a sports bar restaurant unloaded a huge parade of dude-bro yuppies all wearing the same corporate logo yellow baseball cap who crowded in, over and all around us and then proceeded to drunkenly yell the lyrics of the song on repeat the whole way back to San Francisco. Christine and I weren't into Nirvana, but regardless, we both knew what it meant to all music subcultures. Punk rock had hit the mainstream.

"Care for a drink?" she asks, motioning to a vintage drink cart. These were originally made to be rolled out onto the patio, preferably poolside, like the one in *The Graduate*, but in this scenario it stands at the ready next to her half-made bed. It's getting awfully vibey in here, so I start off for my next stop on my Haight route.

Next is back over to Haight Street and down to the block-long border between Buena Vista Park and where things pick back up business-wise at Divisadero. MacKenzie and Joanna live in a ren-ovated 1930s art deco apartment building stocked tall and wide with units, where I get buzzed in, then skip the ancient mechanical elevator for the carpeted stairway up to their fifth-floor abode.

They are a very attractive couple in a lesbian relationship but both also bi, which tended to make my mind wander some but I never let that show, despite receiving unacknowledged invitations to let it wander, which I guess is flirting, but we have an unspoken agreement to let that pure energy permanently float in the room like a soap bubble, and it's fun to see how long we can keep it floating by gently blowing, which is a good energy to always have to play with, rather than pop it and then that's the end.

MacKenzie is the hunter-gatherer here and the tomboy type, literally, with a scruffy red bowl cut and often wearing little-boy clothes like overalls or loose sweatshirts with rolled jeans and "tennies". These choices all succeed in hiding what is, underneath, quite the opposite.

Joanna has almond skin, large brown eyes with long matching and usually slightly disheveled hair, fine and floaty. Every time I see her, it looks as though she's just woken up, but in that good way that people who exude youth do, not needing much grooming or fashion effort, a plain white T-shirt and jeans is more than enough.

They are both in a bad mood today, taking turns dealing with being nice to me while the other is slamming doors and talking under their breath to themselves, all the while Mazzy Star's "She's My Baby" blasts from the stereo system. Normally I'd stay a little while until they either asked if I wanted to go along to wherever it was or gave me a hint to split, but today is a no-hint-required day and I'm just going to take off.

Then down to Buchanan and Page Streets, just across from the housing projects where I used to live on the other side of off Webster. It's a simple buzz-down and handoff through the ornate iron entry gate situation, which is good because I don't really know this girl, except that she goes to State and is a friend of one of the others in my small business bubble.

I guess as a favor I've let her become my "I'm not a dealer" internal deal breaker, which I know is something I shouldn't do. "Everything was going great, and then the next thing you know…" *Zip*.

Walking the block back over to Haight Street, I remember the time I'd actually had a gun put to my head on this block within my first two weeks moving into the neighborhood. It was after midnight and two guys who'd obviously been waiting to trap someone closed in on me from both directions. I didn't have any real money on me, nor did I for the subsequent muggers the next two times it happened over the following months, and by the fourth time I'd experienced the scenario enough to be able to rationally explain my way out of losing another palm's worth of coin or getting shot or something.

In the Jingle Jangle Jungle

All of this at the time just felt like life and nothing much more, just the unlucky shit that happens to people, because somebody has to be in the wrong place at the wrong time or there would be a lot less to talk about. Maybe.

Cymbal

The Brian Jonestown Massacre are going to play in the basement of the apartment I've just moved into for a roommate's birthday party. By now the original BJM lineup had quit and after some revolving-door work new members were just starting to stick in the right way. Anton had been bringing over band gear in borrowed carload increments all day, and as he was leaving for the last time, already halfway out the door, he turned around and after taking a second look at a pair of maracas on top of the fireplace off-handedly suggested, "You live here, why don't you play maracas or something?"

Maracas? I thought internally while hearing myself say *"Sure!"* outwardly in response. Regardless of the method, this sudden totally left-field invitation to have another chance playing with the band is one I would accept by any means necessary, even if it was for just one night shaking the maracas.

That night I discovered that maracas were actually harder to play than they looked. When spontaneously shaken without a sense of time, they change from being a Latin percussion instrument synonymous with 60s beat groups into a useless baby's rattle. To find the method forced me into a concentration that when mixed with rum and black shades gave an outward appearance of disengaged nonchalance. I found the key to timing wasn't by playing them from an outside perspective—not by trying to imagine hitting on something or finessing an outward method—but playing them from the inside. It was the unseen beads within that had to be in time with the rest of the instruments. The goal was to learn how to *feel* the inside, not play it, to *be* what it is to be inside only without thinking about what it is to be it, *man.*

The next morning Anton invites me over to watch the video footage that manager Dave D had filmed from his position in the corner of the basement right in front of me. Dave D has a stoner slow-draw Cali accent and looks more like one of Metallica's guitar techs than BJM's manager, but he had an educated healthy cynicism toward life and was most importantly dedicated in keeping the band going with his college fund. I could barely make myself out smoking and casually shaking my maracas in the near total darkness. With all of the guitar amps the band had kept blowing the antiquated Victorian's circuit breaker, leaving just my maracas and the drums together in forced drum-break percussion grooves until someone would eventually flip the power breaker back when then suddenly BLAST! the whole room is back out of the party deprivation chamber as a one-light bulb lighting job flick-flickers back on and all four guitars come back screaming, all still in time together and at the right point in the song.

We watch the footage and suddenly, the power goes out again. Taking camera angle advantage this time, I'm crouching down like Jimi Hendrix and squirting some lighter fluid I'd spied among the cans and bottles of basement household items. I light up my maracas with my Zippo right in front of the camera. Now my face is the one single visible onscreen object lit in flickering firelight. I rise up playing flaming torches in the pitch blackness.

CLICK. Anton has turned off the video.

"We're doing a warehouse party on Saturday, you should come!"

"I'm in!" I answered.

"Really?" he asked, smiling. It was his way of getting you to add on enthusiasm rather than actually being a question.

"Yeah, man! You say when and where and I'll be there!" My enthusiasm level was legit.

One week later, on a foggy night along the Bayshore section of the San Francisco waterfront, a condemned shipping warehouse is booming BOOM...BOOM...BOOM...BOOM...BOOM...BOOM... BOOM...From out of its walls gaping holes and half-broken windows flash multicolored lights spinning in fast interior orbits as the entire building continues to BOOM BOOM. The Golden Gate Bridge fog-horns blow off in the distance like woofer party horns while seagulls circling in the sky above squawk-shriek like referee party whistles. They both join in the mix with the BOOM BOOM. Fast-whipping sea winds gather up large portions of the emitting BOOM BOOM and spin-cycle it back out to sea and away from the ears of potential "good citizen" narcs, prolonging the survival of this illegal rave. Suddenly, there is the rare BOOM that is not followed by another BOOM and there is now silence...

They will return after tonight's scheduled live music band performs when then they will continue on nonstop until whichever comes first, the sunrise or the cops. These two forces race each other pretty regularly these days in mid-1990s San Francisco.

On the water's edge side of this old dock distribution center, filing into a large loading door are The Brian Jonestown Massacre, carrying guitars, amps and drums onto a small makeshift stage. Inside the wet and cold warehouse, odors of rotted wood, slimed steel and cigarette smoke are tonight's modern equivalent to childhood's carnival sensations. They whisper in the wind "anything can happen".

The underground rave scene is one of today's major subcultures, and tonight its San Francisco Bay Area guard are currently holding ceremony on the outer edge of America. Not just spiritually but also physically, all the way at the tip of the continent's furthest west razor's-edge. They are here to engage in epiphany-seeking through dancing, music and drugs.

When an illegal rave party like this reaches its late-hours peak, it's a sometimes thousands-strong vortex of openness, heightened awareness and enhanced connection. Everyone is tuned into the same invisible space grid. No longer a sea of individuals but one singular being. The cells that make up the whole. The tribe of "one". This is what it is all about tonight in this wild dank yonder of possibility.

No one here tonight could know yet that their original directive is about to mutate from underground subculture into controlled mass culture, going down as the last pre-internet gasp of the California Wild West.

In the Jingle Jangle Jungle

The Brian Jonestown Massacre's Lee, Levi's and Wrangler'd boho brigade are now ready and start to emit loud bulbous reverb-infused wailing waves from 60s vintage amplifier speakers. The die-hard ravers in the crowd are instantly bored by this "obsolete" musical obstacle. Just this month the biggest English music weekly declared their new electronic dance music to be the permanent replacement of guitar-based rock 'n' roll, and the dayglo mob is already restless. They are eager to get the glow sticks back out for good.

Center stage, I'm as drunk as the speed will allow me to be while beating my tambourine slower than I should, yet harder than I need to. Most all of the songs we will play tonight are written by our lead singer and songwriter Anton. The music's sound tonight is based in English post-punk, like a Joy Division + Spacemen 3 dual-action angst mixture spun through an indigenous surf music machine that's wired with exposed raw nerves. Its circuits are sparking.

With face facing forward from behind dark bubble sunglasses, my eyes are actually sideways watching Anton belt out the song. It could be considered a sonic version of its author—driving, urgent and intense and with all the drama that comes from an unwillingness to give up for anything. He is the one flying this musical ship and is dressed appropriately for the part, head to toe in white cowboy denim over thick sailor's knitwear.

I switch my eyes to the other side of the stage where Matt Hollywood bobs back and forth. He's following Anton's guitar part closely on the bass, which much like in his own songwriting keeps consistent style with Anton's. The addition of his ever-present pout plus thick framed eye glasses push for an indie rocker stereotype, but this is ultimately averted by his over-extended mop haircut.

Next to him playing the guitar is Dean Taylor. Dean is a "face", which is a mod term meaning young, fashionable and good-looking. An elfin version of a young Robert Redford in a black velvet blazer and brandishing a natural kind of "cool" that makes you stay in check with your own.

In between and just behind stands Jeff Davies, somehow equal parts goth, hippie and rockabilly with lipstick stuck to his teeth braces. He's playing what could be considered a simple guitar melody part which is technically beneath his extraordinary ability, but like in his life itself he is often content to remain in safe places where he can just "get high".

As is typical of the youngest of the young, Brian's real-life purpose is a search in progress. In the meantime, he will hit these drums until his eureka moment arrives. His dirty blond pushed-back hair, plain white T-shirt and cuff-rolled blue jeans give him the James Dean effect, though he didn't mean it to. He leans into the ride cymbal, pushing the song further.

It's starting to get hot in here despite my ten degrees below zero-fucks-to-give internal temperature. Even with the perspiration that's just now threatening to exit my skin, I know I've teased, ratted and spray-frozen my Beatles-gone-bird's-nest as well as the best of the female 60s hairdryer gun slingers. If it sounds like I'm kinda "full of it", I am—but it's not ego that I'm full of, it's the drugs. They add that something else which after going two nights straight can turn me into the wild card of our deck.

A glimmer below catches my eye and I look down the length of my all-black kitted frame to see that aforementioned ride cymbal wobble-rolling past my Chelsea boots. It breaks my trance and I suddenly realize we're already on the last song which is now officially ascending into outer-space chaos. I pick up the pace on my "better late than never" tambourine beats and turn my head around to see Brian dismantling his entire drum kit.

I am surprised but excited that he is actually taking it there and I want to go with him. Matt's already left the stage and now Brian, with his kit spread out across the stage floor, joins him. Anton is crouched in front of his amp turning knobs and riding feedback. Now Jeff sets his guitar down and stride-skips across the stage to jump off the side with the others.

For my exit finale, I throw my tambourine down hard and it bounces and falls. Then, I stand it on end like a miniature Ferris wheel and smash it to bits in one great stomp. Its jingles sprinkle off the stage periphery like slot-machine coins. Looking for something else to destroy, I lift up the fallen cymbal and then as if leading a gonzo marching band bang a maraca against it five hard times. Then with full body effort, I whizz it up into the air hard on a high-flying trajectory. Even in the state I'm in, I know this thing needs to land behind the stage where no one can get hurt and the cymbal reaches its peak high in the air and with a backwards curve as intended. What I don't know is that just a moment before one of the party promoters had made his way back there and unknowingly positioned himself right beneath my high-flying vertical saucer cymbal now spinning back down to earth like a buzz-saw blade.

He didn't even see it coming.

Back on the stage in shocked horror, I watch helplessly from over my shoulder and follow its downward trajectory until it lands directly atop his head. He goes down and hits the floor in perfect time with the cymbal which crashes loudly next to him like the tablecloth trick didn't work.

Still intensely focused on the music and unaware of this, Anton has since moved on to adjusting his guitar effects pedal knobs and is now bringing the spaceship down onto the runway as I jump off the rear end of it. I hesitate for a moment and watch to gauge the scene's unfolding severity. A pair of girls have already run over and are escorting my buzz-saw victim out of the loading doors behind the stage. He was walking. I run over and by the time I get there he's already on the ground, flanked by the two girls who were now tending to his wound.

"Man, I can't tell you how sorry I am! Are you OK?! You just appeared out of nowhere back there!" He had a three-inch gash on the top of his head that one of the girls was dabbing at with a tissue. Though obviously in deep pain, to my great relief he seemed to be mostly alright and was actually somewhat forgiving.

The sound of fresh BOOM BOOMS return. No one else has seemed to have been at an angle to catch the backstage carnage. That is except for Matt, Dean, Jeff and Brian who had been watching the whole thing from side-stage. Not only had I trashed a piece of Brian's drum kit, but I'd laid someone out hard with it. He came at me and got right in my face.

"What the fuck were you doing?!"

"He's OK," I asserted guiltily, "Man, I feel like an asshole, but I didn't know anyone could go hang out back there! It's OK though, I just talked to him."

"*OK?!* It's not OK! You're throwing my drums around and fucking hurting people! I saw it—you coulda killed that guy!"

"He's *O-K*" I repeated, now realizing he wasn't going to let it go.

"It doesn't fucking matter—that was fucking stupid!"

Of course I knew he was totally right. No matter what the damage level, I am totally in the wrong—but his harsh, unrelenting tone now mixing with my own guilt and embarrassment career together and right through the barrier of my "no hassles allowed zone". It triggers off an unexpected detonation.

"Well, FUCK YOU then, man!"

Just then Anton comes outside "What the fuck are you guys doing?!"

"I'm quitting! Fuck this shit!" I yell now, letting adrenaline, alcohol and the amphetamines do all the talking. I turn around and march away into the night. After only walking a couple blocks, I'm lured in by a line of orange plastic safety road cones leading up a Highway 280 Interstate on-ramp. I pick up the last one in the row and plop it on the top of my head like a giant dunce cap and wear it for the rest of the long highway overpass shoulder walk back toward downtown.

Tambourine Person

I'm meeting Anton in the Mission District where he says the best tambourines are. We both arrive at the 16th Street BART station at the same time and I see he's had his hair cut shorter, to The Beatles' *Revolver* specs, or as he'd probably prefer, The Zombies' *Odessey and Oracle*. His all-year-round parka has been getting the summer off so far, today leaving a thick blue and white stripy top with white Levi's uncovered.

There's something weird about our timing being so perfect, with me coming from my place in the Western Addition and him from the far end of Cesar Chavez Street where his rehearsal room slash sleeping-bag spot is. My initial apprehension is immediately dissipated by a friendly smile and that gleam in his eye, which is so disarming, and now I'm no longer worried about having already quit the band last month after only a couple of shows.

We start down Mission Street under the breezy palms and sun-shine blue and after a block he points across the street to a big Latin music CD store. "Here's where we can get the real ones." *Real* meaning made of wood. Plastic is artificial, a fake material and quite literally not *natural*.

He starts laying it down as we rubber-neck for an opportunity to jaywalk across the street. "I want to do this thing, just put all the music on the internet for free, every single song, y'know? Just have like fifty number ones at once because nobody else is willing to do that with their music. Just make it 'free for the people' style, y'know what I mean?"

I smile in excitement for his excitement, but I don't really know what he means. Why would people listen to music on the new internet thing?

"I mean, it's overload as far as everyone is concerned, but actually that's nothing..." (Let me just point out now that in scenes with Anton he is usually doing the talking. Not small-talking or supposing or just filling spaces, he's like a conduit for a constant flow of ideas, random facts and esoteric history and theory, and often with in-the-dark company, exaggerations. It's all at the flow of relaxed conversation, articulated with method and certainly never just "running on". It's like his mind is in a constant state of brainstorming and with a level of interesting that is remarkably high, but sometimes this never-ending flow allows for much to not stick, to not get the light it deserves before the next idea comes along. So just always have on your reading radar that when Anton is in the scene, it's pretty certain that he is saying something most of the time while you and I are in here inside my head together. When you're getting my internal shakedown of the goings on, everyone else over here in this world is most likely listening to the stuff Anton is saying. Now some of you are probably feeling like you're missing out, getting the big "Whatta gyp", as it were, and I apologize, but I also can't spend my time notating everything the guy says all day because that would be a full-time job, and as you can see I'm kinda hung up on my own trip in this thing, which if I weren't then he'd have no need for me and we wouldn't even be here together stuck being me, so let's go back to the scene still in progress...)

"...and so here's the thing," Anton's tone personalizes into a more direct, instructional one, "if you break all the tambourines, then you don't have anything to play." The presently sober me fully understands the science to this.

Now that I am the only tambourine-playing frontman on earth, here is what I know about rock 'n' roll tambourine players. Gene Clark from The Byrds, the West Coast's direct answer to The Beatles, was the initial face in 1960s popular music who stood center stage with his single instrument being the tambourine. He was also one of the three singers in the group and in the beginning was the band's only original songwriter, instilling jealousy in his bandmates with his huge songwriting royalty checks. Musicians ironically are often not the grooviest bunch when it comes to money, and it was the new competitive jealousy from some of the others in the group that caused Gene to quit the band, leaving them with the parting gift of one of their best songs, "Eight Miles High".

Then there is Nico from The Velvet Underground who after The Beatles are the most important band to happen in my life, yet one gets the feeling she couldn't give a good gosh darn or a golden arm for the instrument.

Mark Volman of The Turtles had big frizzy hair, was fat and wore thick-rimmed nerd glasses, but despite his lack of rock-rebel cool, he was one of the best there ever was. He could even do tambourine tricks like roll it off his head, down his arm and into his hand for a fast palm spin, his quick-flash moves always ending just in time for the chorus change. He was also the harmony vocal guy backing the lead singer on mega-hits like "Happy Together" and very much the "class clown" of the bunch, all of which was a perfect fit for their carefree "sunshine pop" sounds.

Davy Jones from The Monkees was absolutely essential in bringing new tambourine players en masse into the two-car 60s garage of rock. His double fists full of four maracas each looked that much more impressive in his tiny ex-horse jockey hands, but his skills in the role were ultimately eclipsed by his good looks, "Beatles" accent and favoritism from the teenybopper girls. While it's true his whole romantic ballad routine gets pretty annoying, in my book of jingles he (and the whole band) gets a raw deal.

By the beginning of the 70s a tambourine was something that could appear in any band member's hand at any given time during a performance, but by the mid 70s it was pretty much just down to Stevie Nicks. With the exception of a handful of fleeting here and theres, the tambourine disappeared from public view.

I guess I shouldn't forget to mention Bez, the maraca player from Manchester's Happy Mondays, mostly because he's the public's only point of reference in the 90s music world. While I certainly enjoy the party mission aspect of them, it's pretty clear BJM aren't paying attention to that kind of music. I also don't dance onstage. Oh yeah, and Liam Gallagher from Oasis plays a tambourine too, but to my eye he's just wanting something to do during the many guitar solos.

Jerome Green was the original "maraca man" in rock who played with Bo Diddley from the 1950s until the early 60s, when all the burgeoning British Invasion bands started picking up what he was putting down. He made it a "thang" in the first place and was plenty enough foundation groove for Bo's three-piece band to not even need a drummer. He was not an "add-on". He was stone cold necessary and a totally self-sufficient power onstage. Now that I was back in the band, that's what I was going to be.

With BJM, every night was tailored to whatever situation happened as it happened, from song to song, tuning to tuning, cheer to cheer, hip to hip, heckle to heckle. There was never a plan, it just was. Having a 60s-style percussion guy who didn't play something else like keyboards or sing backups is no longer a thing and I was already taking a lot of heat from "real musicians", whatever the fuck that's supposed to be.

In 1967 the song "If You're Going to San Francisco (Be Sure to Wear Flowers in Your Hair)", written by Papa John Phillips of The Mammas & the Papas, was actually not created in San Francisco, but down in Los Angeles as the unofficial commercial advertisement theme for the first-ever rock 'n' roll festival, Monterey Pop, which also thankfully enough launched what would be long and lucrative careers for many a now-legendary San Francisco band.

This "turned-on" advertisement was such a massive success that came with the unforeseen side effect of being a pied-piper-beacon song that inspired thousands of change-seekers to heed the call in one mass convergence on the small neighborhood freshly dubbed the Haight-Ashbury and its new utopian dream.

After a few victorious mass gatherings under the bright Owsley Orange sunshine, the continuous worldwide pilgrimage to join the Summer of Love quickly went on to only succeeding in overpopulating the movement with ill-equipped teenage mindsets that lacked emotional maturity, with many becoming lost in the festering hive of various desperations and psychedelic vultures who preyed on their naïveté, sending them down the brown acid hole or much worse. This all quickly suffocated the dream they came here to find, and the Man couldn't have killed off the whole thing better himself. Unless that's exactly what he did, or something.

The actual original real-deal San Francisco "hippies" were forced to abandon the groovy freedom Eden they had created and mostly fled the city to create the "back-to-the-landers" commune movement, far away from Haight Street where everybody got tired anyway and went home to forever live in a fantasy of a fantasy of something important. It could, I will say, be argued that it was those LA music business musicians who'd injected a slow poison into the organic musical purity through their commercialism lab work that ultimately chemically transformed the whole thing into a fad, which could and would, like all fads by definition do, go out of style.

Whether all that legendary love and peace was the actual on-the-street aesthetic straight upon new arrival I will never suppose I know, but despite all those who apparently remember it, yet could somehow still be there, that always want everyone to know you "just had to be there" to get what was going down, seemingly, it was the run-down broken vibe directly following the Summer of Love that became that street's permanent installation. Despite the great generations-long efforts of implants and vacationing tourists alike, this has remained at its heart the unshakable true "norm".

Like trying to live a fantasy reality, like we all do whether it's Disneyland or Las Vegas, but you can see the maintenance sheds through the bushes on the other side of the chain-link fence. No matter what your trip, reality is the discarded pick, the wheelbarrow, gloves and the ladder in the back of your mind you always know is behind the scenes.

Despite all this, like, major bummer talk, man, there has been one type of music scene or another around here ever since, and the long-term results have become far better than worse, with good ol' Haight Street and its youth-centric world continuing to morph into whatever incoming underground music culture relevant to the times while essentially retaining it's hippie Sesame Street sheen of yore, still ever applicable to our new wave of local artist-musicians.

40

We, The Brian Jonestown Massacre in particular, were gonna bring it all back home, again, because the point of really, *really* digging something is to be so inspired as to create your own definition of it that expresses who *you* are and hence metamorphizing it into something new.

As for the original "heads" of the 60s, the 80s had been a great reckoning, and in trying to stay "relevant" in an era that would come to be remembered as America's most musically irrelevant, for the times had gone a' changing yet again, this time virtually none of the same musicians recognized that it was the worst time in the US's musical history to actually know what time it was. As a result growing up in the 80s meant being introduced to all of the worst sides of those 60s artists first and that was the main thing that delayed my total embrace of the 60s aesthetic, while also helping to sweeten the discovery of the post-punk sounds coming out of the UK.

Anton and I walk into Ritmo Latino, the Mission District's largest music store, to the high-volume sounds of Vicente Fernández. The long walls and islands throughout are packed with rows of CDs consisting of all things past and present in all genres of Latin music. A TV hanging in a far corner plays an old Cantinflas movie. Among the explosion of randomly displayed items behind the cash register are tambourines, five to the row and all identical, wooden with nickel-plated jingle-jangles gleaming under the fluorescent lighting.

We combine our crumpled green and pay for two tambourines, which will actually turn out to be the last time we do so in this double quantity as it will be revealed at the next show that the insurance of a backup just promotes more reckless abandon.

The System

After the advent of the compact disc, Reckless Records of London on Haight Street inadvertently became the most peaceful record shopping experience in San Francisco. The practice there was to separate the actual vinyl, cassettes and compact discs from their covers, which were then filed on shelves behind the store counter, while the LP jackets, cassette inlays and CD booklets were placed in the shopping bins for browsing. Though originally an anti-theft method, this process came with the welcome side effect of sparing everyone the incessant CLANG CLANG CLANGING racket of plastic CD cases being quickly flipped through from all genre sections of the store. The shop itself had an all-glass storefront, a wooden interior with sections of brick and three large columns that supported an open balcony second floor giving the shop an extra-high ceiling. The full-frontal view of the Haight and Masonic intersection with all its natural light added to the overall feeling of openness within exposed early San Francisco brick.

Of the many things I was just starting to wrap my head around these days, among them having recently joined The Brian Jonestown Massacre, was the fact I had scored my dream job working at my favorite record store. I was now first in line to intercept all the new sounds coming over from the UK, whether purchasing my favorite new music with an employee discount or just listening to whatever I was curious about in the store for free. Of the handful of record shops in the area, it was here and down the street at Rough Trade Records (with its CLANG CLANG CLANGING) where most all of the incoming Anglophile delights were circulated into the local record collections.

Busking for cigarette money on Haight Street in front of
Reckless Records

Because the shop was only a block away from the famous corner
of Haight-Ashbury it was an essential visit on a to-do list of any
60s-enthused touring UK band. You could almost check the club
listings just to see who would be coming into the store next, usually
in the early afternoon before their soundcheck. I'd developed a
system for any time a Bobby Gillespie-type known partier came into
the store. The "system" was simple: after ringing up a music purchase
for a celebrity "head", along with their bag of records I'd also hand
them back a Reckless business card with my name and telephone
number written on it with the instructions: "If you need any E's,
speed or weed—call me." It never failed to get me on the guest lists
with VIP treatment as this would be required to make the delivery.

Today I had a bit of a hangover. Last night I'd gone to see the
first of two sold-out Jesus and Mary Chain shows at The Fillmore
in support of their latest album *Stoned and Dethroned,* an album that
provided many of my summer anthems. I was such a huge fan that
over the years I'd found a way to see The Jesus and Mary Chain on
all five of their previous San Francisco tour stops, even while only
being sixteen years old for the first album *Psychocandy* tour stop at
the "twenty-one and over" I-Beam club. Somehow despite my not
having blond hair or blue eyes like in the photo on the driver's

license I'd borrowed the bored-looking doorman hand-stamped me in.

The JAMC were formed by Scottish brothers Jim and William Reid and to me they were the definition of cool. They made perfect 60s-esque pop songs shrouded in loud screeching guitar feedback, talked about snorting drugs in the lyrics and in interviews and looked like tousled versions of a '66 dandified Dylan who'd joined The Velvet Underground.

Working the cash register behind the counter, I saw in the growing purchasing line someone I'd seen from last night's first show. He was hard to miss, as he had been standing up on the side-of-stage after the performance and seemingly was in charge of letting all the VIP pass holders, friends and connected industry people back through to the upstairs dressing-room area. He was tall, thin and wore a shorter version of a top hat and an above-the-waist blazer giving him a sort of rock 'n' roll carnival sideshow barker look which to me suggested that working on a rock 'n' roll world tour must be something like being in a traveling circus. As I work through the customers' purchases and he gets closer to me in the line I stealthily begin writing out one of my cards. Now just got one more customer to go befo—

"Hey, Mister Record Store! You look like you're into the 60s—'96 Tears', best garage rock song ever?" I look up to see next in line is a fat, tie-dyed, grey frizzy-haired, Wavy-cold-Gravy, Haight Street hippie guy.

"Umm...'96 Tears'? I'm trying to remember that one," I say, not really trying to remember or even process what he was saying. I'm just wanting to get my card written out and ready before one of my co-workers will have to stop pretending that they haven't noticed the line is getting long and open another register. My tour carny barker is next after this guy, and if I don't hurry I'll lose my chance.

"Hold *ON!* You don't know *'96 Tears'*?! And you work at a record store?! *Huh,* OK—'96 Tears' by ? and the Mysterians, ever heard of them? It's only probably *the* seminal garage rock tune as dictated by history!"

I realize that I did know the song, just not off the top of my head who'd done it. What, just because I work at a record store I'm supposed to know everything? I'm only twenty-four and it wasn't like I could just plug my brain into a lab computer or had some super information device where I could just look up any piece of information whenever I wanted. Everything I knew about music I had to search out on my own or get turned on to by my circle of friends.

He hands me an album by The Ultimate Spinach, then taking his tone down momentarily he mutters, "Ya can't go any lower on that, huh?"

"No, I don't price them," I say, already quickly ringing his purchase up.

"Yeah, I do freelance writing. Had my review of Nirvana's *The Existence of Chance Is Everything and Nothing While the Greatest Achievement Is the Living of Life, and So Say All of Us* published in *Freakout* magazine a few months ago, and NO—not that horrible new grunger or whatever-they-wanna-call-it band, Nirvana—I mean the original 1960s Nirvana. Did you know that? That there was a 60s Nirvana? They were British. *Very* psychedelic." He hands me a twenty as he continues, "Anyway, right now I'm composing the liner notes for the new Sundazed reissue of It's a Beautiful Day's first 1969 album. You MUST have heard of them, right? San Francisco band?"

"Oh wow," I reply to the cash register while making change as quickly as possible. My obvious sarcasm doesn't register, which makes me realize he must be so used to getting it by now that he doesn't even recognize what it is anymore. Now that I have his change and actually look up at him I see he's sweating, which doesn't seem to bother his face dandruff much but still it in turn then alerts me to the smell of his BO-infused tie-dye shirt. As if on cue he unloads a deep sigh full of bologna breath straight into my face.

"Ran into Neil Young at the Giants game on Saturday—he blew up right in my face! Just for asking for a lousy autograph!"

"That's not very groovy," I offer while jerking my head out of his brown acid breath cloud. "Did you inadvertently become the first person to break him the news Kurt Cobain's just died?"

"Who?" he asks as I hand him the record in a paper Reckless bag. He was now waiting for some sort of further recognition, a question or some sign of interest in what he'd been talking about.

"Next!"

Two minutes later I'm calling my dealer friend Chris on the work phone. "Hey man, we're on the list for The Jesus and Mary Chain tonight—and with backstage passes!" Then I whisper in the phone excitedly, "I got us on with the tour manager because Jim wants a bag of snorts!"

"Duude! Holy shit, maan! I just picked up a new batch of some righteous stuff!" Chris had an "old army buddy" quality about him. He was a type of "man's man" but not in an excessively macho way and together we made for something closer to a wily and mischievous *Anchors Aweigh* Gene Kelly and Frank Sinatra film-musical kind of vibe. It was always about fun and when we'd have stand-out plans like this he'd be rubbing his hands together like he was about to hit the town on shore leave. Chris was twenty-eight and hence a few years older than most the rest of us in the scene but you really couldn't tell. Still, no matter how many times I'd have to reassure him of this it never seemed to help and he eventually succeeded in making me feel that when I was a few years older it would really matter. I still had all the time in the world before that happened, though.

Early on at the show that night I run into Matt Hollywood, which somehow causes Chris to disappear so I watch the performance with him. The show was just as solid as the night before, perhaps only made better by William Reid's very impressive all-in-one beer chug during the noise solo section of the yet-to-be-released "I Hate Rock 'n' Roll".

With that song the show is over and as the floor begins to clear I see Chris striding toward me with both arms stretched out wide. "Dude, man, did you see 'Bill' Reid go full-tilt boogie on that beer?! AHH-HAA!" His grin was huge and he brought one of those hands down slapping me on the shoulder. It was impossible not to have fun around him when he was really into it like this. As we walk in the opposite direction of the exiting crowd I see the tour manager side-of-stage. He's doing some serious rubber-necking over the gathering VIP crowd before seeing who he's been looking for. We make eye contact as he waves us right through with an actual carnival style greeting "Step right up, gentlemen, the boys are upstairs". As we pass through the stage-barrier portal and into the elite side of the stage we momentarily exchange a quick glance to ensure we've got our "cool on".

I start up the steps leading to the balcony backstage area but only get about halfway up the narrow stairway before I see William Reid and Hope Sandoval from Mazzy Star at the top waiting to come down. Mazzy Star was not only the opening band on the tour, but Hope sang duet style with lead singer Jim Reid on the new album's single "Sometimes Always". Apparently somewhere along that process she and William had become an item. They were both famously antisocial and must have been making a quick escape down the stairs before the backstage VIP area was overrun. We press ourselves up against the wall of the slim staircase to let them pass and I look down to Chris to share a mutual smile, but not one too long as to break "cool guy" composure.

At the top of the stairs the VIP balcony area is filling up quickly with all sorts of who-knows-who's and soon the tour manager suddenly appears and hands us each a beer before tipping us a wink and going into the closed dressing room and shutting the door behind him. We wait a few beats and Jim comes and walks over to accept our excited yet decorously reserved "Hey maan!" He's nice but reserved, as expected. "So, how much does the speed cost?" he asks almost under his breath while adding a few extra E's to the speed.

"Ahh man, for you, nothing," Chris says, "we're huge fans, man. It's my pleasure to give this to you."

Jim smiles slightly in response, an expression I've never seen in any of the photos or TV interviews. I'm impressed with Chris as I didn't know he was going to make this gesture and I smile proudly, joining in on his generosity. He then elongates his arm somewhat upward and brings it down, popping the tiny but very pregnant plastic half-gram head-shop baggy into Jim's cupped palm. This style of deployment gives it a ceremonious air.

The *obvious* thing to happen next is for him to take us with him in the dressing room so we can all do some party lines, but instead he only offers very drolly, "Well, I'd like to invite you back to do some, but, uh…my mother is here so I can't bring you back. Thanks for the speed." Without waiting for a response he's already turned around and vanishes back into the now closed dressing room.

"*Huh?*" I look at Chris. We reflect each other's disappointed expressions like mirrors as I whisper, "Man, couldn't he have thought of something better than that?"

"Jeeez man, I know, right? Definitely just received a 'get lost' message here."

Deflated, we eye our beers and take long pulls in order to quickly move on from this rejection scene. I'm a close first at finishing when suddenly the backstage door bursts back open and a short old lady with a bottle of whiskey in her hand shouts in a thick Scottish accent, "WHERE'S WILLIAM GONE?!"

Chris and I look back at each other, this time with a very different mutual expression of shocked amusement. We quickly gain composure. "Ahh, he left down the stairs, ma'am," Chris informs in an overly polite animated tone, as if the information relayed was filled with great mystery. Eyes wide, he moves up close to my face and shout-whispers "*Dude*, he really *can't* bust out the snorts—his mom *IS* here!"

"Man!" I answer back in the excited relief of not being rejected by one of my musical heroes. Still, the situation did leave me with a strange new feeling, like they were normal human beings or something.

High Tide and Green Hair

"You didn't have permission to finish my song! It's MY song!" Matt yells. He then coils back like he's going to kick the seat in front of him but catches himself, realizing it's not Dave D or some other dude, but our superfan friend and sometimes benefactor Diane sitting in the driver's seat. Instead, now even more frustrated by this add-on denial of his first choice of car tantrum move, he flails himself around in the backseat where I am currently trapped next to him on a not-so-warm San Franciscan night.

Anton had been up half the night finishing what Matt thought he'd be working on tonight after having left the studio the previous evening, having only cut the basic guitars, bass and vocal. It's ironically titled "Cabin Fever", which I am having more than a large-scale dose of stuck in the back of this mobile metal cage. Whenever Matt reached the kicking or rolling around on the floor and crying stages, you could usually just sit back and let him run out of steam, but this would change soon.

"I think it sounds good, Matt," Diane offers by way of keeping the peace rather than taking sides. She wasn't lying, it did sound good. Despite Matt's display, Anton is still excited about his work. He's sitting turned around in the front passenger seat smiling at Matt, seemingly still expecting him to "get it" at any second as each new audio addition debuts through the runway speakers. He was excited to collaborate and just wants him to like it. The child's playground "na-na-na-na-na-na" style of the vocal melody if nothing else makes it the perfect soundtrack for this conniption fit.

"LET!...ME!...OUT!" he shouts, each word with its own headbang against his window.

"But we just got you and you guys have a record to finish!" Diane pleads.

"Sounds to me like it's already been finished for me," he mutters. I can feel the volcano beginning to prepare for another eruption.

"If he wants out, let him out," I say, chiming in for the first time.

Diane pulls over just as we are approaching the Bay Bridge Rincon Hill entrance. After the door slams, we resume our way onto the bridge where Larry Thrasher's recording studio lies just on the other side of San Francisco Bay in Emeryville. As we make our way across the bridge, I gaze out into the darkness of the empty unlit south side of the Bay, thinking about the first high-end studio experience I'd only just had a couple of months ago. It was the kind of Bay Area "ROCK" spot where you'd find Sammy Hagar and Huey Lewis recording anthems designed to destroy intelligence on a mass scale. A sterile cedar-lined temple to when the 70s got the 80s "modernizing" makeover transformation to a high-end frozen-in-tacky state where music is "business" and time is money and money is music. It was the lure of free studio time that had brought us there but I just felt out of place while Anton struggled to carve something out of the session. In the end, none of the versions the producer tracked could be used from this square-shaped black hole. It would be the first and last time Anton would ever let himself be put in the hands of a stranger.

Diane drops us off at the massive multi-unit warehouse space; she has to get up early in the morning for work, probably around the same time we'll be finishing. There's no set plan or schedule and I have no idea how long, if not for days, we will be here. I know enough to assume it'll be as long as Larry Thrasher will leave the place to Anton. Larry plays in the current lineup of Psychic TV and is a fresh convert to the BJM cause who is now loaning out his studio to us for free.

We walk up three flights of refurbished industrial warehouse stairs and go down a large hall where Anton unlocks one of the doors. "You ready?" he says, flipping on the rows of overhead fluorescent light tubes. The flickering spreads like a wave across the ceiling, illuminating the wide-open white concrete largeness. I'm immediately drawn over to the wall-spanning, chicken-wire-lined industrial glass windows that start at stomach level and go up to the ceiling. It's a lit-up, drive-in movie theater-sized screen of San Francisco Bay and the city beyond in full view. There's no control room or isolation booths in here, just one huge all-in-one recording space.

"Check this out."

A new track, "Monkey Puzzle", booms and the spirit of the 60s fills the room. Originally constructed to be filled with large things, the former shipping warehouse room is now being filled with huge sonic creations that stuff it full to the ceiling, its intensity giving the feeling of further pushing the walls in every direction, blowing it up like an enormous balloon. This is one of the latest tracks I had missed participating in due to my most recent bender. At the same time this song was being tracked, I would've been back across the Bay at The DNA Lounge watching Supergrass perform, the latest in a long line of hot bands coming over from England.

Anton then begins to mix down tracks and so I'm left on my own. It's a familiar feeling I'd grown up with as a child, when I'd get dragged along with my dad to the massive pick 'n' pull automotive recycling yards. He'd be climbing over and under the massive rows of discarded picked-apart junkers while I'd drift off into my own fantasy world, venturing around the junk labyrinth imagining I was in one of the many "dystopian sci-fi" movies of the day.

I had nothing to get high with but I wasn't at all bothered by this. Recording sessions were one space where I didn't care about doing drugs. They weren't needed here. Watching the music being created was a far superior drug and anyway, while jacked-up enthusiasm was welcome out in the streets, in the recording studio environment it could easily become simple intoxicated babble getting in the way. I knew Anton enjoyed psychedelics from time to time, smoked weed and drank but not to excess, at least not that I had seen. He was too driven to be intoxicated all the time and if anything was the ultimate specimen of a person that "didn't need drugs". Listening to him mix new less-shoegaze and more 60s-esque sounds was a better high, something I couldn't help feel that I had helped to inspire.

The next morning I wake up on cold naked concrete. I turn around rolling off of my angry right hip and see Anton is sleeping a few feet away flat on his back and with his head resting on what looks to be a thick antiquarian book. Every inch of the huge white space is now blast-refracting bright light. I get up squinting and hobble into a walk over to the windows and take in the big expanse that is a sunny San Francisco day. It's a rare sight for me from this other side of the Bay and it gives a feeling like I'm still at home looking into a full city-length mirror.

Anton, who was up I don't know how much later than me, sits up scratching the back of his head, "Fuck, I wish we could get coffee. Oh *well.*" He then looks around the room, "C'mon let's make a song." He sets up a stool and a mic as I wander around the room trying to locate where the tambourine's gone. Soon we're settled together behind the mic where I stand and he takes half a stool. "OK, watch this," he instructs while giving me a sampling of the guitar rhythm. I watch his hand downstrokes and hit my beats on the "one" along with him. In teaching myself how to keep time without drums, I'd learned to watch his hand on the "one" downstroke. Watch his hand. No matter where any other band member's timing is or isn't, he and I will still be together.

We run through it once and it's not until it's over that I find out that was the take. Now he goes into his internal work space. He finishes another part and then it's never much of a wait, maybe as much as a few minutes to see what will come out of the space next—a lead guitar part, bass, keyboard, from here the list can get pretty long.

He invites me back inside of the space. "Here, sing this with me, 'Ooh yeah, ooh yeah'." I pull into the lane next to him and we continue together, "*Ooh yeah...ooh yeah.*"

"Great! OK, let's record."

He goes over to the recording console, comes back and we do the vocals together live:

"*Ain't it like I said, they're fuckin' with your head...*" I'm right over his shoulder in repeat to the backing vocal and beat, "*Ooh yeah, ooh yeah...*"

Now fully in the internal workspace he's got to keep up with his own idea flow. This adds in a bit of haste to the mix because he has to stop and take the time to get each track set up while the juices flow at high tide.

Soon he's doing toot-runs of a harmonica track idea as he moves back from the console to the mic. By the time it's set for a take, the idea is completed inside the internal work space. Now just to repeat what has just been forged in the creative mind and utter it into the physical world for the first time. It's just another day in the internal work space and this space *is* the place. Afterwards, a lead guitar part is added, then a thunder-rolling fuzz bass part.

Time for a rough mix to see where it's all at. Now the song plays back with all tracks together for the first time. The wide empty room of solitary nothing is suddenly fully blown with a sonic Big Bang instantly and invisibly devouring all empty space all the way up to the oh-so high ceiling which then bounces the volume back down to the floor where they both refract to infinity as do all four walls like an audio house of mirrors.

This will become the title track for BJM's next and third album, *Take It from the Man*. An hour ago it didn't exist. Now it does.

We break for lunch and go to the only "restaurant" for miles, which is the chip and soda machines down the hall. Fishing through every pocket between us, we pile all our contents together and then sift the coin through the lint, stray matches, guitar picks, torn-off cig-arette butts, bits of folded washing machine-pummeled paper scrap, then blow away the loose tobacco-like sand from our silver treasure pile. Its coin-op only in warehouse world and folding green means nothing here. Anton is surprised to find Diane's television remote inside a parka pocket from our TV crash party at her apartment two nights before. This wasn't the first time and I start to laugh and he clicks me "off".

Oddly, the payphone down the hall starts ringing.

"Think it's the Man?" I ask half joking. We walk over to it and Anton picks it up. It's Larry saying he unexpectedly needs his studio tonight.

"C'mon let's go finish the song," Anton says with the wish for more time in his voice.

"We should call Diane first and tell her to come pick up her TV remote after work," I say playfully.

He smiles and hands me two dimes.

When we see Diane again she is insisting "We *HAVE* to go see this new band from Portland! They are supposed to be amazing!" So about a week later her, Anton, a now chilled-out Matt and I got into her car and drove to some artist warehouse space in SoMa. Over the last few years Diane's been one of the biggest benefactors for the BJM boys, from finding Dean Taylor for the band to countless rides and little favors to keep us alive and swinging another day. A pint of beer at the club and, for me more than the others, plenty of late-night bumps.

We walk into the place, which is on the smaller size for this sort of thing, and take a section of wall along the low-lit. There is no stage, not one that I can see anyway, but the view from where we are somehow still works, meaning that because they immediately sound and look so interesting, I'm craning my neck in all necessary positions to maintain a constant vantage point.

They are cartoon characters like us, but more of the vintage sporty '72 Munich Olympics goes Pacific Northwest old dive-bar version. Courtney's dirty blond bowl is tight around the edges, and his super-erect posture under the current self-implemented fashion circumstances gives him a shirtless man-gazelle gait. He's lean yet rugged, with muscles taut while in the bar-chord gripping posture. It's a square-jawed kind of handsome that the girls must love, and this makes five kinds of sense. I'm sure we all insta-crush out on Zia, who by god is bouncing a tambourine off her hip while playing bass on the keys. She wears librarian glasses and her hair oomphs straight up in that hair product-less child's way. Peter, with blond head down frozen in moody still-life is somehow still always moving at the same time.

Courtney adds lots of wordless vocals from the classic pop wordless dictionary, ba-ba's and ooh-oohs abound, indirectly inviting the group here to sing along, if the too-cool-for-school people you find at most shows these days did such a thing.

They were playing the best music I'd seen from people my own age since I first saw The Brian Jonestown Massacre at The Peacock Lounge four years ago. Something totally special, not this plus that plus that at all. It was fresh and new and exciting and at the same time, we were still a little better, and that made me like them even more. After the gig we launched into them, but they already knew who we were the moment we appeared in the room and started noticeably digging it.

I've never seen Anton so interested in a band, and we all immediately became interchangeable band friends, with Courtney and Peter riding to the next party with Diane and Anton, while Matt and I climb in the very back of the band van with the rest of The Dandy Warhols and their live visuals artist, who is introduced to us as the Dandy's first "superstar", as in "Andy Warhol superstar", Jeffrey Wonderful. He looks like an enlarged little kid whose appearance does in fact fit the superstar bill, but what these people don't know yet is that they've just locked themselves inside a cage with SF's modern answer to Ondine and Lou Reed's sister's cousin's brother's cat vet who plays guitar and raids the animal pharmacy there, and me and Matt's switches are flipped to very on thanks to Diane. We immediately go to work on closing the walls inside the dark and crowded van.

"Hey baby," I say louder than necessary, "I like your green hair, I can't believe I'm hanging out with the righteous cat-kid from *The Boy with Green Hair*!"

"The boy with green hair? What's thaat?" This Jeffrey Wonderful sounds on the crossroads of going snobby, but thinks better of it and takes the pretend-to-be-interested route as his internal clock tick-tick-ticks in anticipation of getting out of here as soon as possible, but there are no windows with indications on the other side of where we are or for how long.

"YOU, man! You mean to tell me you're a boy with green hair who's never seen *The Boy with Green Hair*?" Ohh, *man*, it's the like original movie about the lone outcast against society's judgmental evils! You gotta *dig* that shit, baby! Your hair's green!"

"Yah, my hair is green," he agrees, sounding uncomfortable in what is maybe an East Coast accent.

"Well, I don't want to give the whole thing away, but hold on to something heavy Mister Groovy Green Hair the Second, 'cause guess what? His green hair turns into a symbol for world peace for all the children of the world! His green hair and all the whys and what-fors of its greenness are so righteous that it implements into the consciousness of the people's people a new and better world of non-violence. Then some bullies cut it all off and the dream is over. SH-*iiit*, I just gave the ending away. But he had green hair! Like you! We need to get you back outside so you can start using your powers to save the world!"

"Ohh, OK," he offers, sounding not sure what else to do about this situation.

"Yeah, I hear ya. The Man would just take you out anyway, as usual. The movie got the guy who made it blacklisted, but then he made some *fuck*-ing fantastic movies in England in the 60s," I conclude, realizing I'd started shouting at some point, but I don't know when.

"This is not how I pictured this ride going. I gotta get outta heah," he says nervously out loud to himself regarding currently being in his own band van. I take it down a notch and Matt sees this as his cue to go into his Shaun Ryder vocal impersonation while bouncing back and forth: *"Picked ya' picture, now I'm gonna eat ya', picked ya' picture, now I'm gonna eat ya'..."*

I remember we all hung out at some house and partied until I was too fucked up to remember, but Diane comes away from the evening with a cassette dub of tracks from their upcoming album. We will all listen to it constantly.

The next night I'm at Matt's where we are to be picked up for rehearsal. As we leave it's dusk and it's a sharp-turn weaving-way through the Mission district's grid. I look up to the starless city sky, feeling only the bouncing from the road below and wind everywhere else when Matt's elbow nudges against my leg. He's grinning mischievously while reaching over a pint of whiskey, that first sip now deep inside that brings the transformation from being stone-cold sober to having those first little fluttering buzzies now inside my center. It's a feeling I think is in fact better than the being completely drunk feeling, and I always feel like I'm chasing that first sip-upgrade feel, but it's a one-time a night thing and until science finds a way to make every drink feel like the first, I'll just have to settle for getting totally wasted.

56

The one buzz better is playing those great songs we play and that is what time it is as we pull up to the rehearsal rooms and park inside the stillness of the outside night. It's San Francisco's take on suburbia out here, with all its rows of "ticky tacky" track houses.

We all climb out and adjust our wind-blown everything, then head inside. Like most band factory rehearsal spaces, the pay-by-the-hour rooms had a little extra, usually in the form of a foot-high stage in the corner and often a mirrored wall seemingly so you could rock out children's tennis racket-style into adulthood. Regardless of room tier, the one thing they all came with as standard-issue was worn-out old office carpet that had probably eaten a forest fire's worth of cigarette ashes and drunk a good day at the breweries worth of beer-bottle spillage. Cigarette burns are generously sprinkled throughout like an extra black starry carpet night. Look over there and you can see Orion's Belt.

Still, a small mixing board stand and a few chairs have been rearranged in a tasteful distance around the space for us, the next paying customers. Out of nowhere a couple of six-packs of beer are added to the furnishings and another pint of bourbon is passed around. Anton to Dean, to Brian, then Jeff, Matt and lastly me, which I gulp a little more greedily than the rest. Anton sets the remaining two fingers' worth of booze on his Twin Reverb amplifier unknowingly for me to revel in evil thoughts.

In a large rehearsal space no one has to vie for an outlaw-style back-to-the-wall position, so I wind my way to a corner of the room and watch the swirling intent-filled movements as heavy amps are lumbered one-handedly into position, cords are unwound from their snake coil formations and pedals are pushed and twiddled.

Only one of the four light switches is flipped leaving the room ambience to an appropriate level of functional darkness. A single window adds gashes of streetlight to the floor as Anton burns incense he bought at an Indian bazaar store.

Although everyone in the room are as individuals on their own fully developed planet, it's Anton who was the source of gravity which we revolved around. His power was like a strong undercurrent that held everyone in its grip. As the run-throughs continue, he gives metaphysical, scientific and poetic explanations to each succeeding song, which he somehow always manages to spin into a humorous aside that gets us all smiling and chuckling from around the room.

As the rehearsal wore on, the in-between song laughs became more regular and in turn the smoke breaks came sooner. Jeff and Matt would make sure to add on a point here and a quip there. Brian would stretch out his long gangly arms with a yawn, then resettle back into position, wanting things to keep moving at a reasonable pace. I'd take a sip of beer while looking at the whiskey...

"...minimalism and repetition that's not overproduced. It needs to be similar to the old way of doing things, that's the magic stuff. It's like 60s style but not retro. Psychedelic music and the blues, like Zulu warriors chanted the blues so they could go into battle and die, so they were like, this is all we can do, you know?"

We knew. We were from a messier world, a world of antiestablishment and romance for the underground and we all spoke the same language.

There is also a new unspoken but palpable buzz in our inner-band atmosphere, Matt, Anton and I jazzed on thoughts from the bonding with our new brothers and sister-in-arms and legs, The Dandy Warhols. It's a land-ho situation for exciting times, and as Anton conducts his compositions, I feel invulnerable against everything else, all of it against us, except now one other band in far-off Portland.

Countdown

I hit the record shop floor, but before finding a task to get into, I scan the current scene around the store just to make sure there isn't something to distract me from finding a task to get into. That's when I see a girl outside leaning up against the front glass. What's really grabbing my attention is her hairstyle. It's a blond version of Björk's in one of her more recent music videos, "Big Time Sensuality", in which her medium-length hair was parted in zigzags, then piled and pinned into little hair tower buns seemingly randomly positioned across her entire head.

In the video, Björk prances around the full length of a huge empty flatbed semi-truck driving through the streets of Manhattan. There's plenty of room left on there as if in an open invitation to join the party of new 90s optimism of a kind not felt this strongly since the 60s. Unfortunately, also like the 60s, this was all to end by the decade's close. I stood watching her while infusing these romantic notions into a stranger because...well, she had the hairdo.

So, I decide to walk outside "Just to take a look around". I only make it two steps out to the other side of the glass before two young Haight Street "Deadhead" denizens cut off my forward motion as one laments to the other in a beat-down tone of disbelief, "I can't believe Jerry's dead." The fashion of the zombified mantra-esque delivery implied that the words had been on repeat for a while.

Directly in front of me across the street, painted on the hippie grocery store was a giant Jerry grinning right back at me. Jerry's dead, that's what he said. I looked around but suddenly the girl was gone.

And so it was randomly repeated throughout the rest of the day. "I can't believe Jerry's dead," the Deadheads would say in a whole new kind of daze while walking back and forth up and down Haight Street. This melancholia brought on a rare type of Haight Street day when the quiet stillness of early morning lingers long into the afternoon, like a day that never really gets going.

The day funk lumbered along and while lazily flipping through the local *SF Guardian* music section I saw Oasis listed in The Bottom of the Hill venue calendar ad. That band name crammed in the tiny schedule with all the local what-have-you bands just didn't look altogether right somehow. I'd first heard Oasis a few months ago while rifling through a stack of new releases hoping to find some new single or album I'd just read about. That's when I found their first three-song CD single. I had indeed just read about these guys in the *NME* last week and by the sounds of the single's review it was supposed to be right up my alley.

From the photo on the cover, they honestly didn't look all that cool. Kinda frumpy and arranged haphazardly in a typical beat-down, band factory-style rehearsal room. Still, I was never opposed to finding "sorta cool" UK bands and so I put the CD on top of my allotted playlist stack. An hour later when the rotation came to my turn, I let loose the track "Supersonic" on one of its first-ever stereo system playbacks in America. I liked it, but didn't love it, and as Anton would later say when he heard it, "The guitars sound like Tom Petty. They need vintage amps for the kind of music they're trying to do, not Guns N' Roses Marshall stacks." He was right and had perfectly diagnosed the problem. The real tune here, I thought, was the last of the three songs, "Columbia", which was incredibly vibey along with cool attitude and swagger. To me it sounded like a sonic beacon transmitting from across the pond that "we were not alone".

More EP singles followed every two months like clockwork and they quickly transformed into the right band at the right time, filling the void left by the unfulfilled promise of The Stone Roses. Taking over the controls of "what the world was waiting for". To us Americans and the rest of the world it was Oasis who'd now slid into pole position as the coolest band in England.

What I knew was that we had to play this show and there were plenty of lesser choices around town who'd be seeing this same ad today. Not wanting anyone to beat us to the punch I immediately called our manager Dave D on the work phone and asked him to set it up for us with Ramona who owned the venue. Of all the many clubs we played on a regular basis, Bottom of the Hill was the closest thing to a home base for BJM. Ramona was very down for our cause and would give us special treatment, just as long as another band hadn't gotten themselves in there first.

The day of the gig the whole band drove in Dave D's van together all the way out to the Potrero Hill district where The Bottom of the Hill was. Being the only one really looking, I saw the huge Oasis tour bus parked in front of the club from two blocks away. The debut Oasis album, *Definitely Maybe*, was now just two weeks old and as I'd predicted the band's popularity had exploded. The gig was now an oversold hot ticket that suddenly overnight could've been bumped up to somewhere triple the size of this 350-capacity club.

My English brothers in white lines were in my hometown and I was anxious to show them how we did things here in San Francisco. I climbed out of the van along with the others and while they all grabbed their gear and headed into the venue, I marched straight over to the giant tour bus and knock-knocked on the door.

To my surprise and relief it was the songwriter and guitarist Noel Gallagher himself who opened the bus door. I knew it was weird to be suddenly presenting myself like this but I was also currently powdered up on the California enlightenment that I was about to bestow on them. I was certain they'd never snorted lines like these and they were about to be forever upgraded thanks to me and my international snorts of goodwill program.

"Hey man, I've got some of the most righteous speed you are ever gonna do," I say, then immediately begin to size up the bus steps for boarding.

"No thanks," he replies in a Manchester deadpan, "we only do coke." He waits a beat and then hits a button that shuts the door, leaving me staring at my own jaw-on-the-floor reflection in the dark-tinted glass door.

I go back into the club where the guys are setting up the drums and amps and tuning guitars for soundcheck. Still dazed, I join in briefly to stake my little stage territory out. If I don't, with six guys all crammed on this small stage and four guitar necks pointing in various directions, I'd find myself onstage later without even enough room to spread my tambourine hands apart.

Dean looks up at me for a moment, then goes back to tuning his twelve-string hollow-body guitar while asking in his familiar tone of annoyed yet humorous disbelief, "Did you hear we're being kicked out of the venue right after we're done soundchecking?"

"No, what do you mean?"

"Those guys told Ramona no one except their people could be inside while they soundchecked."

"Wow, that's kinda fucked."

Bottom of the Hill was one of our regular venues and this was our turf.

"Yeah," he chuckles, shaking his head in agreement while still looking down, tuning.

The Bottom of the Hill was probably the best small club in San Francisco but if it had one downside, it would be that its location was in the outskirtsville part of SF, so after being kicked out of the club along with everyone else I had to walk three blocks to find another payphone. I call Diane and let her know that if she comes to the club now, there is a good chance Oasis will be hanging around, but actually I'm moreso wanting to arrange for her to start snowing down more artificial generosity on me sooner than later. I forgot to mention to her that the headliners were camping out in their bus and had also arranged for us to not have access to the backstage rooms.

Diane ends up arriving at the club faster than I expected while I was just killing time down the street having a cheap pint of beer at some lame bar and grill spot. She loiters outside of the venue listening to Oasis soundcheck and just as soon as they finish there's Liam, who had no idea about my earlier offer to Noel, heading out the front door of the club. Diane then quickly offers up my speed and he is apparently quite "mad for it", and takes her with him on the bus just before I come back down the street. Seeing no Diane with my drugs

I poke my head inside the club to find we've been given the "OK" to hang inside again. Ten minutes later I anxiously poke my head back outside for the third time to watch her getting off of the bus. Before I can say anything she immediately goes into a wide-eyed recounting of who said what and the massive-sized lines they'd insisted on doing.

"I gave it all to them but don't worry, I'm getting more. I told them not to do anymore for a while, but I don't think anyone was listening—man, they're already gonna be whacked!"

"Didn't you tell them you have to do small lines with this stuff?"

"I tried but they wouldn't listen! I think because I was a girl they were showing off a bit," she says, thinking wishfully. It was obvious in her lingering faraway state she had been too starstruck to take command of the situation. It's easy for bands, especially visiting from abroad for the first time, to get caught up in the San Francisco folklore, like Jim Morrison walking down Haight Street taking everything that is handed to him on the spot without even asking what any of it was.

We went back inside the venue for good this time and all of Oasis came striding in just a few moments later. Moving swiftly through the small rock club surrounded by crew, it was as if we were all potential paparazzi or some form of riff-raff, to which...fair enough. They were then all escorted out the back and up the stairs to the backstage area from which we were prohibited. This wasn't Barrowlands, this was Bottom of the Hill.

It was becoming time for us to go onstage and no one had seen Jeff since soundcheck. "Where's Jeff?" Matt asks, becoming the fifth band member to do so as he joins the rest of us side-stage. Jeff was hard to miss. His face was ghostly white with make-up and usually glowing like the moon. His lips would then be done up in a shaky-hand lipstick application and his eyeliner always looked a few days old. His hair was very long, but in a move I'd never seen before, it was piled high in a huge pompadour on the top and then pinned flat in the back with a bag of hairpins. It was something between a skinny, freshly dead Elvis and Alice from *The Brady Bunch*.

"Nobody's seen him," I answer. We all knew where he went. Back home to score.

"We'll just have to play without a third guitar until he gets here," Anton says without irony. Matt points toward the corridor to the pool room "Well, I just saw Justine from Elastica playing pool with Damon from Blur over there. Maybe we should ask one of them to play with us," he says in his half-morose, half-kidding way.

Somewhat bizarrely, Blur and Pulp were also on tour together promoting their new albums and had played across town at Bimbo's the night before. Then earlier this afternoon local radio station Live 105 had the supposed "rival" bands Oasis and Blur in the studio together for a double interview. For one weekend in 1994, San Francisco was the Britpop center of the world.

Despite being up for a second night straight, the amount of valium pills I'd taken along with whiskey and beer plus the fresh-from-the-garage-lab snorts added up to an equation that now has me slightly hovering above the stage floor during our entire set. As the openers, we couldn't be on for that long and you could feel Jeff's time running out fast before he would be officially turning in a no-show. Suddenly Anton, who must have been keeping an eye on the doors, saw him enter the packed-tight small club.

"I see you, Jeff!" he shouts into the mic. "You've got ten seconds to be on this stage with your guitar plugged in or you're out of the band!" He then immediately begins a rocket launch-style countdown, yelling into the mic:

"TEN!

"NINE!" The crowd joins in like its New Year's eve—

"EIGHT!

"SEVEN!" I see Jeff is desperately trying to make his way through the over-packed club...

"SIX!

"FIVE!" He's making headway but his head is bobbing in and out of view like a drowning man trying to swim to shore...

"FOUR!

"THREE!" He's crawling onstage now...

"TWO!" Guitar awkwardly thrown on with strap around more neck, then shoulder, he stabs his guitar cord into his hollow-body guitar, instantly releasing a feedback squeal so loud it drowns out the entire crowd along with Anton as they all yell together:

"ONE!!"

In a still moment of "what's going to happen next?", Anton simply looks down at his own guitar and starts into the opening chords of the next song. Though that night Jeff was a real loser's loser, he was still a next-level guitarist with the good goods and truly a guitar player's player. His fingers began dancing a fast-motion can-can up and down the fretboard doing this rockabilly country twang thing that then suddenly spun around to show bare, ferocious garage-rock fangs. A fusion of both gorgeous melody and rotten trash that traded off and combined into metamorphosed melodies fluttering all around him like vampire butterflies. I was happy for him in my pilled-out whiskey speed buzz-ball, stumbling and shaking away. I scan the crowd reaction and that's when I see mid-crowd center Jarvis Cocker along with a mixture of other Pulp and Blur members smiling up at the action.

Having gone straight up and down we then turn it sideways as the guitars begin to drone large and Brian goes into the Bo Diddley beat on our closer "Hyperventilation". It's a hypnotic, narcotic ride that trades off slow burning with flash-fire and goes on for seven minutes and it's just as this freshly erected sonic skyscraper's up for a total demolition that Anton sets down his guitar, pulls his shirt off and begins to prowl the stage menacingly while chanting *"Sniffing glue, in my room!"* Then, the only time I've ever seen this before or since, he takes the microphone, sticks it down his pants and begins rubbing it inside his now open fly.

Forty-five minutes later when Oasis hit the stage Anton and I watch them together as they start up with the new album opener "Rock 'n' Roll Star". You can feel the new optimism of the times shooting around the room like streamers in a victory parade as the crowd all celebrate together in these birthing days of a new musical decade. Then, halfway through the song Anton leans over and whisper-shouts in my ear, "Look at the way he's singing," and sure enough, there was Liam in his signature singing style of resting his upper lip right on the mic. The same mic that was just buried down the front of a certain someone's pants.

They end their set with a cover of "I Am the Walrus" and Anton and I sing along with each other, filling in the missing "Smoke pot smoke pot everybody smoke pot..." outro, before I then find myself almost becoming mesmerized by guitar player Bonehead's jaw that is in a constant tick-tock rotation like a hypnotist's watch trick. He's wide-eyed riding that train a lot higher than on cocaine. Despite all the antics relayed here, the main thing was you could see and hear the magic as the band brought to the stage all the things they were already becoming huge for.

With Oasis finished, the two of us went out front for fresh air and cigarettes and to catch random friends in the mass exodus being told to go home. After the last of the crowd left the building, Anton and I went back in just as Noel, now flanked by security again, was across the club quickly beelining toward the exit. As we began to pass them in the middle of the now empty floor, Anton suddenly flips his direction and begins walking with Noel and talking right up in his ear. They now moved at an even faster pace toward the doors. Similar to the treatment I'd received earlier, he seemed to only be concerned with being back on the bus.

Anton came striding back up to me looking proud of himself.

"What did you say to him?"

I told him that for the kind of music they're doing they need vintage gear. I'm just trying to do the guy a favor because it's true." Whether or not Noel was listening, the next and even bigger album was indeed recorded on vintage gear.

The next night BJM opened for Oasis again in Sacramento. We'd gotten half of the scheduled local suburban shoegazer's opening set time basically because Anton just told them that's what was happening. I loved these Viking invasion meets zen Jedi mind trick moments of his. Beyond Diane having been allowed on the bus again to drop off more of the SF crystal meth persuasion they'd requested, Oasis very much kept themselves to the bus that night, which is understandable when the gig is Sacramento, but then they weirdly seemed pretty reserved onstage later, especially considering everything they had done the night before and would continue doing straight on through up until the next gig in LA before temporarily breaking up. Oops. Liam never went to sleep, and it was on night #4—which is *after* the shakerbreaker of your mind that is night #3—that they played the famous Whisky a Go Go in Los Angeles. As the legend goes they just blew the whole show. Noel quit and disappeared. They had to hire a private investigator who found him holed up back in San Francisco with a girl he'd met. A few days later the band got back together and finished the tour but as they say in the Oasis documentary *Supersonic,* things were never the same between them after that. I wish they'd given me a chance to give proper skiing instructions on these very high white hills of San Francisco...

Toppermost of the Poppermost

It's departure day for our first out-of-town band trip on a mission to court the record industry at the annual SXSW music festival and industry convention in Austin, Texas. Dave D will drive Anton, Dean, Brian and the gear in his van, while Matt and I are riding with Diane in her compact white speed-mobile. Dave D has booked us two gigs en route to Austin to hopefully financially break us even on the trip. Once there, we have two shows to wow the biz, the first in one of the scores of live music bars in the downtown area and another in a bowling alley.

What could go wrong?

As Matt and I prepare to climb in the car, Diane suddenly has an announcement, obviously pre-prepared ground rules to lay down for *Withnail and I*. "I can't afford to buy enough speed for you guys to party on this whole trip," then adds, "but I'll give you guys some for the first show—then you're on your own!"

Once over the California border, the drive to Phoenix, Arizona officially breaks down to a full-time diet of the senses consisting of desert and sun, with the occasional break for beer, gas and weird looks. After the show that night Diane's promise comes true, then on the second night in Albuquerque, New Mexico so does her previous warning.

Left to our own vice devices, Matt and I's search for snorts actually pays off in the form of a pile of biker crank, compliments of the sound man. The clumps of sticky pink chalk are nowhere near the territory of decent stuff, but there's so much of it one can't be anything but happy. Turns out to be very wiry stuff and after having never been to bed the night before I must confess we were both totally gaked out.

Luckily (or at least it seemed at first) the bar does so well that night they give us a bottle of whiskey to celebrate the healthy turnout and performance. Then half a bottle later outside in the parking lot Matt suddenly snaps because he doesn't think I'm listening to what he is saying or I'm acting like his opinion doesn't matter or maybe both. He pushes me and suddenly I'm drunkenly wrestling someone who isn't playing. We are both whack-amped up on the biker crank we've been snorting piles of and the whiskey has served as the rocket fuel to launch us both straight out to planet *An-drama-duh*. We drunkenly roll around in the parking lot while Dave D, our manager, chooses to film us killing each other rather than "managing" the situation. What he catches on camera would later go on to be one of only two shots in *Dig!* not filmed by the documentary filmmakers. It was *that* good.

I get Matt down and climb on top of him, then using my weight to hold his arms down so he can't hit me, I plead, "Matt! You are my friend! We should NOT be fighting! I'm going to get up now so we can figure this out!" I cautiously push off him, crouch backwards a few steps, then get down on my knees. He's writhing back and forth on the pavement with his hands over his face. Then I spread both my arms out as wide as they will go until my hands are fanning out behind my back, and close my eyes. "Matt! If you really want to do it, then just do it—kill me right here, baby!" As I stick my chin out and wait, I play this out in my head while Matt simply comes over and sits down beside me for a bonding session that renews our vows as brothers. I was that *fucked* up.

Instead, what happens is whacked-out whiskey-wasted Matt goes into such a football style wind-up kick that it even includes a run-up step and he kicks me right in the face as hard as he can.

I wake up gasping at hot air and covered in sweat inside what last night had been a cool, dark van, but now after a few morning hours under the New Mexico summer sun has turned into a dirty fabric- and plastic-lined metal oven. It's then that consciousness delivers the double reality death-blow in the forms of the mother of all hangovers combined with having been boot-kicked in the head last night.

I squint out of the large side windows like Clint Eastwood on squint steroids to find I'm in the middle of a sprawling empty motel parking lot. It must be a million degrees out, and gazing (itself an agonizing exercise) beyond the burning asphalt it's nothing but bright dirty desert as far as the eye can see. I have no idea what rooms any of the others are in nor do I think I have the physical ability to find out. I begin to fall back down onto the bench, but the sharp pain in my head is impossible to ignore. I touch it and stinging shockwaves electrocute my entire head. I push myself up and slow-crawl my way through the van, over the other hot leather benches until I've scaled up the brown plastic and carpet dashboard to inspect myself in the rearview mirror. There is a half-inch gash on my right temple that looks bad—that is, until I raise my eyebrow. Then it looks *real* bad. I lower my eyebrow, then raise it again. I can actually see exposed face muscle move to further expose white bone. I lower my eyebrow back down—*muscle*. Raise—*bone*. Lower—*muscle*. Raise—*bone*. Lower—*muscle*. Raise—*bone*. Fuck—*me*.

The other emergency situation is I *really* need to pee I guess what is commonly referred to round these parts as a "whiskey river", and so I climb out and proceed to do so while leaning a shoulder up against the side of the van to hold me at rearview mirror height while continuing my eyebrow exercises in disbelief at my new ability to, by mere facial expression, flex the exposed glistening meat muscle to open a portal to my skull.

Now that I'm whatever relation I'm going to peak out at toward consciousness, I remember why I'm out here. I'd not only turned down going to the hospital last night, but I refused to even come inside the motel. Matt and I needed to be separated which had then imposed a sudden curfew on the whole night, and in the cool of the evening it seemed like an OK idea to have some personal space alone in the van. I'm also pretty sure having a volunteer watchdog, even a delirious and injured one to protect the band gear, probably helped to forestall arguments. Now this watchdog needed some hair of the dog that ripped me a new one last night. It's sweltering out here in this desert and asphalt hell, and starting with majorly dehydrated, I'm every hangover symptom in the alchy-mess cookbook times ten.

I climb back in the van, careful not to touch any of the blazing-hot metal and roll down the front windows, which only serves to allow more hot air in. I crawl back through the toaster-oven van and re-stick my wet body onto the rear bench. The wall of packed-up amps and drum cases provides some shade from the rising blaze of the New Mexico summer sun. For some reason, there are red rose pedals scattered around the floor. They're wilted, trampled and twisted into the dirty van carpet.

It's not long after that everyone piles into the van sounding fresh with rested conversation and the crinkling of paper pastry sleeves and the smell of morning coffees. Dean taps me on the shoulder. "Hey buddy, you alive back there?"

"I hope not," I return, slightly animating my response in an attempt to keep it light, despite it all.

"OK, he's alive!" Dean shouts to the front and we pull back out onto the road. I wake up I don't know how many hours later to the sarcastically shouted words, "Oh boy! The airport La Quinta!"

We all get out and Dave D and Diane go to check in while Matt finds me to apologize.

"I'm sorry," he says timidly. "Are you feeling any better?"

"Maybe if you kneel down and let me kick you in the head, then I probably might," I say with a lighthearted inflection that signals to him he's semi-off the hook. It's necessary in the grand scheme of things but that doesn't mean I care to put any conversation into the subject. *Next.*

With last night now officially flushed down the sewer and into that river that takes all bad memories under that fabled bridge, I show everybody my new head trick. Then, after some concern-tinged amusement we break up into two-room groups where I reside in the party room bathtub for the next hour. Afterwards I find the rest of the hotel room empty but Dr. Dave D has dropped off some aspirin, ointment and a box of band-aids. No Western movie whiskey antiseptic though.

By the time we hit our late-afternoon stage inside one of the countless honky-tonk blues boogie-rock houses along the main music strip of Congress Avenue, the head wound patient is sufficiently sedated. Standing in my center-stage position I can almost get lost in a type of tipsy meditation, with tambourine beats bringing my hands together, then out again, as if I were a conductor. Not the conductor of the music, that of course is Anton, but the conductor of the vibes. Maybe I'm just concussed.

Despite having come all the way out here to Texas, our performance is, as always, not a display to impress or attempt to "win over" a crowd. It is not a bid to be accepted. We are here to spread the good word and you either get it or you don't. There is nothing to mold here, nothing that will bend if you try to make something more stable out of it. It is a highly explosive compound of energy in simple need of a launchpad so it can detonate into the world. What we were in search of was a music business rebel revolutionary explosives expert. There aren't too many of that kind around these days, still-employed ones anyway.

That night our wristbands get us into the VIP party going on in the grand ballroom of the Driskill Hotel. Iggy Pop is headlining the entire weekend on a stage constructed in the intersection down on the street below. I walk out of the cool air conditioning onto the heated balcony and somehow find a spot to watch him strut and flail around. Standing up here on the balcony of the oldest and most lavish hotel in town while looking down on the streets filled tight with people gives the proceedings a ticker-tape celebration feel. This is my first-ever VIP la-di-da industry convention schmooze-fest, and Matt and I, now back to being co-buzzspirators, do the full-tilt-boogie on our free-drink mischief.

With all the other thousands of VIP wristbanders crammed into downtown Austin, we arrive too late to become one of the maximum capacity crowd at the George Clinton P-Funk gig, which apparently went on until 4 a.m. We instead console ourselves with the newly discovered cheap regional beer Lone Star and work on our hangovers until about right after George would have taken his final bow.

Day two begins with more booze and so on and so forth until our second gig at the *Alternative Press* Magazine party taking place in a bowling alley. There is tension. We are three songs in so far and somewhat strangely, when one song ends, Anton immediately starts the next one right up and with no banter or crowd engagement. He immediately segues into the picking lead intro of "The Be Song", a set staple by this point. Matt starts shaking his head angrily to himself. That ol' scowl is back again and when the song finishes, he starts to take his bass off but Anton, not seeing this, goes right into the *jang jang jang jang jang jang jang* start of "Caress". Now Matt's looking incredibly frustrated. Leaning forward over his bass with face pointed straight down, he's punching violently on his bass strings, putting all his weight into it and completely ignoring his participation in the "oh yeah" call-and-response style vocals. I keep a watchful eye on him while I play, just in case anything like a bass guitar or something suddenly gets launched through the air.

Soon enough we all *jang jang jang jang jang jang jang* out the same door we came in through and Matt quickly unplugs his bass and proceeds to walk straight off the stage with it still strapped on.

Anton looks up and sees Matt marching across the bowling lanes toward the opposite side of the building. He leans back to his mic and queries, "Matt, you're just leaving? You don't want to play anymore? Fine, I guess you quit again." Then addressing the audience for the first time, "OK I guess Matt's done playing. Sorry everyone but the bass player's mad so I guess that's it."

Everyone else in the group is in a synchronized group headshake as we all put our instruments down and head out front to smoke on the cement benches lining the entrance path. As we all light up and prepare to bitch about Matt, he suddenly pushes his way through the glass doors and is coming our way in a purposeful stride as he then lifts the bass up and starts charging while holding it by the neck like a battle-axe.

Apparently, Matt had discovered that he had to pee during the first song. When Anton kept going straight into song after song without noticing Matt's comfort level, well, it pushed him over the edge. Now he has snapped again and is charging the far end of our gathering where Anton is sitting.

He comes at Anton, swinging the heavy Jazzmaster bass down hard as Anton quickly slides forward and off the cement bench while simultaneously leaning out of the way just as the bass slams down where his head was just a split second ago. Now on the ground at Matt's feet, he leg sweeps him onto the ground and as soon as Matt makes it down there he's on top of him. Anton roars, "Fuck you, man!" causing Matt to go into his writhing and crying routine. Anton gets up and as he walks away Dean looks over to me and quips, "Somebody better get a stretcher over here, we got more wounded."

I shake my head, roll my eyes and sigh. My head hurts again.

Walk the Earth

"I thought you said you had to be at work at eleven?" Anton says as he parallel parks us under some trees just around the corner from Reckless Records.

"I do," I sigh with heavy weight. Eleven a.m. was fifteen minutes ago now. We'd only just arrived from our all-night drive down from Portland hanging out with The Dandy Warhols. After copious partying on my part, we'd embarked on six hours of desolate night driving until around Mount Shasta when the sun came up quite brightly for the car-crowded other four.

In order to even be able to go up to Portland in the first place, I'd called in sick from a payphone one block away from Reckless just five minutes before I was supposed to be there. Now three days later, I was not only off my rocker but had cultivated a taste of *On the Road*, with nobody pushing my buttons but me and in the way I wanted them to be played in my own life-jazz solo. I was set free. Free all the way, free to be one of the few that knows it, isn't confused about it, isn't looking for it. I was there and I was it and I was now, baby! Blast off!

Despite this star-spangled inner revolution, I had to hustle to work now. As I slowly made my way toward Reckless the sun was absolutely blinding and instantly burnt away anything that I thought I had left physically. Another five steps and my mind went. I was dead tired and I had no idea what I was going to do when I'd be required to articulate words in mere moments.

As I enter the store, the first thing I see is the manager Andy hanging behind the shop counter which was unusual. He was a prim and proper Englishman and the nicest and most understanding boss

I'd probably ever have. Today he's waiting for me. As I get closer, I start to feel even worse and so much so that his face starts turning green. Closer still and further worrisome, as I get right up to him his face just starts melting. I was more fucked up than I thought.

"Ah good," he says in a tight-lipped and not at all in an "ah good" tone. "Come with me."
I follow him up the stairs and toward his office. On our way, we pass Dracula sitting at the small employee break table. He appears to have decided to "go public" and was not only letting his sharp teeth show but also displayed the fact he'd recently been sucking someone's blood by leaving it trickling down his chin. I knew I was seriously sleep-deprived, but I was really starting to hallucinate. Dracula gives me a sympathetic look as we continue on our way to the gallows.

We walk into Andy's office and he wastes no time in handing me already prepared termination papers. Without even giving them a glance I sign. There was no argument to be made.

With the deed done, Andy's regular and familiar friendly tone re-emerges. "Sorry Joel, we really do like you," he says as the green melting drips on his face jiggle. Now that I was able to look him directly in the face I could see that the green skin tone was actually thick crusting make-up and the melting drips were glue-affixed rubber dollops. "Good luck to you," he says, and as we shake hands, he picks up a tall witch's hat from his desk and pops it atop his head.

That's when I realize that for once it wasn't my drug-addled brain hallucinating, it was Halloween.

On my way back down the stairs, Tonya Harding in her Olympic ice-skating uniform completely ignores me as we cross paths. For some, the nightmare of my work ethic was over.

Despite my only living a block away from work, I was late every day. I loved my job and didn't want to lose it, but it was slowly starting to make less sense that I would skip out on the type of life experiences I was having in order to go to a job and listen to people sing about the life experiences I had to miss in order to keep the job.

I walk out of Reckless Records with a couple days' back pay and a serious need to escape the current reality situation. I decide that this is a job for the truest and greatest escapist drug, the movies. I pull a *San Francisco Guardian* out from a sidewalk dispenser and checked the showtimes. *Pulp Fiction* was playing at The Vogue Theater, which was just a fifteen-minute bus ride on the 43 Masonic line. The film's popularity had been so overblown that it had put me off seeing it, but by now it had been out for months and was doing its last rounds. Nothing else sounded good so I thought alright, let's see what all the hype is about.

A few hours later, I walk out of the single-screen movie theater now no longer having a job to make money to pay my rent. Still, I was no longer worried. I'd just received an instant-karma message from the cinematic universe. I now knew what I was going to do with my life. I was going to *Walk the earth, meet people and get into adventures. Like Caine in 'Kung Fu'.*

BJM are doing a noontime in-store for a record shop in the South Bay. Anton is picking me up at the address in the Excelsior District I'd given him last night, because I knew that this was going to be another all-nighter. What I didn't know then was that I would be in rare totally demolished form. Unemployment had by now led to not being able to come up with my share of the rent and I was now basically homeless, bouncing from party place to party place, and it was getting harder and harder to even keep customary bender lengths in check.

Still, everything had seemed to be going fine or whatever it was, drugs-booze-drugs-drugs-booze style, but then these big blue oval science-fiction looking hits of ecstasy came out. Not long after the orgy started and the next thing I find out is that despite my enthusiasms for all things 60s, I'm just not an orgy person. Not that I'm in any way against it, mind you, but joining in the naked group grope just wasn't going to float my boat, seemingly. There is no peer pressure greater than that of an orgy situation, let me tell you, for those who do not know this already, and so one must choose to either be naked or be clothed on the couch, the problem or the solution as it were, depending on which side you are on, and I decided my side was outside.

Couchsurfing

From the grey stone apartment steps I watch the cement sidewalk roll back and forth like a confused escalator as the grey sky above twinkles oddly while the ornate grey Victorian houses across the street march toward me, jerking from side to side like Atari *Space Invaders* until just as they get up close they suddenly flash-reappear back where they'd started across the street and start the whole process again until I stop looking when then again and beyond that, there's not much reasoning or rhyming on offer this time, as this was all weird and whatever else and anyway why I was feeling so fucking unnecessarily high was the real mystery. Mystery has a knack of turning into misery and after that settles in for a while then Anton pulls up.

Unstable condition remains stable, and it's way too late for displays of normality now. I can't even formulate an explanation to Anton, fresh faced and sipping to-go coffee. Something else must have been in the drugs, and I certainly wouldn't put it past certain people. "Hi-i," he says in a tone I take as not totally sure he wants to spend the next forty minutes in a compact car with me in the state I'm in.

I start gingerly but end landing hard into the passenger seat, then use my body weight to aid my arm in shutting the door, then rebounding back, I fall flat up against it, cheek to window glass, and not even trying to hide the fact that I am fucked.

He has his parka on, which fences his neck in mod fur and his front bangs give a half-inch before lush eyebrows pick things back up and help to frame his handsome and gentle-with-driven intent features. He is exasperated in vibe tone, because it's the first thing in the morning and here-we-go already, but still a tolerant and a patient friend. I was certainly not making for the most attractive scene, sweating bullets while physically having a hard time not pouring out of my seat and onto the floor of the car, and I knew it. At least I'd made it though. No matter how bad things ever got for myself as a result of myself, missing the boat was always a non-option. He takes a drag off his now down to stubbing size Camel non-filter and blows it out the window with a hard sigh. Thankfully, this is as direct as the call-out gets, because I know I'm a wreck right now and it's already embarrassing.

The medium-sized record store is very white and filled with long island racks of mostly CDs, the popular physical music form of the day. I'm still feeling pretty rank but Matt has a pint of hooch and I take a good pull. Dean is in heaven in moments like these and signifies so upon first drinking in my demolished state. "Not feeling so hot today, huh? *Huh huh.*" He casually smiles, only barely hiding his relish at my current plight with all the effort of frisbeeing a trash can lid onto a overflowing garbage dumpster. Still, it's nice to be entertaining, even on this level, and all of these different shades of support are welcome. It's a fertile ground where I can begin to make amends rather than face judgey vibes that would make it all way worse.

Brian is preoccupied with setting up the drums at the front of the store, looking detached and serious. Jeff is in the nearby corner nodding along to Del, the store owner and once BJM manager for a night. Del has sort of a parrot-shaped face, with long thin purple hair and a high shrill voice that stays that way even in casual conversation. He knows a lot about music and has a lot of opinions that go along with all that and we hear them fly around the room like large squawking cartoon birds until we can finally drown it out with our backwards window display inside the shop's all-glass storefront.

Matt is melodically moody, Dean in shades of in-play serious and serene, Anton sings and strums the ship forward and Jeff now begins to wail a solo with jaw clenched, poofing pompadour threatening to float him away like a bouffant balloon when then it hits me, the lights at the tip of the shrapnel that signals the very beginnings of being led back to feeling normal. Coming down while coming up on the music is a metamorphosis most true and I'm soon to be fully inside the safe confines of the spirit thanks to the band and the music, *this music*, now in a horizontal sonic avalanche rattling the rows and rows of plastic CDs, with us all together on the pulpit of sorts and it's this spirituality that washes all badness away. The largess of the reverb and the bomp and twang dancing over it as I keep the chiming beat with the drums and soon enough the inner lights grow brighter within the damage like a salt lamp being dimmed up, and I am free again.

Despite being saved, for today anyway, I'd very soon be disappearing again, this time all the way out of town. Blasted drugs, in a few months from now I'd be back fresh-faced and yet wind up doing more of you than ever.

Taken days before my first "disappearance"

Arrival

Bang! Bang! Bang!

On the door for the tenth time and many more buzzer rings. I look sheepishly back at my father who was casually leaning against the side of his white pickup truck with my two boxes and sack of worldlies in the flatbed. "He said to show up at two o'clock," I say, knowing he already knew this as it had been the plan for the last week. My main concern now was making my old man loiter around a San Francisco south of Market Street alley for what was now over half an hour. Despite this being a rather open and sunny side-street alley comprised of mostly living and office spaces, this part of the city could still be pretty sketchy. What was mostly making me antsy was the zombie-like wino duo doing a slow-motion lumber-waltz off in the distance, slowly swaying in a zigzagged orbit getting increasingly closer to us.

Checking again for signs of wear on his expression, he actually didn't seem bothered at all; with his arms folded casually he readjusts his stance, then repositions his lean back up against the side of his truck. He was in his daily middle-aged uniform of Wrangler jeans, blue nylon faux fur-collared jacket and perma-Mike Nesmith hairdo that he'd had longer than I'd been alive. These days it was shorter and smaller compared to its 1970s blow-dryer glory days. Both his overall features and personality were ironically equal parts Clint Eastwood and Alan Alda.

I hover the bottom of my fist up to the door for yet another attempt when suddenly from up above I hear a very casual and familiar "Heyy maan". I look up. It was my in-moments-to-be roommate Nick visible only from the neck up and sideways directly above me from a small window on the next floor.

Finally, I'd turned the engine over. We then hear an unrhythmic downstairs trample as Nick appears at the door with no apologies and a look of almost hidden bemusement during my introductions.

He was more rugged than most of my other male friends in his look of crumpled white T and rolled blue jeans. His beanie was angled a little more sideways than usual as he'd obviously just woken up and gotten dressed on his way down the stairs.

From here it takes only a few minutes to have my belongings deposited into my new small room up on the second floor and then goodbyes. I could feel my father's head-scratching on my own as he pulled away for the three-hour return trip back up to the sticks, but he was used to head-scratching by now.

For the last two months I'd been living in a 1970s-era camper parked on my parents' tiny property. I had always promised myself I'd leave San Francisco if I ever had to lean on my friends too hard or was tempted to let "desperation" affect my decision making. After working my way down to the level of a couch-surfing twenty-four-hour party person for the last six months, I had finally started to teeter dangerously close to breaking my code. Finding a J.O.B. within the San Francisco city lines was not on my menu and I had become completely busted. So, I pulled the emergency cord of family and five hours later was riding to where my parents had moved, up in the California Sierra Nevada foothills to "get my shit together". I was twenty-five and for right or wrong, to all my friends and even more pretend-friends, it was a disappearing act. I told no one. I was gone, baby. To be continued.

Through an acquaintance of my mother's, I had gotten a job working the front desk graveyard shift at an eighteenth-century gold rush-era hotel. It was famous for being haunted, but I was too busy wrestling my own inner demons to notice any of those rumored in-house residents. I was finally all the way off the snorts and had made just about enough bread to call action on "San Francisco: Take 2" when I saw Oasis perform on *Letterman* doing "Morning Glory". Right then and there I decided "fuck this" and immediately started thumbing through my little red book. My finger-dialing went all the way to page "Z" when an excited friend, Zee, invited me to move into a new warehouse space she was setting up with another one of my friends, Nick.

Nick takes me out to breakfast a few blocks away at Rocco's Italian Cafe restaurant. The food was the most vivid proof so far that I was really back in San Francisco. The deal was he was now in the final processes of having completely refurbished the whole building. He had not only partitioned out new rooms on the warehouse ground floor, but had connected it with the circa 1930s two-bedroom apartment living space on the second floor. The last and biggest project was to build a full state-of-the-art recording studio with adjacent sleeping quarters in the back where bands could both record and lodge. This was the ultimate goal for the place, to be built piece by piece as the revenue came in. He didn't mention where the revenue sources would come from, but I could venture some pretty good guesses. In what would ultimately be a practice to protect me, I'd have to get used to venturing guesses.

Having finished breakfast and paid the check, we push up from our chairs. He gives me a once-over and smirks, "Man, you got fat. Wanna line?"

Many hours later, blue dawn gradually overtakes the room's electric light as the switch into day mode fades in. Nick breaks the silence with the drawling opening chord of Verve's *A Storm in Heaven* and the album's lucid vibeyness fills the room.

Suddenly, the whole place starts to shake along with the rattling of the large automatic steel garage door below us beginning to crank open. It's my other new housemate Zee returning from who knows where in her 1960 Fiat convertible. The sound of the motor moves from the street to inside the garage where it reverberates loudly before switching off in time with the garage door now starting to vibrate its way back down. Immediately we can hear double-stair prancing that rises fast as it gets louder.

"Jo-el!"

I'm there at the top to meet and catch into a big double-swing-around hug. She's dressed in all black from head to toe in the 1950s bohemian intellectual style of turtleneck sweater, Capri pants and flats. I move in close to her pixie-like face to rub noses while adding tousle to her foppish black hair and she then excitedly grabs me by the hand and we run back down the stairs for a grand tour of the ground floor that she presides over. There is one room multi-locked and off limits, but her warning comes with a grin of a *Lion, the Witch and the Wardrobe*-style mystery and so therefore is not a serious matter.

"You have to fix your room!" she excitedly declares by way of tipping me the wink that I can do whatever I want to it. My room upstairs was very small and in contrast to down here had that old-school San Francisco apartment feel that comes from decades-long rotating tenants coming and going by way of misfortune, change or death. Its latest coat is freshly painted and this time in darks of deep grey, maroon and black. The kitchen is next to my room, leading out the back door onto a black-tarred roof which could immediately drop an unobservant one down through a skylight. Beyond that and all the way back to the street-side corner of the building are four rope ladders in individual piles. *In case of what?* I wondered but didn't ask. *Alien invasion?* The current number-one television show is *The X-Files*, and the number-one movie this week is *Independence Day,* so I decide to go with my first instinctual explanation of aliens. These days extraterrestrials had become such a big part of the everyday media machine that it was starting to feel like we were all being groomed to take them on as the next big worldwide propaganda scare threatening our way of life. In hindsight, I wish that one would have gone down. The full extent of my concerns with aliens was that I just wanted to dance with them at full-moon beach parties while on ecstasy.

After a trip to a nearby hardware store, I paint my whole room black from ceiling to floor. Then I line each wall with three Rubbermaid outdoor garbage can lids. These particular lids had the same circular indention specs as the British mod symbol, so I paint them in the classic red, white and blue formation. Then, with my mod garbage complete, I lie back on my mattress for the first time after a first two-days' night and sleep while being enveloped in the wall-to-wall wet paint fumes.

The next morning, I return from the corner liquor store to find the garage door wide open, which is kinda like having the whole front of the building open. Inside Zee is rifling through the glove box of her convertible. The canvas top is up and she appears to have entered through the opposite driver's side as her body is fully extended in dark shadowy silhouette visible through the rear window. The click of my vintage Florsheim zip-boot heels on the concrete broadcasts my arrival and she turns her head around.

"Hey!" she calls out. She has one foot still in color dangling out of the open door. Then, reversing herself back out and squatting on the door frame, she shouts, "Do you have to get a job?"

"I hope not," I say smiling.

"I know something you can do—it's easy! I'll meet you in your room in ten minutes!"

"Cool!" I shout back and head up the stairs.

About twenty minutes later she appears at my doorway just as I'm flipping over my Marvin Gaye *What's Going On* cassette to side two. The opening piano and flute on the track "Right On" starts up and before the seven-and-a-half-minute song is over, I am fully schooled in my new household duty. Making sheets of LSD.

On the mutually agreed-upon day, she would deliver to my room a little glass medical jar of the clear liquid mix and twelve sheets, or a "book", of ever-changing design blotter paper. My tools consist of just gloves and a small plastic syringe-type applicator. I clip each clean sheet onto a small easel, dip the applicator into the jar and paint the LSD onto the paper as slowly and evenly as I can make myself. She'd designed her own artwork for the blotter sheets, so in order to use the designs she'd bring her perforated blotter paper to be specially printed at of all places the Kinko's copy store on upper Market. To have a Xerox clerk personally print your LSD blotter paper was bold, especially as it had the individual dose perforations on it. I ask her if she was worried about this but she just smiles. She just thought it was funny, which of course it was.

I had to apply the acid onto each sheet meticulously and thoroughly from top to bottom, corner to corner, edge to edge—no drips. I would then carefully place each wet sheet in my vintage gold-wire vinyl LP display rack to dry. A few hours later she would wander back up and take away the dried sheets, and with that all my household bills would be paid for the month.

Reappearing

"Anton's here," my inner secretary suddenly informs me from the frontal lobe office. I'd tracked him down via telephone yesterday and I was now to join him for three different performances on various outdoor stages around town for the all day, city-wide Noise Pop Music Festival. The odd part was we were going as a duo. *Where'd the band go?* I very much wondered but did not ask.

Conveniently already dressed for the most part, I simply zip on my leather boots (never pass out with your boots on), scoop up my leather jacket and slide it on as I stumble down the stairs.

"Hi Joel," Anton says with an almost hidden air of relief as the door swings open. From bright blue skies above, the sun is in partial solar eclipse position behind his head as a burst of light escapes through a puffy white cloud and refracts from behind an arched eyebrow.

"Hey man!" I shout with excited yet expected surprise. This was our first face-to-face meeting since my returning from the unannounced "disappearance."

At his hip he's holding the upside-down neck of an acoustic guitar that's strapped across his back. On the sidewalk next to him is another guitar in a weathered leather case.

"Listen, let's go play some music," he says in a simple fashion that suggests an invitation into intrigue. I pick up the other guitar case and we begin to make our way to the first performance which is just a few blocks away on a stage constructed in downtown's Civic Center Plaza. Despite the sun we're both dressed day for night, him in a white knit sweater with a bar of blue decorative Scandinavian folk design around the chest and me in black denim, wool and leather.

As we walk, I can hear the rat-a-tat-tat of military drums in my head as if we're marching off into battle.

For the second time a full lineup had quit all at once. "I don't care, people can come and people can go and I'll just figure out a new way to make it work," he explained matter-of-factly. I was grateful that it didn't seem necessary for me to explain the details of my months' long unannounced disappearance, so I didn't ask questions either. It was time to get back to business.

Grunge was still the music king and although we had a feverish Britpop movement in San Francisco replete with the fashions, optimism and chemicals that fueled it all, it was still an underground society. Big things could happen for the band and quickly if there were only some way to break past the traditional label business process or regular press channels and directly share the music with people, especially in places like the UK. The only tools we had available to us were handmade demo cassettes and the post office. For an unsigned band, there are no shortcuts to this system. No way to bypass the record syndicate and reach people directly.

Anton has a pint of Old Grand-Dad whiskey on him which had been a popular choice for us mainly due to a low price point that could still render a merciful flavor, and at this moment, also a nice "welcome back". We each take a good pull to push the edge back but not enough to take it away as it's going to be a long day of running around San Francisco.

From the urban cement Civic Center "park" I can barely see the Ferry Building clock tower all the way down the far length of Market Street (also the final stage location of our one-day music tour) where both hands are pointing straight up to our noontime showtime.

Performing in the stark light of morning under the reality sun spotlight is out of my regular comfort zone and I don't even know the new songs. There are about two hundred people scattered around waiting for us to start while outside this free-entertainment perimeter it's the "just another day" realities of sleepy homeless people—"Hey, knock off that racket! People trying to sleep here!"—representing all vertical movements while horizontally it's officially the lunch hour time hustle and bustle of people rushing to and from work in every possible direction.

We are this stage's first of the day and it's time to start rubbing two sticks together as the sun is blazing and we climb up onto the stage. I look around and make a "how did I get up here" face for the audience as if I've just been tricked into this as Anton clips on a capo to the third fret of his guitar neck. Ready, we then discuss what the plan is for the first time.

"Just watch me," he says off-mic, then with a single nod he goes straight into a song I'd never heard. Its immediate strumming is what seems like a small intro but I can't be sure so I hold while internally searching for where the beat is going to be. Then with his lips moving toward the mic he quickly changes his strumming pattern, *here we go* and I cast off on instinct into my beat pattern flow which is in time as he pulls his quick-draw vocal.

"She said, I love you
And I know it can't be wrong
'cause I've waited for so long"

From behind dark sunglasses, my eyes are following his strum downstrokes on the "one" beat. *Watch the hand.*

It's a bouncing tune floating on a romance cloud no one is enjoying more than I under the hot sun. As I beat the tambourine against my upper thigh, I feel the rare immediacy of hearing an unheard song that is familiar, like it had always existed but no one had opened its portal into this world yet.

That familiar feeling is back and coming on strong like a fresh injection with the potency rising and rising as we journey through the song's two and a half minutes. This stripped-down earthy presentation of just the two of us performing brought on a "do or die" feeling of intimacy that made me feel like it was us against the world. In the absence of voltage, these new acoustic folk-based songs of Anton's and the naked power of this current presentation scenario creates a magic swirling vortex all around us where no one could deny its beauty, humanity and its rightness, regardless.

"Where now?" I ask after our twenty-minute set.

"Alamo" is his simple response and in keeping with the mission: least information as possible theme.

When we reach the four city-block-sized hilltop park, we begin to weave our way up through the carefully laid haphazardly arranged picnic blankets and random bodies spread throughout and all along the way up to the top where the sectioned-off performance area lies just inside the border of treed shade. Our view while playing will be a big ol' blue sky which is at its fullest up here on the hill above the surrounding blocks of living structures making us level with the city skyline beyond.

It's an easy breezy grassy green that decorates this family-friendly portion of our day tour and they are represented throughout the three tiers of descending lawn leading down to the row of famous "Painted Ladies" houses. I get us halfway down the hooch bottle while gazing toward the side street where Dean's apartment is just out of view over the other side of the hill.

What happened to those guys? Like birds that would leave the fold but couldn't quite get their own nests built right, they would be back. Again. For myself, I may have just had my own time-out, but unlike the rest, it was the result of self-induced destruction rather than just getting fed up with everything. Asking for things that go beyond normal existence, and at the levels we were after, not only required being capable of handling every emotion on the spectrum chart but also going beyond the breaking points of every one.

Mara had been my fill-in during my absence and had also brought with her along to the stage keyboards and her lead vocal on one of the strongest songs "Anemone". It always made sense to me that she'd be a well-fitted BJM member. Firstly, we weren't standard "Duuude..." rock guys, and Mara was a real musician. Despite her Monica Vitti-esque good looks, she was well beyond the bubbly stage candy you'd just hand a tambourine to. Wait...

There's lots of multicolored flannel flapping in the breeze up here like grunge rock flags tied around waists and unbuttoned body trunks. Regardless, when we go into "Free and Easy", everyone seems to agree it's a fitting soundtrack for all the extras present in this scene.

The sun is starting to set as we make it back down to the beacon of the San Francisco waterfront that is the Ferry Building. As we finally enter the darkness of live music's correct time zone, the

Ramadan-sized festival of GE lightbulbs lighting the thousands of offices in the financial district refract off the Bay's water.

I breathe the sea air in deep while walking up to the bronze Gandhi statue standing pedestaled in the center of the gathering audience. From below him, I investigate his life-sized feature curves and gleaming angles while the Ferry Building's clock tower rises tall and large over his shoulders.

Back on the large rental stage, the sound woman and Anton are getting the guitar soundchecked so I decide to sneak off for a toot. This was actually the first time today that I'd even thought about it, this day of music was a much better high, but there's just something about the city lights at night that start turning on all the "why not?" idea lights.

I walk around and behind the stage to a long stretch of pier railing, then find a spot to lean against not occupied by the many seagulls lining the top and tiers of the old wooden fence. Letting myself settle into a publicly visual "nothing going on here" scenario, I watch a ferry boat make its nearby approach as another is off in the distance bobbing away in the opposite direction.

Watchin' the ships roll in...

Looking above it and up to the Bay Bridge, I make the panoramic observation journey across its huge span, starting from the faraway end that's buried deep into Yerba Buena Island and all along its vantage growth spanning over the chasm of glistening ocean water until it nestles its firm largeness between the confines of city buildings and out of view.

With a toot-toot I then give the scene one last goodbye when suddenly I see spread along the railing next to me a gang of rough-and-tumble-looking city seagulls who are each in nautical fashion-style combinations of striped shirts, vests, cocked navy caps and mariners hats, one even has an eye patch while most all have lit cigarettes hanging from their beaks. *What was in that stuff? Are they waiting around for the music?* As I walk back to the stage, I'm overcome with a feeling like Anton and I were once again two wayward dreamers up against an indifferent world, like in *La Strada* or *Midnight Cowboy*. I can't help but feel he *must* think the same thing. Maybe I'm just high. Maybe...

Later that week Anton had Diane's car on loan, as he would from time to time on her days off. He picks me up at the warehouse and we drive out to "The Compound" recording studio where he's going to play me the newly completed album *Their Satanic Majesties' Second Request*.

Upon climbing into the passenger side of the crappy white compact, the car stereo is blasting the intro to "Straight Up and Down" from the brand-new *Take It from the Man!* CD, the album recorded before I left and released on legendary garage rock and pop punk indie label Bomp! Records during my "disappearance". In addition to *Their Satanic Majesties' Second Request*, Anton was now preparing a stripped-down album of four-track recordings made from some of the songs we'd played at the all-day festival. *Not too shabby.*

Right as Anton hits the gas the chord progression begins its thick chugging strums and he starts a PowerPoint presentation. "It starts off like 'I'm Waiting for the Man' backwards in a different key but then it's going on and the change comes in and you're like OK, they say they want us to *be ourselves*, great. But *wait*, you can't be yourself unless you free yourself. OK? Then it breaks down and all of a sudden it's like the fucking Righteous Brothers with a 'Get Off of My Cloud' vocal style. Then it switches again and all of a sudden it's like 'Sympathy for the Devil' and 'Hey Jude' at the same time and you realize that the four-chord progression in the chorus is the exact same as 'Sweet Jane', 'Sympathy for the Devil', and 'Hey Jude' and they *all* came out at the *same time*. They can sue each other for ripping each other off, but they can't sue me—I'm the only one who created something new out of it. But it's just to show a thing. Y'know what I'm saying?"

He's excited (rightly so) and begins to break down other points of the album for me, maybe just in case I'd forgotten since I'd been gone, or it's him that's already forgotten I was there at all, but most likely he's getting amped up to talk to the press about the three new albums coming out before the year 1996 is over. "...but this was de-producing. People lost track using all these modern recording techniques..." he continues while crushing out a filterless into the maximum-capacity filled ashtray of half-buried stubs. His hand comes back up with a Horseshoe Cafe to-go cup which he sips off of carefully. Being just before noontime it's probably only his fourth large coffee. These two items are his "usual" when sitting at his permanently reserved table "in the zone".

We pull off the 101 and head into the southeastern section of San Francisco, Hunter's Point. Originally an old naval shipyard area, it's currently a low-income neighborhood consisting almost exclusively of black families originally mass-relocated from one of the most historic old-school "hoods" in all of black culture, the Fillmore district. The Fillmore was the West Coast epicenter for jazz and blues in the 1950s and 60s until it fell victim to "urban renewal" in the 70s in which the city wiped away shops, clubs and over thirty thousand residents in the name of creating more convenient thoroughfares for predominantly white neighborhoods to commute to and from their downtown financial district jobs. It's also possibly one of the most toxic places in the entire country as in actual toxic waste, which the government had previously mass-buried here. Today the military aspect is long gone and crack is king in this dilapidated area where stop signs are to be treated as only at-your-own-risk suggestions while we travel deeper into it and reach The Compound.

We pull up and get out on the trash dumped-off parking area dirt, where you can see the Bay close by as well as the top of the massive sports stadium Candlestick Park, where in 1966 The Beatles played their last-ever concert. Ramshackle as any structure can be on the outside, once through the fortress-like door, it's a studio nerd's wonderland of state-of-the-art up-to-the-minute equipment, almost to a science fiction level. We enter and head toward the control room, our way low-lit yet lined with warm multicolored console boards and rig lights.

"Jeff's gone so we need to find somebody until he comes back or something," Anton laments as we drop into the two rolling chairs in front of the giant mixing board.

"And shows are coming up," I offer so as to have something to offer.

94

"I know, but it's fine. We'll get somebody." He gives the thought a single shrug while loading *Their Satanic Majesties' Second Request* for playback.

The opening album track "All Around You" starts and it causes me to react by envisioning Peter Max rainbows beginning to flow out of every speaker, then multi-curlicuing around the room until they all meet at my head and flow into my ears while leaving crimson audio hallucination trails of clover dangling around the room. My eyes have turned into spinning kaleidoscopes and I become hyper aware of this being the first completely successful attempt at a legitimate *Sgt. Pepper*-style album opener since the second attempt was made less successfully by the Stones on their, ahem, "first" request. More exciting was it being a modern experimental version of classic experimental sounds; it didn't sound like any other band from back in the day and especially not now. It felt as if my smiling head detached from my body and floated upward while slow-spinning round and around. I was instantly listening to one of my favorite albums that I'd never heard, encoding itself into me in real time. Any and all campaigning I'd ever done was toward this exact kind of result and these results went even beyond my impassioned evangelizing. This was a completely different experience from *Take It from the Man!*, as in that recording process you would listen to each song over and over again for days and weeks as new tracks are added and tweaked upon. This I was listening to for the first time completely finished from top to bottom, side to side, inside and out, as a fan.

"Soo groovy, Anton. This is way more righteous than I even expected!"

He just smiles. "I *told* you."

Left: Holding court with "Anemone" Mara Keagle

Below: Dean and I seeing a CD copy of the freshly pressed *Their Satanic Majesties' Second Request* for the first time

Left: Our manager Dave D

Anton and I backstage
at Bimbo's 365 Club
for our first non-duo
performance since
my return to San
Francisco

Animal Pants

Something called "Burning Man" was going on in the Nevada desert and the warehouse door buzzer had been going off every few minutes all day. On comes the next wave of commotion via Zee parading up the stairs with a kite string of about ten ravers parading behind her who are all very dayglo deep in it. First in the Fellini-esque line and holding hands with the kite herself is an older probably thirty-something girl with long bleached white dreads. What's most noticeable though are her pants. They're made completely out of small factory sewn-on stuffed animals. This is the first time I've ever seen stuffed animal pants.

In contrast to the dress of this brightly colored crew, they're all in a bad mood apparently due to the strip searches and anal probes received by everyone at the San Francisco Airport. I piece together the situation through the random complaints while watching them all file past and to the left into Nick's large bedroom. As soon as they disappear and the door closes behind them, it reopens and the stuffed animal pants wander back past me and straight into my room. I follow her and by the time I get to the doorway she's already flopped onto my mattress.

Her legs of smiling stuffed animals are now stretched out and lining the wall creating a similar arrangement that a child might make on her bed.

"Whose room is this?" she queries matter-of-factly and without even looking in my direction.

"Mine," I answer back quickly.

She's visibly annoyed that my response is not an immediate capitulation to her royal desire of my new room for her and her party of animal pant subjects. Her display of obvious dissatisfaction is in great opposition to the gallery of smiles stitched onto her legs, although now on closer inspection, some of the creatures are looking a bit worn and faded. Especially the ones around the knees—faces dirty, stretched and becoming disfigured. The smiles on those faces looked less innocent and happy and have morphed into more crazed and twisted madhouse-like smiles. Balding faces, random missing noses and eyes reveal that they've seen quite enough of this never-ending vagabond life. Pants like these to a person like this are worn forever until no longer wearable and then trashed.

It appears realizing this, some animals have begun secret escape proceedings, unattaching themselves slowly, quietly, stitch by stitch so as to not be discovered and fixed back on. Like tired soldiers in a losing war, they are worn on day after day. They themselves are the draftees to make her "party all the time" statement to the world. The current morale among the party animals looks to be at an all-time low from the day-after-day drug sweats on the inside and the grime of the streets and warehouse party floors on the outside now visibly accumulated within the folds of their weathered animal facial features. Euthanasia for the whole litter was obviously looming.

She doesn't attempt to rise nor even lift a finger, but rather twists her mouth in disapproving annoyance. With her elbow buried deep in my pillow, her hand holding her dread head, she taps her extended foot at the air in impatience, seemingly a signal to let me know it was time for me to retire from her new chambers backwards and bowing.

"Hey Joel, come meet Dill!" I suddenly hear Zee shout from halfway down the stairs. I sigh and go down to meet her. She grabs my hand and leads me back through the white corridors to a free and closet-like all-white empty space.

"This is Dill! He lives here now too!" she proudly announces. Despite the steady flow of artists, organizers, and outlaw entrepreneurs, she could also be the "everybody gets a trophy" type when it came to her curated selection of eccentrics. I don't know what you'd call Dill. He wore a ruffly sleeved, pirate-like shirt and even had tight fitting white pantaloons on. In fact, everything that he owned had to be the color white, and not just everything he wore, but *everything* had to be white, even including what he ate and drank. Needless to say, he had just moved into a closet-sized heaven.

In our brief time together under the same roof, he would only communicate with me in an *Amadeus*-style laugh. The laugh had a register spectrum that started at silent hand over mouth shyness and from there it moved up to varying levels of flittering laughter that topped out with a loud shriek like the one in the film. After a few kitchen run-ins over milk and white bread with the crusts cut off it became apparent that the real fact of the matter was the whole performance was just a judgment call on his part and simply a fake way to not have to talk to people like me who weren't "weird" enough for him.

In order to fulfill his ivory code, his past-the-shoulder length wavy hair and musketeer style mustache were bleached from its obvious-by-the-roots natural brown. Unfortunately, his personal salon skills could only get his hair as light as faded yellow and not technically color-code compliant. Also adding to the image fray was the strength of laundry detergent vs vagabond life. Through his airs of regal wishful thinking he'd elevated himself into a ballroom cake, while in boring reality he was actuality more like buttered popcorn.

Back upstairs I find the Queen of the Animal Pants has moved on from my room back over to the rest of the crunchy ravers who are all strewn around the floor in a 1960s hippie exploitation film formation. Suddenly, a Spin Doctors intern darts up, pupils peeled back to the dark side of the moon and announces, "Man, I gotta sit down!" and then promptly does so. It's then I'm informed by Nick that they are all in the "K hole", or rather, on the latest chemical raver companion, ketamine. All my eye-rolling was now officially giving me a headache.

"Yeah, I know," Nick says agreeing with my expression. "Hey, my brother, let's you and me go run a little errand," he now says rather than asks. Something odd was up.

Ten minutes later, we're in a cab driving in the direction of Golden Gate Park. It's a peculiar move considering he owns a Harley-Davidson motorcycle, but I'm also glad to not be riding on back of its two-man built for one seating accommodations. Nick's fidgety and not just artificially, turning around every minute or so, or messing with his beeper.

We're approaching the wide green expanse of the Panhandle Park, the number two "happening" grounds for the Summer of Love and all manner of things 60s San Francisco groovy. Suddenly his latest over the shoulder turns into a double take.

"Fuck, man. Change of plans, turn left here," he quickly instructs the cabbie while readjusting his beanie cap lower.

Almost as soon as we turn, "OK, here!" and the taxi begins to pull over as his door is already opening. "C'mon!" he says urgently while tossing a balled up bill onto the front seat. We jump out onto Baker Street in between the DMV and the mouth of Panhandle Park.

"Run!"

We start down the sidewalk to Oak Street. It's a four-lane, one-way thoroughfare, and rounding the corner I take my first glance back and I see the car now—black, medium-sized with tinted windows. They are indeed following us and make the turn onto Oak Street. Now committed to the one-way street direction, we start to cut through the four lanes of traffic one by one, forcing the cars to either change lanes or hit brakes. He has an authoritative force about him and the drivers seem to recognize this, stopping for him without honks or window guffaws.

Some people just have it and some don't, I guess, but as for myself I'm cool with wondering for now as I follow the stopped-car path he's carved over to the other side where we then cut running back the other way against the traffic direction. Now whoever is in the car following us has no choice but to either leave their car where it is in the street or continue on to the next block and loop around hoping we're still here.

Luckily, there are always cabs going down Oak and we wave one down as if it were planned in advance. "Castro Theater," Nick commands with our double-door slamming and we then continue down Oak just two short blocks before taking the right on Divisadero Street toward the Castro District.

Even though I'd really like to, I don't ask what the fuck is happening due to the presence of the cab driver and also because I doubt I'd get an answer which is probably for my own good. We make our way over and down into the frozen-in-70s-time fairy tale-like hills and valley of the Castro and pull up in front of The Castro Theater, my favorite art-house and classic cinema movie house in town. Right now it feels strangely more like a drive-in theater, as the sensations I'd normally get watching thriller movies inside it are currently happening to me right outside. As we exit the cab, I look up to read *Harold and Maude* on the marquee, which only makes things worse when its clear we're not going inside the theater to hide out for a while, as he heads in the opposite direction to an apartment gate nestled between storefronts. He pushes one of the numbered buzzers and we wait while I take turns rubber-necking the street view and trying to read his face for signs of my future.

Bzzzt—

"Hello?" It's a young, male-sounding voice.

"Heyy man, it's me, I'm sorry to drop on you like this...ah, but I need to come up."

"You came...you're here? Uhh...OKaay, I guess...OK, I'll buzz you in..."

BRAAAMP

Nick pulls the iron gate open and I follow him through the entryway and building door as he whispers, "Go straight through to the back and out the trash door. I'll catch you later."

He heads up the stairs and I continue down the narrow corridor past the staircase leading out the back of the building and onto the smaller and very peaceful Collingwood Street. Unlike the hustle and bustle of Castro Street, it's so still and quiet back here it's almost like walking through a portal back into a pre-day drama dream reality. I pause in all its tranquil breezy bushy green linings around rows of Victorians in rainbow colors.

Suddenly, a black car with tinted windows pulls out from down the street and is slow-rolling toward me. I turn right up the sidewalk and the car casually cruises up alongside me, then slows further down matching my walking pace. The windows aren't moving so I sneak a look to assess the possible intent but I only see my reflection in the glass as the car holds my speed. I'm trying to look casual outwardly, while inside adrenaline is flash-flooding my entire being.

After the eternity of walking only a quarter of a block, it's pretty clear it wants me to know it's following me.

On the corner the street narrows into a forced merge lane onto the busiest street in town, Market Street, while for me the sidewalk veers into an inward walkway path with stairs down to the Church Street underground MUNI station. I take the steps down two by two and get on the next train.

Cookie Jar

I wake up into the night and begin stumbling around to confirm what the silence and unlit stillness indicates: I'm alone. On completion of my first second-floor lap, I begin a second, this time going deeper into Nick's room and over to his dresser where his large glass drug surface lives. I know due to its heavy abusage that at any given time there will be enough disregarded built-up residue stuck onto the glass to make for a healthy line. With a little housekeeping, I'm all set. There's a party at a friend's apartment in the Western Addition and I need to wake up.

Also atop the dresser is a new video security monitor the size of a portable television. It's turned on and broadcasting a boxed-in black and white view of the building's front door area. The image is heavy with black shadow except in the corner closest to the front door overhead light, which is blown out with white illuminated sidewalk.

Nick's only advice for how to feel about the car that was following me the other day was, "Don't worry about it, brother, the less you know the better it is for you," which echoes again in my mind as I take the razor resting next to the excavation site and go after all the cloudy caked-on mirror residue. As I unearth the glaze, it reanimates into powder. Despite wanting to get my hand out of this cookie jar situation as quickly as possible, the black and white screen keeps stealing my attention back to its foreboding subliminal home paranoia.

I roll a bill, then do a quick pass over the mirror surface, which takes my gaze upwards to the view outside the large front window. There's a girl standing alone in a doorway directly across the street. She looks to be waiting for someone or for something to happen, but what makes it odd is there are much better places nearby to do it. Say, two doors down on the busy corner for instance, not in a shady dark alley doorway. I get dressed for the party, go downstairs and open the door while simultaneously lighting a cigarette using my Zippo trick. She looks at me from across the street and smiles. I smile back.

"Hey, can I bum one?" she calls. I nod as I drag and keep my momentum going into the street. We meet in the middle and I give my pack a couple of upward shakes. She takes the tallest standing one, then I light her up.

"You waiting for someone out here?" I ask.

"Not really," she says. "No one I'm that I'm that excited about anyway." She's attractive and despite this whole scene being random, it somehow feels staged.

My first ever crush was in preschool. She was sitting directly opposite me in a large cross-legged circle of my class of thirty or so four-year-olds. She was wearing an emerald felt jerkin over a white turtleneck with matching thick cotton leggings. Her hair was quite short and extremely deep, dark red. If we had been older, you'd think that it had to be dyed.

We were all in the middle of singing the infinite loop that is the children's song "Who Stole the Cookie from the Cookie Jar", a game by which one kid would single out another and then the whole group would sing, in unison, an accusation. The only way to get out of it, which also served to keep the song going, was by narcing out a different kid. She was popular and her many friends often picked her out when their turn came, but then each time this happened, she'd go and choose me next. She'd done this now for the second time in the song, which only on rare occasions ever happened and when it did was usually between two close friends. Repeats of this nature were in fact kinda frowned upon in general by the teachers; I guess so everyone could have a chance to learn how to sell someone out.

So now once again everyone sang my name in unison and pro-ceeded to merrily accuse me of stealing. At the end of the chorus, I could then free myself again by way of naming a name, so I threw it right back at her. To mine and everyone else's shocked surprise, she then proceeded to just throw it right back on me again. Now the whole class began singing in much louder surprised amusement at this unprecedented raising of the stakes.

After song time, there was a recess during which I saw her standing on the other side of the playground. Her patent leather toes were pointing toward each other, while she clasped her hands behind her back. She was watching me, waiting for me to come over, but I never did. That's when I learned for the very first time that sometimes all the signals in the world are not enough.

"Hey, can I get some drugs?"

"Uhmm..." I was caught off guard. This wasn't the type of place people were just sent to randomly.

"Ahh...I wish," I answer, with my voice now having gone up a register. "Actually, I was just leaving and then I saw you out here and...well...be safe!"

I turn the immediate corner where there is a cleaning van with two guys inside just sitting in silence. The van had been out of my field of vision but to her the two guys inside were in plain view the whole time. They both watch me as I pass.

I arrive at the party and head up the wide wooden steps to the open front door exposing the large Victorian human sardine can. Pulp's *Different Class* is blasting from the living room down the packed hallway. I begin to squeeze my way through the various conversations.

I see Matt talking to a couple of girls. "Hi Joel. I was just telling my friends here about how you quit after every show we play. How are you even still in the band?"

"Simple. I suffer from terminal temporary amnesia."

"Well, hopefully that's what Brian has. You know he just quit, right?"

"Ah fuck man, no I did not. No Jeff, now no Brian and we've got those shows...Fuuck man."

"Ye-ah. So where's the snorts?" he whispers in half-joke.

For Matt and me the days of wrestling around parking lots were long gone. In fact, it was because of those shared dramas that we'd by now formed an extra-strong bond having gone through such heavy scenes together. *We'd been through some shit, man.* To strangers, outwardly he would be the seemingly stoic no-nonsense one while I was the more animated wide-eyed cut-up. It was true Matt to a degree had surrounded himself in a protective wall, but he had shown me where the secret door was. By now we'd built up such a large catalog of inside jokes that there was too much material to pull from when life tried to get "serious". His "resting face" is in a permanent scrunch look of disapproval, as if he'd been "not having it" since birth. Eventually, he'd always catch himself complaining too much and then make a point to talk about positives, as if consciously taking care to keep the scales balanced.

Our party days together now informed his songs. His gifted song-writing ability had expanded from the point of view of a morose moaner about loneliness and failed relationships to the confident cool guy, and I was the Neal Cassady figurehead through whom he could "party all night long".

Despite my room at the warehouse, lately I was finding myself more and more wanting to wake up on the floor next to Matt's bed. Then we'd spend the rest of that day together and regardless of who currently had the meager means to acquire booze or drugs (food always coming in third), we never competed over who got more of whatever supplies we could muster. I'd be the one to have a lighter for a few days before losing it, then he'd have a matchbook to last maybe a day, there were infinite sparking combinations other than us both having our own light source at the same time.

"I ain't got no snorts to bust, buster. Hey, you seen the lady of the manor?"

"No, not in a while, but she's here."

I continue on squeezing my way through the packed living room.

I see Dean with a small group.

"...anyway, it was four-thirty in the morning and he was shouting at the top of his lungs about how sober he was, then he just leans over and pukes right in her basket of music magazines...what a dope—oh, hey Joel, what's shakin'? You know these here losers already, and this one here is Brad."

Brad Artley has a Brian Jones haircut. He gives me a forced "hi" while his right nostril flares upward as if connected to the same invisible string as his curled lip while giving me a once-over. I get the impression he could be more impressed. Some folks already seemed to "know me" before meeting me and lately to my dismay I'd been getting the feeling that the negative buzz amongst my local scene cynics was getting Dean's attention. Somebody or somebodies were trying to flip him. I continue on my quest having no way of knowing Brad will soon be BJM's new drummer, and my being responsible for it.

Finally, I reach the other end of the apartment and the kitchen where I find Romy. She was my part-time necking partner, an almond girl with skin the shade of the flesh and eyes and hair the color of the skin. Her nose was slightly upturned like mine and her upper lip would appear to be under its upwards pull, if it didn't look so perfect paired with its bottom. The act of simply necking for prolonged periods of time is one of the most divine states created by the universe. We headed back through the party crowd to do so in her bedroom.

Staying over the whole night wasn't usually on the house program and her waking up with a hangover and a destroyed apartment is saintly enough as is, let alone having to face it all with an ultra-alert Lady Chattery's Lover. By the time I exit Romy's room it's now very late and I can't locate any booze. No Matt or Dean either and despite the jovial bounce of "Parklife", most of the party is winding down in general. Guess I'll just split.

I wake up into the morning light and begin stumbling around to confirm what the silence and unlit stillness indicates: alone. On completion of my first second-floor lap, I begin a second, this time going deeper into my roommate's room and over to his dresser. It's dollars to powdered nose doughnuts that at any given time there will be a fair amount of disregarded lost crystals sprinkled in the general area around the hardwood. With a little housekeeping, I'm all set. Popscene is happening right now and I need to wake up.

I roll a bill over my dig and crush the crystals into white powder. Then as I'm tapping a razor on it, the black and white screen again keeps stealing my attention. Suddenly, the same girl from last night walks into camera view and presses the ding-dong door buzzer. It echoes throughout the halls. She spends the next ten minutes ringing the door buzzer while I chalk up, watching.

Armed with Shovels and Dangerous

"Just pull right up in front!" Anton says, pointing urgently.

"But they might want us to load in through the back alley!" Our manager Dave D stoner-drawls in his usual way of always suggesting an alternate possibility, no matter how needless it was. He always did it.

"There's no time, we're supposed to be playing right now," Anton returns, with sub-zero patience for making a conversation out of it. He was right, we were supposed to be already performing on the Popscene stage, not barreling up to the front doors to start unloading the gear.

As we pull up against the curb, I turn around in my bench seat to share one more secret headshake with Dean before we all simultaneously kick open the van doors and with the unified authority of a Viking invasion begin charging the double doors with guitar cases. "Hold on, guys, it's waay too late now," Aaron Axelson pleads while blocking the doors with puffed-up faux-authority. Aaron is the program director at LIVE 105 Modern Rock Radio and one of the head promoters and DJs of Popscene. He's kind of like an urban bleached surfer-bro. Trying to add on to this blip of control momentum, he rapid-fire states, "Our music permit doesn't allow for live music past 11 p.m. and that's in ten minutes from now. Your set time will be over by the time you get your gear up."

"Then we'll only play one song," Anton says, completely serious. I know he secretly just wants to get us set up on that stage where we can then wreak maximum havoc on the permit conditions. Once plugged in onstage, we would control the room with our own laws and Aaron knew this.

"No way, man, not this time," Aaron returns, then looks back and nods to the club security. Security guys 1 and 2 move up and flank his shoulders, then squint at us menacingly.

"This is fuckin' bullshit man!" Dave D says now that he can see the situation is over and safe for him to start up his manager act.

Our battle is quickly forgotten for the consolation prize of a camera crew heading right for us. A young woman and a guy with a video camera on his shoulder move in for a close-up.

"So where is the show tonight?" she asks by way of introducing the current scene to an audience that won't exist for another ten years.

"*Right* FUCKING *there!*" I respond while pointing at Aaron off-camera standing in front of the doors. I give it a dramatic flair, the dreamer in me immediately imagining whatever this is up on the big screen.

"Who are you?" Anton wants to know before this goes any further.

"I'm Ondi and this is my brother David. We're making a documentary on bands navigating the music business."

"Hi, I've been waiting to meet you."

He has? I wonder to myself.

"What about the show tonight?" Dave D says as if he wasn't yet done with the done situation. For once Anton didn't ignore him, and this was only because he wanted to answer back to the camera.

"It doesn't matter. We just booked a show in LA and every record label is coming to fight over us!"

My eyebrows perked up at this new-to-me information announcement. *Finally*, I thought. The world would find out what The Brian Jonestown Massacre were all about.

We all go to a friend's small party in the Lower Haight, and for the next few hours everyone hangs out sans cameras and gets to know each other. Mostly, it's Anton holding court and laying down his master plans, and once his keynote presentation is complete, he and Dave D and the documentary siblings all split in different directions.

Meanwhile, the kids stay up getting into trouble of the wee-hours persuasion, into the very wee-est of hours, all the while with senses sharpened by chemical know-how, yet all concerns diluted with booze and always, always the taste of tobacco. Hours of cigarette inhaling to the point of tripping smoke alarms on the opposite side of this very large shared Victorian apartment. Lights are left low as some sort of compromise with the sun, which is currently making its way around the other side of the planet as we get further and further out of sync with the clock on the wall.

Dreams are shared, plans made and future bonding deals done. Silences of every stripe, uncomfortable or otherwise, do not exist in this flight terminal lounge between yesterday and tomorrow. There is always something to say and something to hear from every part of the room. What would normally miss the ear entirely is somehow full, rich and interesting, and even if you know it technically isn't, it's important to respect the pact you've all made. The pact of the night being duly agreed to be spent together. We're "all in" and need to share this "safe space" together until the lights go up. It's an agreed "no dilemmas allowed zone". That is until dilemma's mother, the sun, rises up from the bottom end and as it comes up, you ironically come down.

When Matt was incredibly wired his lips would protrude out repeatedly in a type of emotionless kissy face and at a rate of about 135 bpm. I think it was because he couldn't stop moving his mouth while waiting for his turn to talk again. Maybe he wasn't even aware that he was doing it, but it gave Dean and me endless entertainment taking turns imitating it behind his back as he traded his focus between us, which would in turn determine whose turn it was to render exaggerated secret mimics of him doing it while he was looking at the other actually doing it. We were all indeed brothers, and this included the childish angle where loyalty could flip on a dime. I would spend all day with Matt but then Dean or Anton would show up and suddenly Matt bore the brunt of the jokes. We all loved him, yet none of the rest of us ever seemed to fall victim to this style of coup. If it bothered him he never pointed it out or even acknowledged it, outright anyway. Then again, there is that little scar on my temple.

The three of us had the rest of the room at a disadvantage as we were able to not only gossip and rag on what bugged us in our lives but also ponder the new horizons and possibilities of what new opportunities were currently there to excite about. We're in a semi-huddle in the corner on an awning, an easy chair and one of its arms as Dean continues our conversation, "Well I heard someone from Interscope Records was at the last show."

Matt adds to the mystery-solving, "I saw Anton talking to someone at the bar I'd never seen before, maybe she was the person setting up this big show in LA."

"Well, this is all the first I've heard of it," I add, "but nothing new there."

"I know, right?" Dean scoffs with bemusement.

Little did we know that earlier tonight Anton had also made plans with the new documentarians to make an even sooner trip down to Los Angeles. We had our *third* album of the year about to come out, one which this time featured me as the solo cover star. Not only did he have business with his indie label head Greg Shaw, but now we could add the rest of us to play a party in Beverly Hills. Back-to-back trips to showbiz town. Shit was starting to go *down*, seemingly.

Suddenly a hallway door swings open, "Pleease, It's 4 a.m. and I have to *work* in the morning!" the shirtless white male pleads. He shuts his door, then we all just laugh. What a dope.

The Life

I wake up on my mattress which is like a life raft floating on stilted wooden waters of hangover, where my dreams switch from the experimental film theater of sleep to the daytime real-world matinee kind, continuing on now in Technicolor-awake scope where I am suddenly in control of where they go.

Hovering next to my head on my fourth black wall are The Small Faces in '67, Marianne Faithfull in '68, '65 Keith Moon, '71 Marvin Gaye and others who pose knowingly moody for the cameras. They inform me how to use my head and I wirelessly connect and gather information, which is then relayed into my system's passion program. I light a smoke and lie there a good while, body shut down, eyes wide open.

It's wild how little I actually need. I have a library card, a portable turntable and a tiny black and white that can tune into a fuzzy PBS, and this is enough to idle by behind what is not only my bedroom door in the warehouse, but also life's game show door #1, where my desires lie on ice until...

All of the above plus room and drugs can be had for a mere errand here and there, and once that bedroom door of mine opens I become a part of the whirl. Maybe to paint sheets of LSD onto blotter paper, or perhaps a trip to a Fed-Ex shipping office to mail a package full of E capsules or, like now, a cab ride across town to drop off a duffle bag of I don't even know what. When they don't bother to tell me it means that I'd probably prefer not to know.

Oh yeah, the "dream"? The dream where I make music? I don't really, myself that is, and yet somehow I know it's deeper inside me than anyone else in the genre-correct bands I see around town, a real feeling, like the push of water when something swims by you. When I watch other bands, behind their posturing and "feeling it" faces, you can see they are internally lost at sea. You just know it's never going to happen for them and I wonder if they know.

Anton makes the music and I've been his main in-it-all-the-way in all of this, but maybe for only as long as these days are, because lately I've been getting too caught up in "the life", that being the life around the warehouse. Between that and partying, I'd begun to spin out in my real life, the band and my place in it.

Still, there is a show tomorrow night so Anton and I spent some good time walking the streets together on pre-show errands, like two mates in school on the sprawling bohemian campus that is San Francisco. Him scheming and formulating next moves, me bouncing back enthusiastic approvals. With *Their Satanic Majesties' Second Request* and *Take It from the Man!* already out and *Thank God for Mental Illness* now about to be released, it's time to roll hard with it, and yet somehow because of the drugs I still find myself currently go-go dancing the line between realist of the for-realest and complete fuck-up.

I tag-team with myself into the aforementioned me, now on another night errand where I'm presently getting out of the cab with the duffle bag. These errands felt more and more like a dark TV show where I knew the storyline, but not the script. The opening credits have now rolled and we switch to a wide-angle camera shot of a dark street in the far south side of San Francisco...

I ring the apartment building buzzer underneath windows blasting house music and it bazzes back a *BAAAZZZZZ*, meaning I need to get the door open before it closes its mouth again. Up wooden stairs to the second floor above a garage, or more likely a lab, and I'm "greeted" at the door by a rough-and-stubble long-hair and tie-dye type who takes me into the living room. There's more of an air of hard crime than party supplier zone, despite the music and dayglo lights. This is one of the second-chance depots of the unsanctioned ones, those trying to beat the built-in order of things.

He takes my duffle bag and goes into another room while I take an edge-of-the couch seat position. Two DJs are huddled over a mixer with turntables set up in the protruding bay windows. They are fully immersed, talking close while spinning and it seems pretty serious to them. They don't look up at me, let alone want introductions. We are a type that has no interest in comparing information on how to potentially narc each other out down the road. Everyone has their masks on straight and I check mine again. Seems right, but I can't completely tell.

This angle of the electronic hippie drug scene is drenched in a vibe of dark energy. This room in particular has a beady mad-eyes looking in from the other side of the wall's "Have a Nice Day" repurposed hippie-era yellow smiley face feel.

Party profiteers like these had acquired large portions of the market that regularly supplied the huge trance-dances held illegally in abandoned buildings and remote fields. Those drugs are then either pumping people's brains with powers of enlightenment, or continuing to slowly erode them, depending on your lot in life, with both scenarios being brought on by the same chemicals. The great deciders.

He comes back and gives me the bag and it feels different now, like there is something else in it. A cab is called for me and I go wait on the front steps.

Everything was indeed getting weirder and weirder and at a pace that was picking up speed with the speed. Beyond the ever-increasing wack-a-doo behavior brought on by long-term chemical compounding, the big bad beginning of the end was the sudden arrival of Richard. I woke up after a near-twenty-four hour Lazarus lay-down after a three-day marbles-blending bender to find this guy and Nick huddled in the darkness of night working on what looked like small computer chips. The small nighttime hiker's headlamps they wore provided the only light in the room, neither of which blinded me as I entered because neither of them bothered to look up as I did so. They were transfixed in a feverish self-hypnosis, or "tweaking" on whatever it was. "Oh, hey dude," Nick finally says, now noticing me. "This is Richard. Richard, this is Joel. He lives here." Richard gives me a silent single nod of hello, careful with obvious experience to keep his head lamp beam shining just off to the side of my face, then goes back to work on his laid-out display of tiny bits of electronic guts. Richard is dressed appropriately for whatever this is, wearing mechanic shop overalls while his hunched posture looks weary in that way that suggests he was probably once strong and sturdy in frame, but now slight by a slighting from life, like a Michelin Man drained of air. The top of his head was plastered with dyed jet-black hair greased back slick and oily, while at the bottom his wide jaw worked like a flat shelf to which his weather-worn and sagging wrinkled-before-its-time face could be piled atop of. Microscopic electrical components and an organized assortment of small intricate tools were all around his desk station. I didn't know Nick was into those things, yet it certainly made sense for him in his growing position to make the big-time upgrade to one of these new drug dealer's luxury items. No one in my circle of friends owned one, nor expected to any time soon, if ever.

Richard, as it is explained to me back in the hallway and with an air of pride, was "ex-FBI" who apparently knew how to reprogram mobile cell phones for resale. I feigned the required impressed reaction, while on the inside I'm wondering, is there is even such a thing as "ex" FBI?

He continues to beam in a whisper, "I got a guy now who gets these for me cheeap, dude." As I nod with a concerned smile he moves in closer with even smaller whisper-tone, "Look, do me a favor and stay away from the downstairs for a bit. Zee is incredibly pissed off these days and we don't want her tripping out any harder than she already is."

I go back to my room and then notice she had left a very old looking *Brain-Washing in Red China* book on my bed while I was asleep, which could have been laid next to my hibernating body anytime since around this time the night before. Whether or not it was her intention, after what I'd just been told plus the overall bad vibes that had started to seem here to stay, I took this odd gift as the calling card that I was officially on her outs now too. Gone seemingly were the optimistic plans of this being a place becoming a legit recording studio and place for painting and photography. Too much business had as of tonight officially crept through the cracks and tipped the scales in the wrong direction, and like the business of business does, had turned it all into something else. The recording studio was nowhere near done and in attempts to fast-track its completion with new kinds of underground entrepreneurial avenues, things were instead coming apart and threatening to fall off the rails before getting to the destination of legal living. It was almost like a microcosm of 60s Haight-Ashbury itself, with things having officially moved on from the innocent early days of E's and acid and having by now morphed into something darker.

A few nights later Matt and I are walking home from Popscene. His hair has gotten longer than I've ever seen it before. It's not technically *long* long, but just on the brink of shoulder length. I get the impression it's never quite reached this length before as he seems to be in a constant state of affirmation by putting enough extra bounce in each step while simultaneously raising his shoulders each time, as if to momentarily feel his hair touch his shoulders. It's like a working mechanism. *High step—head back—shoulders up—touch hair—shoulders down—high step—head back—shoulders up—touch hair…*It gives one the impression he's reacting to his hair never having been this long and it's endearing to hang back a few steps to witness his unintentional marching style parade performance.

We're walking down the last two blocks to the warehouse when suddenly from the upcoming side alley two young Asian-American gang-looking guys pounce. Now blocking our way forward, one commands "YOUR WALLETS!" while the other one flashes a knife just like I've seen countless times in movies and on television, the biggest difference from the TV reality being that when someone is getting mugged, you know in advance there's most likely a hero about to save the day. In real life the last thing you're expecting is a hero about to save the day. Suddenly from across the street comes a-running Richard jumping straight into the action and right on time. With both hands he grabs the arm of the knife holder and shakes it hard, sending the blade skipping into the gutter. Giving no resistance or any attempt at all to fight back, the two would-be muggers bolt back into the darkness of the alley.

"Whoa man, THANKS!" I shout.

"Yeah, we sure were lucky you came along," Matt reinforces.

Richard twists us out a somewhat awkward smile but doesn't say anything more for the rest of the walk back. Meanwhile, Matt and I pounce excitedly around him like six-year-olds getting an autograph from their favorite baseball player.

Back upstairs at the warehouse, Richard beelines straight to his cellphone reprogramming workspace while Matt and I excitedly retell the already enhanced tale to Nick, who has a look of amused vindication while listening to our story.

We were all sold. Meanwhile, Zee, who had been listening to the whole thing from the kitchen, was not. As I attempt to win her over to the fantasy of action film adventure in real life, her look of unwavering doubt only turns harder and harder the more I speak until I slowly begin to realize for myself that yes, the whole thing had been a bit too coincidental, all over with too easily. I'd started on an outward exclamation point, but found myself ending on an internal question mark.

The next morning that cleaning company van was parked on the corner again and the same two guys were sitting in the front seats. Then the day after that there they were again and some new homeless people had appeared sitting against the wall directly across the street. Strangely, all their camouflage, flannel and the rest of their "bum" attire looked to be brand new.

I decide to go upstairs to check for this cleaning company's listing in the phonebook. They ain't in it. I go downstairs and poke my head outside again. The two guys in the van are watching me watching them. I go back upstairs to think about my future, then slide into sleep around midnight, a getting rarer all-the-time normal time and wake up again at 4 a.m. totally famished. I think back and realize I haven't eaten in almost two days. The only thing open at this hour is the twenty-four-hour gas station a few blocks away so I decide to go out into the sleepy city.

In the Jingle Jangle Jungle

The walk there is dark, cool and silent. Thick vampire-town fog blows slow and reflects the streetlight humdrum. The only food options there are packaged things with expiration dates the same as when people will probably live on Mars, and I stand outside chewing under the gas station fluorescence while staring at the artificially lit silence and highway overpasses. The on and off ramps are empty and no one is around. It's eerie out here and is a perfect addition to the growing feelings of dread that seemed to follow me all over the neighborhood these days. If night is "the witching time", then dawn is even worse, when all the demons, aliens, specters and waking evil dreams, all unearthly things, scurry back to the crossroads before it's too late. The big "too late" is scheduled to arrive soon, and I feel its nebulous specter just over my shoulder, waiting for the given moment to strangle my everything. I shiver and take long strides back to shelter.

Timothy Leary's Bed

The blaze of the sun is turned up to eleven as we arrive at Greg Shaw's formulaic mid-century stucco second-floor apartment. He meets us at the door with freshly pressed copies of the new *Thank God for Mental Illness* CD releasing in a few weeks. He's in middle age but with the same young-aged long blond hair from back in his old 70s rock magazine photos as a music journalist before going on to among other things running his own record label, Bomp!

His straight-line bangs look like they were done in a single giant scissor-chop, seemingly causing some of the fine hairs to have been taken by surprise which are sticking out in some sort of shear-shock. They are not quite yet ready to lie all the way down and join the mellowed sleepy spell the rest of his physical form seems to be perma-under. Looking at the CD cover of the third BJM album release this year, there I am on the cover, pictured in close-up while whacked out of my skull and with a bloody mouth doing my best Christopher Lee as Dracula.

As Greg begins filling in Anton, everyone flops around his copious amount of living room throw pillows while I drop at the kitchen table and sit flipping through all the inlay booklet band photos and read the liner notes for the first time. There's even one of my quotes inside: "If you can't dig it, you ain't got no shovel."

Greg was hyper-intelligent, an absolute sage of the cool side of guitar-based music and certainly one of the leading scholars of 60s garage rock. I notice the more Greg's thought stream flows through his mind turbine, his eyelids flutter, making him the only person I've ever known whose wheels you could physically see turning. When Anton is in the right company he has this huh-huh with just enough ha-ha and ah-ha mixed into it that I'd become familiar with it as his most genuinely amused and engaged state. It came out in situations like now, scenes of relaxed natural comfort of innate *now*-ness. His fountain of observatory one-liner commentary would flow, with thought-provoking realities delivered by a quick-thinking sharpness that had its own built-in sharpener. Like how a car charges its own battery simply in the act of driving it. He and Anton are in the kitchen going into deep rapid fire on subjects like the dimension-surfing powers of DMT and the ins and outs of Brion Gysin's theories while my random bits of participation with interjections like "soo cool" do little to forward the esoteric conversation. Still, self-awareness is its own important and rare sign of high intelligence, methinks.

Getting the hint, I join Sophie for a while out on the small balcony patio overlooking the palms and stucco structures nestled among the hills. After sharing the view for a few minutes I notice Anton in the front doorway smoking. I stride through the fellow retro band-dudes lying on pillows to join him in smoking a cigarette, but just as soon as I'm lit he's already done and drops his butt among what is by now a growing collection.

I drag away at my smoke until down to the filter, then flick it, pinging it off a plant pot where it then joins all the others.

"Hey! Who's supposed to pick that up? Do you think the cigarette butt fairy is going to come or something?"

It was Greg. I look down at all of Anton's filterless stubs riddled on the patio like bullet casings in a war movie. Greg had been watching Anton drop butts for the last hour unbothered by it, but Anton delivered the albums, so that all made sense and he could dig it—but I was more like a drug-addled teenage stepson he wasn't excited about inheriting. He if anything had overpaid his psychedelic dues and it was becoming apparent I could only expect to top out at tolerated.

I pick up my single butt and go inside to sleuth out the waste basket.

Later we pull into Ondi and David's driveway just a few blocks off of Melrose Avenue. Overly excited hellos and welcomes as she invites us in and through their small 1930s-era apartment house and out into a large backyard.

As we settle in for what appears to be backyard blabs, Dean and I exchange furrowed brows and wander back inside to look for whatever music we can find. Back through the house in the front living room there in the corner is a stereo system and accompanying CD display storage tower next to it. It looks not unlike a miniaturized under-construction tacky high-rise apartment building made of cheap plastic with many more empty unfinished floors than occupied ones. I kneel down for a closer look with Dean right behind, then start at the top and move down the selections as if giving a PowerPoint presentation, using my finger as a pointer:

Red Hot Chili Peppers' *Blood Sugar Sex Magik.*

"Gross," Dean says.

Mother Love Bone.

"Ugh."

Jane's Addiction.

"Eck."

Soundgarden.

"Oh man."

Blind Melon

"Barf."

We stop to give each other a look and laugh. Then Dean further chuckles in his part-amused, part-annoyed way, "How is she making a movie about us when she listens to all this crap?" We both laugh again, this time shaking our heads before I continue down the CD tower.

Pearl Jam.

"Jesus. Don't tell me, Spin Doctors?"

Bob Marley *Legend.*

"Well, we could definitely listen to the earlier songs but the chronological order's all mixed up. What else?"

Funkadelic *Maggot Brain.*

Finally!

"Let's play that!" Dean says with consciously animated excitement. I pull the compact disc out from the plastic tower, flip open the case and hand him the shiny plastic disc. He inserts it in the player and sets it on "repeat" mode.

Just then Ondi comes in. "Hey, you guys! You should come hang out in the backyard, it's *gorgeous* out today. Also, I was just telling the others about the big party my friends are throwing at Timothy Leary's house. A bunch of people have been living there since he died last month because the rent's paid through until the day after tomorrow. They were all his young people that he liked to just be around him. He was so cool, he'd say yes to *everything*. A bite of someone's apple, whatever. He didn't turn experiences down."

Now I remember Jeff had met Leary in the audience after we'd opened up for Sonic Boom down here at The Troubadour. I couldn't believe it when Jeff told us Timothy Leary had waved him over during Sonic's set. Now Jeff had moved out of state and Timothy Leary had moved out of this reality.

She continues, "Anyway, you guys playing will be the last thing to happen before everyone is kicked out and the house is put up for sale. One last big mind blow-out."

"Whoa," Dean says.

"Wow," I reinforce. "The *last* thing to ever happen at Timothy Leary's house?"

"...is The Brian Jonestown Massacre playing in his backyard," Ondi returns.

"Far out."

The Matt, Brad, Dean and Joel team spend the following afternoon bummin' it around Melrose Avenue. As we traverse through all the visual interference in between the few record stores and vintage clothing shops, I daydream of what this scene must have looked like back in the day and what it would have entailed playing a party at the house of Timothy Leary, the guru of perhaps all psychedelic gurus. if any of the POW! ZAP! BANG! POP! WHIZZ! of groovy 60s LA still exists anywhere, it would be there? Maybe like an elder version made up of psychedelic sages of the ages still flush with turned-on wages, where I imagine Z-Man from *Beyond the Valley of the Dolls* is the house servant and he can still freak out over his scene unfettered and dignified.

We head back to Ondi and David's house where we find Matt and Dean, and it's not long after that the rest of the BJM gang arrives from Greg's. Reconfiguring our two rag-tag teams into Dave D's van and Ondi's SUV, we begin our convoy up to Timothy Leary's Beverly Hills house and the post-mortem grand finale of a several-months-long going-away party.

As we drive onwards and upwards to the tippy-tops, Ondi describes what friends had said were his final moments, him asking the question "why?", then repeating his own answer to this question *"why not?"* over and over.

Oddly, no video cameras have come out yet, which makes me think maybe they are still feeling out if we are to be one of the prospected ten bands they want to go "all in" on with filming their documentary project, which is to focus on ten bands trying to "make it" in the music business. Either way, it seems like an odd thing to skip. It won't be long until this sort of sentiment is the stuff of fantasy.

We are met at the door by a handsome Burning Man-on-the-Sunset Strip sort of fellow who gives us the grand tour. It's a single-story somewhat modest house of mid-century architecture common yet on the lower-class scale of these highfalutin lands. A gradual A-frame roof angles down to the back wall of the house which is made entirely of glass, bringing the exterior backyard view and hills beyond inside. Gazing out to the next set of hills, the sun is going down, casting pinks, purples and oranges from the other side of the hidden horizon.

The floor is thick with white shag, which leads to white walls in all directions. The whole place has a 1950s modern but worn-in around the edges feel, as if it's a giant object from the vintage store this afternoon.

With the only remains being haphazardly arranged furniture items too big to be easily carried off and built-in shelves with the tipped over less desirable leave-behind books, it's like a canvas stripped of its paint, reversed back to the original pre-creative idea state.

His bedroom has been picked bone dry. Gone are the lava lamps, Hindu god and goddess tapestries, strobe lights, faux fur, framed psychedelic posters and paintings, plastic accessories, smoking paraphernalia, medical-sized tanks, fish-eye mirrors, Tibetan bells, color light wheels, fabric dayglow, decaying garlands and many more multi-random-tandems. In the last few months this place has been a nonstop parade site of musicians, artists, writers, actors, directors, journalists, scientists, politicians, activists, spiritual healers, fellow elders of the movement and on and on, all here to say *bon voyage* and have a nice flight.

Timothy Leary's bed has been moved out onto the freshly fraying lawn next to his old sensory deprivation tank. The backyard is framed by a barrier wall of foliage under towering palms that take my gaze up to the brand-new stars beyond. Ondi declares, "Oh my god! Let's do a photo shoot!"

We all climb onto the bed and arrange ourselves in a skinny pile of heads, torsos and limbs covered in turned-on groover traditional regalia while Ondi snaps at us from above. This bed that only a few days ago had served as a launchpad for the spirit of Timothy Leary was now covered with our unfettered youth.

We then set our gear up in a type of shindig police lineup formation along the glass wall. Why we are not playing in the backyard comes down to our temporary hosts not wanting to incur the wrath of Barbara Streisand, Bruce Willis, Zsa Zsa Gabor, Burt Reynolds, Cher, Steven Seagal and the many others in the neighborhood who would have such loud riff-raffery shut down by police.

Despite these tight performance quarters, I grab the house life-size Clint Eastwood Spaghetti Western cardboard stand-up and put him next to the drum kit. He is looking ready and with fitting attitude.

The anticipation of live entertainment is now spreading through the house and more people begin to gravitate to the living room. Guitars are in the final tuning stages when suddenly unplanned and unannounced Anton begins the performance solo by going into "Spanish Bee". It's a flamenco-esque number that requires patterned handclaps and while we're at it, why not for the sake of going all the way add Cuban heels on hard wood? The room encompassing white shag carpet is the last surface on earth that I can flamenco stomp on, so I quickly scan the area for hard furniture surfaces. A wooden chair from the neighboring kitchen will have to do, and I collect it as Anton continues through the first verse. I climb up onto the chair and begin to clap hands while speed-tapping my Cuban heels. Having established my balance and form in time for the chorus,

I *stomp stomp stomp*, which also serves as exclamation points to each line. Now looking over my shoulder at Anton, I see focused, artistic passion as he ramps it up further.

We settle back down into the second verse and now Brad begins providing minimal rim shots which add to the Latin feel, yet tentative enough to keep his lean off the jazz. Matt plays single bass note accents, furthering the flirtation of full-band integration. Not playing, Dean holds that style of moody reserve that few can pull off as being more than enough participation. This background stoicism continues until broken by the next chorus and now Dean picks up the chords and holds them down as Anton's fingers take off into solo work that evokes Paco de Lucía playing in The Velvet Underground until he lands back into his own distinct brand of slink and twang. As his fingers fly up the fretboard, I from my high perch work as a visual talisman while the audience now joins in with the handclapping pattern. The song ends and Sophie, who has been waiting in the wings, slowly saunters over, Persian cat-style, and sits in the chair as I step off it.

As that ride ends the setting becomes ripe for what music pedestrians might call a "retro" set, but then we launch the bulbous bobbing B-52 bomber made of chrysanthemums that is "Evergreen", projecting its lumbering glide through a multicolored paint-can-splattered ten-story canvas sky.

Doing gigs in your hometown is very much still living your day to day, with everyone converging at the club, be it after work, the dinner dishes, or just getting out of bed after a full-tilt night. Leaving town together on the road to foreign lands was a whole other level of bonding. That was when the adventure started. That's when you become a unit, and for better or worse, a family.

Despite the post-performance genuine good vibes of the gathering, things can't help but begin to slow to a drag as I'm bounced around to various introductions and new conversations that tingle with underlining personal ambitions. The constant schmoozing and feigning is foreign to me, and I don't know the strokes in these "OH WOW" waters.

I go over to the unpopulated part of the backyard where Timothy Leary's old sensory deprivation tank is. Looking inside, it's been emptied of all its sensory depriving submersion agents and is now just an empty tank. I climb inside and shut the door behind me. In my now antisocial escape pod, I ponder the heaviness of Timothy Leary's chemical-fueled solo dimension-trotting adventures that had gone down in this small darkened space place. I sit in silence and wait for a transmission.

Back from LA and a few hours of sufficient mind-numbing later, I fall asleep to the slap bass and frantically flying credits of a late-night TV show. The next day it's all still there—the homeless people in brand-new bum clothes, the cleaning service van whose business isn't listed in the phonebook is on the corner, and Richard the "ex-FBI" guy is back at his bedroom desk working away on reprogramming mysteriously acquired cell phones.

Nick orders a pizza from an old-school Italian restaurant, then passes around powdered nasal aperitifs before asking me to fix us up some tall gin and tonics from an unopened bottle of Tanqueray chilling in the freezer. As I'm about to return from the kitchen, Nick is suddenly there with elbows leaning up against both sides of the doorway. "Hey man, I want you to know things are gonna get *waay* more chill around here soon. I'm working stuff out with our angry girl housemate and things in general are going to start getting legit around here."

"What about those new bums always hanging out across the street? Man, all their flannel and army camouflage clothes look right off the rack!"

"*Yeah?*"

"They're there all day except when they magically disappear around lunch, dinner and bedtime. Don't you think that's weird? And there's a van on the corner with two guys that's been there every day for two weeks!"

"Oh *man*, you sound paranoid, dude. There's all kinds of regular characters around here. It's called living in San Francisco." I hand him a drink and he smiles at me reassuringly, then heads back to his room. I re-tip the bottle for a stronger strong one. There were no "regular characters" around here before and that's what makes them all so irregular. If this is the extent of the response from the observation booth, I'm going to keep my "paranoia" to myself from now on.

I go back to my room, having just self-diagnosed myself as suffering from both paranoia and reality simultaneously. As I lie down, I am thankful to Zee and Nick for taking me in here, this sanctuary from the "real" world of jobs and their time-thieving bosses. It's the true bohemian life for me and it was rendered here with smiles. All I had to do was help out a little here and there, which I probably did less of than I should have, and I was pretty much free to play. Now the wolves had found the nest, and it's time for this little bird to fly before he gets put inside of a cage.

The Johnny Depp Viper Room Massacre

Today I feel there's something deeply ironic about Los Angeles being known as the "City of Dreams", the place where you go to fulfill them, where you come to draw all entertainment industry eyes on you, taking the countless hours of time and effort spent building up to bringing the big "make or break" moment upon yourself. In these moments, these *situations*, there is a peculiar vibe that follows you, or maybe it's just following me, or maybe it is in fact not following, but rather just *is*, everywhere, before you even get here, like the smog. A smog that brings sudden feelings of the impossibility of your dream, like every piece of armor you've earned on your personal winding journey up until this moment when at the castle gate suddenly everything is just stripped away. I look up at the enormity of the castle and the wind blows an ominous whisper in my ear, *I dare you*.

This great outdoor interrogation-room theme park that is Los Angeles, with its perpetual and unmerciful blazing hot sun, arid air and lifeless architecture that seems to be comprised of block after block of strip malls, is not like a Paris, or Rome, or San Francisco, or one of the other settings from old classic movies that got your head dreaming in the first place, but rather the bare "reality" of it all; a "dream factory", an illusion-manufacturing center using its own wares to lure you here only to crush the dreams that were created here in the first place.

Back home in San Francisco there were no career "stakes", or none that mattered, and everything there played out exactly the way you saw it, day to day, naturally. There are no narcing eyes following and watching, ready to put the word out—good, bad or otherwise.

We've been told there will be a bidding war at our music industry showcase tonight, but the battles have already commenced without them.

Things started out so well at Greg Shaw's today. Moods were high as Anton hipped the documentarians to our friends The Dandy Warhols while on camera, but upon moving camp over to Ondi and David's backyard, things almost instantly turned nasty with just a few hours before soundcheck time at The Viper Room. They both have video cameras out and move around the yard looking excited internally, yet stoic externally while capturing all the little fires of drama going on in every corner. Everyone is over-involved and has something to say, as though starring in a disaster movie. It's all perfectly understandable, one person's dirt is another's gold, and my own hard day's life is that it only resembles a Beatles movie in fleeting moments, seemingly.

There is a new guitar player of the responsible type seeing an opportunity here to be just that: the "together" one. Add an out-of-nowhere-to-me college intern-looking agent fellow who thinks he's going to buck this BJM bronco into becoming successful good boys. His new job will begin and end today, but for now he is a part of the constellation of foreign elements festering the hive.

I hear music coming from the backyard which means the fighting has stopped, theoretically, and so I leave my solo living room escape zone and go back to join the others. Ondi had noticed my boot sole splitting off from the leather so she'd taken me into her bedroom and given me some black leather ankle zip boots. They are round toe, but 60s enough. The thing is though, while I'd probably choose Cuban heels to run a marathon race in, these are proper three-inch-heel girl boots that have a narrow fit as well as being two sizes too small. Still, when it comes to rubber souls tomorrow never knows, and they would also serve to further bring Sophie's and my physical look closer together.

I grab my tambourine and join in as the band play a new mantra for the cameras called "I Am Love", replete with sitars, tablas and a tamboura. The title is the whole of the lyric and we follow Anton as he puts the sentiment on repeat while we put on accompanying airs that all is not spiraling out of control and fast, but there is an under-the-radar apprehension, like some are not wanting to move any further toward what is ahead.

This message of love sort of works for the moment, but then after the instruments are put back down Matt becomes eager to air all of his grievances. Cameras don't get bored after three or four negative comments and in fact love them and only want more. Matt has plenty. He's instantly buzzed with this new power, coupled with all the warm backyard beer and the pressure cooker's lid begins to rattle again. In some way, he's gone a level beyond the rest of us in that he's found his own method of dealing with this day of all known rules changing. I guess I should be jealous.

Later outside of Johnny Depp's Viper Room, the sun from the Los Angeles heat sticks on like a napalm-esque physical trait, causing multiple strains of sweat: the alcohol infused, the new impending-doom kind, and the regular sort sucked up to the skin surface by the sun with its countless invisible tentacles.

I'm in a dark room. My head is spinning but in the way a hubcap rolls away from a car crash, then falls over into a wobbling spin that increases in speed until the entire band flatlines onstage in a brawl while the packed house watches in shocked amusement. Amusement was not what we walked out on this stage to conjure, but rather to be desired by every major record label, all of whom have sent representatives here tonight. In the end, our potential bidding war is reduced to just another inter-band war. They all said it was self-sabotage, but I know it wasn't.

Perhaps you've already heard the rest of this story. I hope so, because from here I have a drunken memory blackout.

A simple internet search of "The Brian Jonestown Massacre fight" will bring you the footage first thing, because when the documentary finally comes out, this scene went big time viral, as in seven kinds of breakthrough variant viral.

It's our embarrassing party video that for all involved will never go away, one that ends with us fighting on the stage floor with each other before the curtain abruptly closes, separating my confused head from my body like a showbiz guillotine while all around me the rest of the band are crawling on the stage floor in dazed confusion before being physically thrown out the stage door by club security.

My turn comes and out the side door I go yelling, "What is this, *Planet of the Apes* or something?!", which makes the giant bouncer, if he didn't already, want to kick my ass. Dave D saves me with some level-headed defusing and then keeps everyone a healthy distance from Anton, who's down the sidewalk being interviewed by Ondi. Kevin Haskins from Bauhaus and Love and Rockets appears out of nowhere and helps bring me back down to earth until the van eventually arrives with the gear and guys sans Anton and Sophie, who go to a hotel. We head off for Greg Shaw's apartment to call this all enough for one night.

The following morning I awake to the sound of Matt cracking open a beer can, or as I like to call it, an aluminum rooster. *Psshhhtt.* I look around and I'm lying on a section of Greg Shaw's ocean of hippie pillows. On the other side of the counter in the attached kitchen, Robert, along with a few of the others are devising a written "agreement" for Anton which outlines a declaration of behavioral demands. All are basic and normal human rights, yet I and the rest of us who aren't engaging in it know the idea of demands and signatures would never actually happen with Anton.

Suddenly we hear the sounds of the van doors slamming outside. We all head out onto Greg's front entryway deck and there is Anton, parked behind the van and pulling gear cases out while Sophie stands at the car's passenger's side door, watching him and smoking. She doesn't look our way.

"Heyy Anton," Robert shouts down with lazy reserve, like one does when you have no idea what you're bringing on to yourself, "we've been working on a little band agree—"

"Fuck you guys! I'm moving to Portland!" he shouts, also not looking our way as he pulls the unbroken one of the two sitars out of the van and loads it in the hatchback next to his guitar and amp.

He peels out of the driveway and I have to assume I'm now a band member of the Fuck You Guys. Meanwhile, upstairs there is a useless agreement-in-progress flashing on Greg's home computer screen now waiting to be deleted.

The Rinky Dink Doublethink

Not surprisingly, everyone was fine with leaving LA early, which gets me back to the warehouse around 6 p.m. I have Dave D drop me off at my regular liquor store and then, with bottle, walk the two remaining blocks back. This brings me within the orbit of the fake cleaning van. As I approach I can see a pair of aviators watching me from inside the side rearview mirror. Then when I pass, the wearer of the sunglasses pushes his car-seat-cushion-slept-on-hair-head out of the window and yells at me sarcastically, "HEY! Where's the crystal, maan?!" He pulls an arm out and slaps at the door three times.

Ignoring him, I maintain my pace—though my chest has stopped moving. With the scare is the odd side effect of relief in that the paranoia was undeniably real. I'd just been called out by a cop one-on-one.

I wake up into morning-time heavy on the hustle with a side of bustle in the house. Zee has been waiting with a new kind of errand for me, which is one that doesn't sit well at all. Instead of going somewhere unusually usual, she's asking me to go to the main San Francisco police station at 850 Bryant to un-impound her car for her. The parking tickets had apparently piled high and one of the Man's meter maids had it towed off from a two-hour only zone. Despite this probably being the last thing on earth I want to do considering all of the police action already in effect, I take the mission as this could be my way back into good graces with her. By now she viewed me as an enabler to Nick's increasing drug intake that had led to some of his recent questionable decision making, and while I was if anything trying to interject a voice of reason in where I could, looking at the situation with all honesty I couldn't say she was wrong. I head out toward the belly of the beast about a twenty-minute walk away.

The police station looks like Fort fucking Knox, a huge fortress of cement authority, and is about as inviting as the deep end of an empty Olympic-sized swimming pool from sixty stories up. There's even a giant replica of a police badge on the front. They've got it all here: jail cells, courtrooms, every type of police officer's headquarters, and the automobile impound.

The rub is, I've got to try to obtain the vehicle's release without the car's registration papers signed in my name, which she doesn't have either. I'm not yet fully committed to instigating the situation, but I at least need to attempt getting a read on how stupid it would be for me to try, which I highly suspect is pretty stupid.

As I walk up the cement steps to the giant fortress super-center of the Man, I suddenly remember to tuck the miniature coke spoon hanging around my neck under my shirt.

It's all things serious inside here and they are whirling in every direction, uniforms and ties and high heels and random faces stretched long with unwanted mandatory obligations to be here. It's the ultimate no-fun zone and intent-driven movement festers everywhere inside. Before I can even join in the fuck-this fracas I have to go through the metal detector, which mercifully reveals my micro-spoon necklace is either fake or beyond detection.

Once I've collected my Zippo, keys and coin on the other side, I turn around and am immediately lost. I begin going down the epic mini-marquee letters that make up the horizontal novel that is the building's directory list. I don't even see anything about cars and so I spy an empty bench down a hall and head for a regroup. There is at least some slight comfort in the overt art-deco style of the vintage corridor and its long row of thin wooden telephone booths, each with the little glass sliding accordion doors with period-incorrect modern payphones.

I sit on the bench and start to worry. What in the fuck am I even doing here? I should not be sticking my neck out for this, a high-risk dice roll from someone else's hand that calls my fate. Just then a middle-aged guy sits next to me. He looks straight out of *The Streets of San Francisco* 70s television series, salt-and-pepper blow-dried back which matches the beard and blazer, large aviator eyeglasses and elbow patches.

"So, luck finally ran out, huh? And now here you are. Party's over."

I look up at him but say nothing, trying to assess what's just started out of nowhere.

"When are you going to start thinking straight, man? After some jail time?"

I quickly scan around for an answer that doesn't require engaging in this situation, then realize I'm sitting in the section of courtrooms. He must be assuming that's why I'm here today. He thinks he knows my whole story just on sight, the one missing ingredient being I'm still one small step away from being busted for something bigger than I'd like to think.

He takes offense to my non-participation. "Wake *up*, man, before you're too buried in it to ever get back out." He stands up. "I hope I never see you again, for your sake."

I watch him walk into one of the courtrooms. "*Fuuck* this, man," I whisper under my breath and get up and walk out of the building.

When I get back to the warehouse I head straight up the stairs to gestate on new revelations, but then Zee almost runs into me at the top of the steps. I jump into explanation mode but something bigger is now going on.

"Guess who's here?!" she exclaims excitedly.

"Who?"

The Dandy Warhols are here!" she relays, as if announcing royalty at the ball. The fact that she doesn't seem concerned with the car adds to the fanfare. Despite it being a cool classic one, fortunes were steadily rising for my two roommates and the "I'll just buy another one" days had arrived, seemingly.

"Really?"

"Yes, but they are here to have fun and relax, so you can't tell anybody. They're all downstairs high on ecstasy right now."

"Well, I guess I'll leave them to it, then."

She bounces down the stairs while calling back, "OK, come down later and say hii!"

Happy to see Peter from The Dandy Warhols in the only known
photo of me inside the warehouse

Early evening I go down and find them spread around her large
white room, all sunken into furniture and big pillows. I get a happy
"Hi Joel!" from Peter. Courtney smiles but looks in another direction,
like he's both acknowledging me and not at the same time. Zia just
says my name in an animated, not real way, and then Eric smiles
and nods while parroting Zia in a more downplayed version. They
don't want it to be known they are here, OK, but whatever sort of
statute of limitations this type of stuff gets must be over by now,
I should think.

They had now adopted a "leave them all in the dust" mentality,
having signed with Capitol Records, but oddly, because I live in the
warehouse, which at this time, and in addition to Andy Warhol's

Factory, will turn out to be the living modern inspiration for their own near-future artist's slash party creative space to be called the "Odditorium", I was kept on their radar. Or it was simply due to the fact that there was just nowhere to hide here. On the flip, my history with the band turns my residency here into part of the fanfare and in turn has gotten me off the hook with Zee, car or no car.

That's about it for down here I guess and so I leave them to it until their show at The Bottom of the Hill tomorrow night. Ondi and David are coming up with their cameras so we are all guaranteed to be "on", and hence have a fun time, which makes it even weirder when Anton doesn't show at the club. Zia is wearing a BJM T-shirt onstage despite whatever it is our situation is now, and I'm asked to join them onstage for the last encore. Once I'm up there, it turns out to be The Rolling Stones' classic "The Last Time", which I couldn't yet see as ironic as I shake beat next to a shirtless Courtney.

The famous San Francisco "rock 'n' roll" hotel that is The Phoenix, which we've never had a good reason to stay at ourselves for obvious reasons, is the interchangeable crash site and launchpad for our poolside party crew as we rise from the ashes of midnight and pop more E's at 8 a.m. Sprawled and splayed in beach chairs around the pool, we all lazily converse, but it's more to the cameras than each other, despite appearances. It's like talking to someone at a party or a gig while really only being interested in someone else close by hearing what you have to say. People already do that a lot in this business, but when a camera's rolling it's an unspoken given.

It's weird Anton never showed up last night. I was hoping to reconnect with him, and anyway, he's the one that hipped Ondi to film The Dandy Warhols in the first place, and now here they are getting in on the film. How did it all go so wrong? I haven't seen Anton since the Viper Room blowout and I need to plead my case to him. I drift off and think of better earlier times as I take another sip of cheap Early Times bourbon.

Final Destination

It's a thin (but extremely long) line between being a beautiful loser-outcast in rebellion against everything conventional and just an obnoxious asshole nobody wants to deal with anymore, and the trapeze wire is very high now. I look down and squint at the tiny shapes far below. They are the ones inviting me everywhere. Waiting to see what crazy thing I'll do next, to be there to see it when I fall. I'm wobbling and warping just like a tambourine that's seen better days and it feels like on any beat I could just snap into bits and pieces. This realization causes the high wire to shake under my feet.

No longer a tool for finding good times, I have officially passed the drug's expiration date. Historically, there are no long-term success stories with speed, only the post-use victories that could have only happened by having known when to leave it behind. Like the whole warehouse life itself, you have to know when to get out. There were others in the music scene that had become casualties, and now I could hear my own number being called from the podium.

I drink more and in turn am hungover more, so I drink more. Now my last year's worst possible hangover face has become my freshest possible look. Only when I *need* to, do I glance at my face in the mirror, which more times than not is from below my nose, all I can see is that I am looking older. The vitality in the skin above my eyes that gave my eyebrows that extra arc has begun to drain down into puffy bags underneath my eyes. I smile and it flips on new hidden wrinkles like a light switch. That big smile once full of youth mirroring the carnival of life now has a plastered-on psychotic effect. It's a road sign on the side of a desert highway, bent back and full of bullet holes, it's only there out of public necessity. I'm sure it must be obvious to anyone who sees it that it only exists as an all-in-one skeleton key expression to get me through whatever or whoever it is I am being held conversationally captive by.

Walking down the street I half expect passersby to suddenly punch me in the face for no reason, or for the footsteps behind me to just plant a hatchet into the top my head. I steal reflective glimpses from angled glass shop door entryways to ensure this isn't about to happen. Under no circumstances will I step on a manhole of any kind. I check over my shoulder at busy street corners and especially on subway platforms as rushing trains approach.

Then one night I wake up on a white push bed in an all-white sterile sort of lab room. I look over and see who I understand is my wife, lying on an identical bed next to me. We are both wearing identical white jumpsuits and she is plugged into a small white machine perched on a white stand beside her bed. It hums and makes a slow, pulsing electronic heartbeat sound. Now I see that I've got one too, but unlike hers mine seems to have broken. I unplug the cord affixed into the fold of her arm and she immediately shoots up into sitting position.

She looks over at me and without saying anything, we both acknowledge that wherever this is, we have to get out of here.

I grab her hand and we run out of the room and down a metal hallway to a door. I throw it open and the doorway leads out the side of a mountain into a vast landscape of what I understand is in the deep remote green hills of Northern California. About twenty yards in front of us at the bottom of the slope there is a bulldozer knocking down a small wooden outhouse. The now exposed shit and piss pit is buzzing with hundreds and hundreds of flies, none of which want to vacate the full-up stinking outhouse shithole, even now as it's about to be filled back in with fresh dirt by the bullozer. The flies are buried under it.

Suddenly, coming from everywhere, I hear a loud electric alarm sound and I immediately lose consciousness. When I wake up again, I'm at home in my bed. Another nightmare. Never at any period of my life have I had so many and such vivid nightmares. They are becoming more real than being awake in the daytime.

The next night, in some cosmically crucial coincidence, I get a call from Anton. Apparently things hadn't exactly been going according to plan for him either and I was now officially being invited up to Portland to be his sidekick again. In just the same way it didn't seem necessary for me for me to explain things after my months-long disappearance, I didn't ask any questions. It was simply just time to get back to business and I was grateful.

I slam the phone down. "That's it," I say out loud to my empty room. His timing was of the purest perfection. As for this place, the feathers were about to start flying, and so I begin to pack up my knapsack full of my most needed worldlies. The rest of my stuff I don't expect to see again.

On my mattress I arrange my favorite snorting mirror, which was a detached round mirror belt buckle, my extra large double-sided safety razor blade, tiny single-blast *Superfly*-style spoon necklace, a cut-out section of a crazy straw with one full loop and a unused 1950s two-piece syringe I was saving for some eventual "gotta try it once" day. Time to leave this all behind.

I set the knapsack in the center of what had just been my bedroom and walk down the dark stairs into the expanse of the garage. The big wall-spanning garage door is wide open and the cool, quiet glow of the city at dawn gives a false sense of possible beginnings.

Nick is at his large work bench in a zombie-like state hanging up some tools on the wall—he should have been packing them to leave. We all need to leave.

"Hey man, I think I'm going to get out of here for a few days."

"OK dude," he says with a slight twinge of sarcasm, not looking over at me. He continues with his organizing. I small-talk my way through my trip plans, all the while both of us knowing we were involved in a different conversation, which was me asking for blessings to abandon ship. Among other things, he hadn't bothered asking for any rent money from me these last few months and I was feeling disloyal, even though at this point all my loyalty had left to offer was a one-way ticket out the free world's protective orbit. I finish and begin to stew in the extended pause when he slowly looks over at me for the first time, and with eyes now fully engaging mine says, "You're not on the lease, you don't get mail here, so as far as anyone else is concerned you don't really live here."

This was true. While residing here these months my name had not been attached to anything pertaining to official residency. Even more importantly, I had not become a part of the moneymaking side of this place. I was what square writers said when referring to my archetypical bohemian heroes: "strictly out for kicks".

As I slowly walk back up the wooden stairs, it hits me. He did know. He *had* seen everything that was coming, but after all the money they'd put into this, all the next-level risks taken, having renovated the whole place from the floor up, he had resigned himself to being like a sea captain going down with the ship which right now had him knee-deep in the water. There was no other move left other than to wait for the final end to come break down the front door. It would only take three more days.

I walk into the large open San Francisco Transbay bus terminal with my military knapsack slung over my shoulder. This being an old art-moderne-style building from the 1930s, I stroll straight over to a ticket booth widow and, doing something I'd always wanted to do, ask in my best Edward G. Robinson voice, "Shaay, shee, when's the next bus up to Portland? Shee, meah."

"Two fifteen," the old man answers back, blowing my noir movie fantasy of being able to walk right on board and *skip town*. Man, it's only just past 7 a.m. now. "OK, I'll take it," I say, dejected.

After the cost of a one-way ticket, I've only got about twenty bucks left and no idea what to do for money up there in Oregon. Then again, this was nothing new for me, and Anton had Sophie with him, so between the three of us we'd be able to get some sort of action going. Anyway, if all else failed, The Dandy Warhols lived there, so it *had* to be groovy. Then again, now that I think about it, things between us certainly weren't what they used to be.

Working out the logistics of my financial situation I had enough for a little pint o'sumpthin' for the hard day's wait and bus ride. Ondi and David planned to meet me at the bus station in Portland, which meant I would be stepping off the bus right into their documentary cameras. Best be feeling good. Last night I'd split open all my little empty drug baggies and scraped their inner walls to make for about one good fat line to get me to Portland. A last nasal hurrah. I head out for a liquor store and am back in fifteen minutes with a pint bottle of Smirnoff resting in the inside pocket of my leather jacket.

I sit on one of the twenty-foot long wooden passenger waiting benches. I'm bored about thirty seconds in, but I don't want to go outside again. I have my ticket in hand now and am feeling safe in this giant womb of change and new beginnings. I buy a *San Francisco Chronicle* and hunker down.

After hours of fine-tooth combing the newspaper and imagining how entertaining this station would have been in the 70s when the now shuttered bar, diner and shops were still open and packed with people-watching material, my bus finally pulls into the underground loading area. I board along with all the other passengers and settle in at the back of the bus. I begin to engage my inner self with the impending rebirth and it all starts to become very real. *I am leaving San Francisco.*

The bus engine rumbles up and we slowly pull out of the underground and into the bright afternoon sunlight. The relief brought on by the actual physical movement of escape mixed with leaving the city I love made for a bittersweet cocktail. I slide out my bottle of liquid entertainment and add to the chemistry.

Two and a half hours later we pull into another beat-down bus station as the driver garbles through the bus speaker, *"OK folks, this is a connection stop…we'll be here for one hour…the bus will be departing this station at 9 p.m. sharp."*

Sacramento…ugh. I get off the bus and do some recon around the station for options. Like the one in San Francisco, it looks circa 1930s and long ago gutted of all its vintage hang-out spots. Nothing else on the block except fast food. Fuck it, I'll go the other way. Inside a men's room stall I take out my "last ride" bag and rather unceremoniously do my final San Francisco treat. I go outside and smoke a cigarette, then back inside the station and over to a sectioned-off empty glass waiting area. In the corner on a ceiling-mounted TV plays an episode of *Nash Bridges*, starring Don Johnson. I watch for a few minutes, trying to deduce if it's the episode with our song in it, but it isn't. I watch a little more just to catch some San Francisco location shots, then go back outside and smoke another cigarette.

With nothing going down around here, I get back on the bus early and this time I take the outside seat with my bag by the window. With new passengers about to board, this move will serve as the last line of defense in keeping the row all to myself. Most new riders will usually sit in the open aisle seats before having to ask people to scoot over. As the 9 p.m. departure time draws close, all the other passengers have boarded the dark bus. As everyone is getting settled in for the all-night ride, I see there are a few seats left and it looks like I've held my row. The driver walks through the bus doing his headcount, then returns to his driver's seat. Just as I'm about to stop paying attention to all this, a middle-aged guy with feathered blond hair and a thick mustache appears at the top of the front-door steps. He seems to know the driver and after a quick exchange he addresses us passengers.

"OKaay, I'm with the DEA office, we're gonna get you all on the road here in just a minute, but before that can happen, there's a person on board we have reason to believe is a dealer of narcotics. If you'll be patient, we can get this taken care of in just a few minutes and get y'all off toward your final destination."

What are the chances? They've got some poor fool trapped on here. Purely on instinct I think to reach in my pocket for my little baggie but then remember I'd done it and flushed it down the toilet in the men's room. Wanting to appear as unrelated as possible to someone involved in this type of situation, I remain perfectly still with face forward and watch the DEA officer, waiting for what was going to happen next. The moments pass and he's just standing there, with an elbow on the back of the front seat. He and the driver go into another inaudible exchange. I decide to sneak a scan around, seeing if I can judge anyone looking like a dealer before the officer comes back here and hauls them off. I turn my head and standing directly behind me in the aisle is what must be another DEA officer looking down over my shoulder, watching my every move. I turn back around and sit perfectly still again. This one must have gotten on the bus after we'd all exited, waiting back in the dark shadows. He waits a few more eternal seconds, then slowly walks to the front of the bus and shakes his head to the other officer. After a short exchange they both get off and the doors shut.

I can't be exactly clear on what just happened, but judging by how the situation just played out, it seems they must have been dispatched to intercept me, but at the same time didn't have any hard evidence that I was part of "the ring". If I'd gotten spooked by the announcement and attempted to unload any kind of stash hidden on my person, they were there, surveying right over my shoulder with the cuffs at the ready.

As we pull out of Sacramento station, I am no longer sad about leaving San Francisco. I will return someday, and for good, no matter how impossible it seems from where I am sitting now, but like in *The Wizard of Oz*, I had almost lost my way by falling asleep in the poppy field. Now I was wide awake and back on the road. This would by no means mark the recovery into sobriety section of the story, as my days of being a partying explorer are to this day far from over, but from now on I would be officially dialing it down from "speed freak" to just a freak.

Sixteen hours since leaving San Francisco and in the early morning the bus pulls into the Portland Greyhound station. As I slowly make my way down the aisle toward the door, I see out the windows that a camera is rolling and waiting to greet me at the bottom of the bus steps.

"Action."

I walk off the bus and David Timoner is standing there in a stationary position, camera rolling. I ask, "Are we on?"

"Yes."

"I'm in Portland now, kids. It was a rough trip."

"How long?"

"*Six*teen hours."

"From where?"

"...*none of your business.*"

He takes the camera off his shoulder and we half-hug our hellos. "C'mon, let's get over to the hotel. Ondi is there with Anton and Sophie for the convention."

"Convention?"

"They didn't tell you? It's the North by Northwest music convention all over town this weekend. Like South by Southwest, but wetter. The whole thing kicks off this morning at The Benson Hotel."

Talk about getting right to it. We climb into the documentary SUV machine and head to the convention kick-off summit.

We enter through the large entranceway of this turn-of-the-century grand ol' dame of a hotel which is packed with people having hundreds of different conversations echoing throughout the huge lobby and corridors, in a cack of phony cacophony. Everyone in the entire place is all at the exact same time freshly high on their first of the day communal hit of caffeine and the biz talk is bouncing back down hard from off the ornate ceilings. Aged but not faded crystal chandeliers hang and glisten with electric light that refracts in the ebb and flow of decorative lines and curves carved and finished into the mahogany walls.

The laminate warriors are psyching themselves up for battle and their corporate sponsorship is everywhere, but by the number of representatives from the scraggly indie tribes, there is still a local-centric feel of the type faded from its more accomplished older sister living under the bright Austin, Texas sun. The massive revolving doors at the front of the hotel are the one single thing in more constant motion than Anton as he prowls in excitement, not knowing where to start with the mind-blowing. He puffs on his cigarette, scanning, but it's next to impossible to tell by outward appearances who here is looking for something new, innovative and dangerous, and who has become impossible to impress and will just show you the wall for even suggesting that they don't already know everything.

He's had his hair cut since I last saw him the morning after the band's Viper Room demolition and is now back to his more mod angle, wearing a simple navy-blue wool pullover and white Levis. He sees me from across the room and messages me a bemused smile. Time to get back to work.

David has just freshly loaded his camera with a new tape and is now rolling. I lead him over to the center of the lobby where I pull the largest flower from the massive centerpiece bouquet and garnish dirty looks. I'm too high to care. Not *high* high, though I haven't slept yet—I'm high on my escape from Alcatraz. Just a couple hours ago I was watching the sun come up from the bus and with it a new way free from harm.

Feeling free on the morning of my arrival in Portland

Anton's lawyer is here, representing the cool California schmooze where all news is good news, whatever the question. Hand me a stick and I will pass it back a piece of licorice. Music is a multimillion-dollar-a-second industry and here we are at one of the biggest pop-up pop shops of it all, coming in third after SXSW and CMJ in New York City.

Friends from the Dandys' circle are present, but no Dandys proper. There is a buzz for their show tonight with support from more mutual pals Swoon 23 and Anton's planned "solo" performance backed by members of the Dandys. Whatever it is he'd thought up for tonight will apparently not require my tambourine skills and I don't let that bother me as apparently the stage show theme had been decided upon before I'd been invited. Tonight's being advertised as "after hours", which for me means with the minus sleep that I will officially be opting out of the hang.

I was expecting to see a big "scene", which there was, but not for us. To be fair, Anton had come to conquer, and they surely would have sensed that and known he had the goods to do so. The choices were to put your hands up or board up the town. I guess this was part of the reason he called me, which played the complementary role of having saved my ass. I'm dropped off at what is to be my new home with Anton and Sophie, Suburbia Studios. It's a punk rock-style band factory where he's been recording and they've both been sleeping. It's raining and as every band in town is either playing somewhere tonight or watching friends do so, not a creature is stirring, not even a mouse with a Mosrite. I'm taken up to a dark studio room, and with the light provided by the windows and open door, I'm directed to the large mattress in the corner. I pass out smiling.

Bande à part

Sophie, Anton and I lie across the king-sized mattress in the darkness of unlit midnight listening to the radio:

...farmers from a village there have—CRACKLE—formed nighttime vigilante squads to track down the flying beast that has been dubbed the goat sucker...we're telling people to keep the women and children locked up at night. This is real. There's something out th—ZZZT—it may be very old, it may be very new, I really couldn't tell you—but I can certainly tell you it's out there. So, coming up in just a few moments, I've g—HISSZZZ—BUZZZnd is as much an expert as you are going to find these days on chupacabra, which is some kind of horrible new animal. Here, somehow unimaginably, either something new, something from somebody's lab...something created...or something that has come through the veils...the openings to elsewhere. We don't know...

We are tuned into the Art Bell Coast to Coast AM radio show, which starts at midnight and goes until either when one falls asleep or the program naturally ends at 2 a.m. Tonight and every night it's accompanied by rain pitter-patter and wind-blown tree branch tips tapping at the windows while Art Bell does extended raps, interviews with experts, then listener call-ins, who stoke the flames of belief in all things paranormal ranging from extraterrestrial visitations to the end of the world itself, which we'd only learned last Thursday was just a few months away now. For us, listening to Art Bell is like campfire ghost stories, nursing us to sleep from the old school's oldest tool when it comes to electronic media entertainment, the broadcast radio show. Once the radio is turned on, that's the way it stays the entire night, left alone through the wee smalls, talking to itself while feeding our dreams lines until every morning when we awake to the speaker sounds of the morning-boring "real" news.

I've been here in Portland with Sophie and Anton for a couple of weeks now. Us engaging in secret permanent unlicensed residence inside a "punk rock" music rehearsal room complex is technically against the law, but we make sure to maintain a discreet outward presence. Whenever a physical place is described as "punk" that often just means that it's a dump. Suburbia Studios is very punk. There is only one bathroom in the whole place and while it was conveniently located just opposite our door, the toilet had layers of grime and filth that over time had acquired different shades and dimensions, textures of browns and grossness that you could see were of different eco-fug-scuzz families. A better word than punk or dump is *squalor*. It beats jail though.

As I lie hearing about new monsters that I never really expect to see in person (probably), my feet are throbbing. The high-heeled zip boots Ondi had given me after my Chelsea boots blew a heel had felt OK when I'd left San Francisco, but being two sizes too small they were now officially hurting my feet all throughout the day. It's too late now and their three-inch heels have me flexing my toes in my sleep.

"...let's take another caller, West of the Rockies, you're on the air."

"Art? Uh, hi, I, uh..."

I wake up the next morning into white-walled dinginess. The pair of large second-story windows casts a blinding grey light that still very much commands a squint of respect. I see Anton on the other side of the mattress asleep, but no Sophie. I get up and carefully step around and through the guitars resting against amps, scattered percussion instruments, the multitude of different-sized bottles and cans and other consumption objects that are repurposed as ashtrays, various keyboards and children's musical toys, microphones and cords piled high like spaghetti and through the drum kit over to the windows. It's still pouring rain on this industrial no-man's-land area of Portland, Oregon. Nothing public whatsoever. Offices, warehouses and nothing else to make out except the crummy Burger King off in the distance. Grim. I know the wide expanse of the Pacific Northwest lies just beyond, but it's thickly veiled in grey and damp.

"Hey," Anton says, now awake. He flips back his hair and starts feeling into his jean pockets, then through the parka he is also wearing, then around the edge of the mattress where he finds his almost empty wilted pack of Camel non-filters. He pulls out the last one and delivers the wrapper to full crumple.

"I need coffee," he announces, then flicks his Bic with a first finger and lights up.

"Where's Sophie?" I ask as he reanimates up from the king-sized mattress.

"She got picked up early to go shower and stuff."

"Must be nice," I lament for my own state of uncleanliness. There were no common areas here, let alone showers, and we had to take sink spit baths in the never-been-cleaned public bathroom of death out in the hall.

"C'mon, let's drive to the store."

When I first arrived here from San Francisco I saw that Sophie had modified her look to one similar to my own, wearing all black, usually tight-fitting jeans, pullover tops and ratted bird's nest hair. "Here's your new tambourine sidekick," Anton had joked upon our one-sided introduction just a couple of months ago. Replacement was more like it, as he had just given up on my growing unreliability right at the same time I'd decided to become reliable again.

Sophie, whether now a new stage partner or band role competitor, was exotically French and I wasn't sure if I should be mad or glad, as she would without a doubt be adding solid cool to the stage image, a precious commodity that one should never get selfish about. Despite the potential spite of this situation, I feel no real threat. I had created this version of the tambourine-playing frontman role with my own personality, which apparently I was still the model for with my unaffected stage presence. I never understood what it was that made people act so excited about playing a tambourine. I was a *serious percussionist*.

We climb into our little beat-up old Honda Civic to do the first group morning ritual of the day, coffee at the nearby Plaid Pantry liquor store and market. I didn't have real food kind of money and even if I did, I'd rather have a pack of smokes or a bottle of beer. I certainly didn't have the kind of monetary position for all four of those things. In fact, by this point I didn't have any kind of monetary position. It was Sophie's family allowance now keeping me alive, and I figured the lighter I leaned, the longer the means.

We return to our space where there is already the sound of some-one here early to jam some morning time "tasty licks" from one of the other studio rooms. Back in ours, whether it be tracking, mixing, overdubbing or just listening, I'll be spending most of the day and probably night watching Anton at the mixing console or moving around from instrument to instrument, strumming on this, banging on that, like in a workman's shop only the product is purely sonic. I keep the tambourine and maracas close, always at the ready. This was the lab, the bunker, where we resided in our self-exile from Portland. Unlike what we would probably be doing in San Francisco, we did not take further advantage of the situation like say, walking the streets as traveling artists with guitars and tambourines, Anton out front, strumming and singing his songs while male and female tambourine twins followed behind banging away. Truthfully, we never had a chance for any of that because it's rained *every single day* since I'd arrived.

Sophie didn't seem too curious about the process of recording, but was always enthusiastic about the finished product. She would usually sit on the mattress in the furthest corner sketching away at a portrait or reading until the inevitable music break would come, then she'd look back up with conversation subjects and relaxed vibes. Her English was quite good but she talked with a French accent so thick it's like she wants to keep it as close to still speaking French as she can.

I'd been on this mission with him a lot longer than her, long enough now through joint experiences and mutual dreams to cultivate a power of unspoken understanding, a state of not needing to verbalize every angle of your points. There had been a merging through all the prolonged silences. Maybe to some degree it was an illusion, but either way it filled the void and the less there was of everything that wasn't band-related, the more there was of what mattered.

Portland is strictly a transitory location for us. Where to next though was not so decided, but we had busted out of our California safety zone and were ramblin' for real. I was broke, dirty, and my feet permanently hurt, but I loved it.

Surprising yet not so surprising was the news that Anton and Sophie had gotten engaged on their arrival in Portland. At the time they'd planned by now to have a proper place to live and have a ceremony, but as it went their wedding bells were to chime here at Suburbia Studios.

Anton and I are dressed rock 'n' roll functional for the occasion, with the groom in traditional black wool pullover and matching Levi's while I, the best man, am in a suede high-button blazer and turtleneck combo. We smoke cigarettes and he is oddly quiet as we wait for the bride to arrive. I catch myself giving him another expectant look with raised eyebrows for the second time in five minutes. He slightly shakes his head in his amused dismissive combo way and blows out a drag of smoke. I'm a little embarrassed at not knowing more of what to say, but I'm also not going to clutter up the vibes with empty comments.

Sophie arrives with Peter, the only invited friend who also plays in The Dandy Warhols, and his girlfriend, whose place Sophie was able to doll up at for the occasion. She makes it a "happening" white wedding in real-deal 60s go-go boots that were made for walkin', a miniskirt dress and faux-fur babushka hat. Then shortly after, the ordained hippie sailor of ceremonies appears and with that, the five of us gather into position around him. He is head-to-toe in bohemian denims with a fade that matches the shade of his long beard.

The backdrop is white drywall, the nails and studs are spackled and whitewashed over, but the wall itself is left unpainted, as if just at the very brink of completion the workers suddenly remembered almost too late that this place was to be punk and not ruined by normal societal finishing practices or past-the-expiration-date carpentry conventions, man.

Our hippie-sailor-of-ceremonies clears his throat and begins to read the prepared sermon of vows when suddenly Anton interrupts with a "Here" and hands him an unopened pint of whiskey. "Nobody will believe it otherwise." We all laugh together as the hippie-sailor-of-ceremonies nods in appreciation, then takes a tipple before restarting his prose to people he's just met. You can tell it's been a while since he's done this, but he bottle-tilts his way through with sufficient success until it's time for me to pull out the ring.

I open the small clamshell jewelry case and hold it out for Anton, who smiles as he pulls it free. Then as he slides it on Sophie's finger, I realize I've never seen her smile so much. Tonight so far probably outweighs all the other times I'd witnessed it put together. It wasn't like she was a depressed or a detached person, she was just "French cool" in that classic Jean Moreau way. Even so, when she smiled it was so natural that I had to wonder why she didn't do it more often. I imagine she got so good at it by growing up somewhere nice in France.

With the deal now sealed the bride and groom get such a rousing applause that you'd think there were more people here than just the three of us cheering to accompanied percussion of a silver sailor's ring clanking on liquor bottle glass. Anton and Sophie raise wine glasses in toast and drink with arms intertwined.

As the official best man I also get to sign the official marriage certificate along with the consecrator and consecrates, which fills me with pride. Anton is back to talking as Sophie places it atop a keyboard leaning against the wall and holds it in place with a vintage 60s troll doll with flaming pink hair. Then with that, the newlyweds whisk themselves away and off in the rain and into the little beat-up white Subaru where they head to a hotel, to be followed the next day by a honeymoon day trip to the Oregon coast.

The next morning I wake up alone. I think of last night and all the smiling and I smile again. Then my stomach growls and I realize that I haven't eaten anything since the previous morning. I look outside and it's pouring rain. My stomach bemoans this realization. There's a payphone out in the hall, but I have no dime. I scan among the amps and gear for discarded change. Nothing in the tobacco-dusted recording area but guitar picks, cigarette butts, empty matchbooks and random bits of torn and wrinkled wrappings sprinkled all around. I check for any possible small change kicked under the edges of the mattress. Nothing but a few pennies and another pick. I begin to wallow in the stillness of what is ultimately self-inflicted poverty.

Now I'm depressed. Not sure if I want to attempt to remedy or fuel it, I look through Anton and Sophie's stack of CDs. I pull out Donovan's *Troubadour: The Definitive Collection 1964–1976* two-disc collection. Track one is a demo version from his early folk period "London Town". Depressed ye shall be.

"Could be he stopped moving, ramble round and round..."

There is a part of me that welcomes the melancholy as a feelings capacity detector, but this emotion brings on a more generous realization helping of the have-nots. Without money to spend on distractions, whether even wanted or not, to not have a choice in the matter extends the pondering moments. Is it like staring down from wherever it is and fondly gazing at your mark on the world, or is it like a jigsaw puzzle that you'd been staring at with all its individual pieces and all the building up of different sections and by the time it's finally done you've been looking at it so long the finished thing is no longer interesting? The pouring rain picks up. No hustles or bustles outside to partake in. I see the Burger King off in the distance. I don't love fast food, but I certainly would on a day like today.

I remember all the smiles from last night and it snaps me out of it. Anton is like a different person now; well, the same person but no longer the fired-up, pissed-off one. Now he's back to being super motivated in that inspiring way that makes you want to arm up for the cause. The version that despite feeling the weight of the enormous amount of task and road that lie ahead, was paired with a positivity and humor that you knew would steer the ship straight.

By early evening I'm getting desperate. I stop strumming, set the guitar down and go back to the window. Sometimes I think the reincarnation assemblers at the reincarnation department got the order wrong and put a cat inside of a human. The rain has mellowed to steady. I look again at that crummy Burger King in the distance. They're closed. It's early, but it's the weekend on an industrial side of town. I look at the dumpster sitting next to the drive-thru. I'm so hungry. A chain of thought begins that wants to justify the impossible to justify. Any unsold pre-made stuff would get tossed out with the wrapper still on. Then I remember once seeing a news story about a McDonald's hamburger not decomposing for years. This thought thread continues to grow and soon I have no control or reason to stop it.

The rain has now lightened to a sprinkle as I creep down in my two-sizes-too-small too-tight boots to the Burger King dumpster. I slow my approach to a stealth-like prowl as if I'm attempting to steal something of worth, not just thrown away garbage. The lid is chain locked, but there is enough play to rise it up about a foot. Now I realize I'm not just worried about being seen by any employees or security guards, but being seen by *any* other human being at all.

I hold up the lid of the dumpster and I can see that the whole top layer is the unsold food items of the leftover hamburgers and other various wrapped devil's what-have-yous. If there is anything going in my favor, which there isn't, it's that right on top there are indeed sandwich items still individually wrapped and hence separated from the bed of straight-up garbage piled below. Regardless of my self-brainwashing, my rational awareness won't sanction a way around acknowledging this being the milestone event of me eating out of a garbage dumpster. This occasion even goes beyond the time I spent the night drunk sleeping on some church steps until a crowd of churchgoers had to wake me up because I was blocking the doors. Now I get to tick this one off the list of how to rock to the rock bottom.

Safely back at my secret crime lair, I lay my three contestants in a row on the windowsill. Contestant #1 is smashed down flat, with four, maybe five kinds of grey-looking gross. I one-two-three loosely wrap it back up and move on to #2, which looks pretty much the same except there seems to be something about it that's trying to say the meat is supposed to be different, like comparing teak to walnut. Contestant #3 looks like #1's older brother, so I go back to #1, close my eyes and take a bite with my teeth only half closed like you do when you have to bite into something that you don't want to but have to for some reason. I spit it back into the wrapper and throw it all away in the garbage can down the hall by the gear escalator. Say I wanna revolution? Well, it wasn't like I had to sleep in the jungle like a gorilla soldier, and even if it's just musical, revolution is not supposed to be easy.

After my shame lunch I leave the rehearsal cell to pee and make the horrific mistake of sitting down to do so on the death punk toilet. There is a weird old-fashioned hump on its bottom base porcelain bowl that has over the years collected pees and scums and god knows what else until it's built up into a thick fuzzy layer of sticky film that I swipe off onto the back inside of my only pants. I don't even notice what's happened until I pull them up and fasten and now they're stuck to the small of my back. My knee-jerk reaction is to run away from this grime monster that's attacking me from inside my pants, but after jogging around the bathroom in a semicircle, I accept I'm just trying to run away from myself. This is the moment when squalor officially defeats me, but there's more. I carefully undo my pants in fast—slow motion and they go reluctantly as I peeeel them off of my top bottom, clinging like when you take a cloth backstage pass sticker off of your denim jacket. It then takes all the powdered soap the little metal wall dispenser has to give before I feel like I've remedied the hazmat zone on myself and my only pair of pants.

Back in the studio room I find a hanger and hang the soaked material up on a loose string of Christmas lights dangling near the rain-covered window which creates a 3-D effect of futility in the key of soaked. I take down an Indian wall tapestry off the wall and wrap it around myself.

The next morning I'm so hungry that I begin to wonder if I should think of a good hunger strike cause while I'm already here. I check my hanging pants. Almost dry. I get back into the mattress bed when suddenly the door swings open and there are Anton and Sophie. She's smiling and holding a salami and a block of cheese. There is a goddess, and she's French.

The Last Hitchhiker on Earth

I snap-awake inside the car. It's very cold. Thick raindrops from the last rainfall hover on the glass like spilt specimens and the whole exterior world beyond looks like a black and white movie made of every tone of grey. Inside here the interior is late-70s tan leather, all of it hard and frigid just beyond my body's border until I rise for a full perspective look down the white runway of the hood and out to the widescreen horizon of brown and deep green soaking in the hours of downpour. White lines grid the hard launchpad of cement ground and I still can't remember why I should wake up in such a place.

I climb into the front passenger seat as Anton pushes out from the gas station glass doors, then briefly stops to light up and blows out a mixture of smoke and morning condensation. He puts his Bic back in his parka pocket with a flip of the bangs as my own breathing begins to cloud the glass inside the car. I think about beginning to roll a window down, despite the cold, but in my moment of indecision he is already here and opens the door. The wind blows in and eats it clear.

He pulls the door closed and begins with a sighed, "*Fuuck*, man," but doesn't finish his thought. With a turn of the key the radio is in the middle of announcing that Dean Martin is dead, a random further dusting of the gravity on reality. We move and the car commences to crumple aged loosening concrete as we pull out of the sopped parking lot, onto the road and into the thick leftover Pacific Northwest dawn fog. We should make it back to Portland by later today.

Our hair is a little oily from the elements while our skin has a translucent shielding tone of survival. Telephone poles and the shore of weeds are the only things close enough to see out on this road. I'm still tired, but it's the kind of tired that doesn't matter, the kind that doesn't have a say in anything, the type that helps no one from any time, space or dimension to complain about.

We sit in silence as Anton drives. Smells of tobacco, old car leather, worn carpeting, aging dashboard plastic, gasoline and motor oil is the only dish on the nasal menu in here and they mingle in familiarity that goes all the way back to my infancy. I watch the thicker rain-drops slow-drag along the side window defiantly while the thinner ones split apart in trails under velocity's pull, an inconsequential battle that plays out just inches away from my face. Far up ahead the now thinning grey slowly turns the aperture level up.

There have been times where I was the one who could provide us with the regular meager means to get by, but it's starting to feel like it's been a while ago by now. I go to pull a Kool menthol from my leather jacket, but then see I'm down to my last three. Best to ration further until something happens that might lead to more smokes...

Fuck this, man, I repeat out loud now to myself as I stomp onto the Hawthorne Bridge walking path. My two-sizes-too-small boots have my feet joining in a call-and-response inner performance of that sentiment with each and every step forward. It's nine o'clock and officially the shittiest Christmas Eve ever. With the whiskey flowing through me I'd just snapped back, "Fuck this, man! I'm going back to San Francisco right NOW!" and split our punk rock live-in studio right then and there. Who needs it? The argument hadn't even had a clear cause to start with, but what was surely clear was we were all getting hung down low in that one-mattress room. I've been here for two months now and it has rained every single day, that is until today which is in itself the big Christmas miracle.

Well, Sophie and him can stay and live here, *I'm* hitchhiking back to San Francisco tonight! I'll get a ride soon, probably have to switch a driver or two along the way down from Oregon to California and be crossing the Golden Gate Bridge before noon tomorrow. Diane will be off from work for the holiday and she'll be so excited by my sudden materialization down from Dandyland that I can just see her now falling over herself to put together a big spread and get the exclusive on just what the heck had been going on up here. Plus, I've always wanted to long-distance hitchhike at least once in my life. This will be my *Five Easy Pieces* ending to all of this.

Man, this bridge is a lot longer when you walk across it. It's supposed to be only a quarter-mile long. I still don't know the lay of the land all that well, but what I do know is this is the right direction to all the highway interchanges and not *that* far of a walk. Besides, it's still early and this bridge is always busy. I'll probably catch a ride before I even make it to the other side. I'm prime material for someone's *It's a Wonderful Life* holiday do-gooder deed worth many pats on the back. First come, first serve, baby. I'll get a ride, probably from the first car I see. *It's Christmas.*

I feel a combination of freedom from the prolonged months confined almost exclusively to the rehearsal cell and never feeling so alone ever in my life. Unlike in San Francisco, I have no network of places I could go and am at least a day's ride from there or anywhere else familiar. Tonight is also fighting cold as I gaze along the dark water while I walk. It's glimmering with the uniformed constellations of bridge lights reflecting off its tiny waves. As I make my way further to the west side of Portland and its larger buildings, I can see it looks pretty dark for a downtown, its "closed for business" holiday mood lighting provided by just a few of the office buildings now serving as giant nightlights.

The other side of the bridge is getting closer now and not one single car has passed yet. Not one car. *It's Christmas.* Man, what was I thinking? Nobody's gonna be on the road now, they're all already at wherever they need to be for the night.

Suddenly, with a *pap pap pap* count-in it's pouring rain in a shower-faucet-turning instant. The Portland rain has awoken from its nap and with it quickly begins the washing away of my buzz. Now I'm really in trouble. I pick up my pace. Larger slow plops of water run-off from the steel truss girders above start dropping on my head out of time with the faster pitter-patter from the sky. It reminds me of the times I'm too loaded to stand, let alone play a live show, and

I can hear the rest of the band all playing ahead of me in the right time signature. Luckily I'm at least wearing my leather jacket so I won't get totally soaked.

As I get closer to land I start scanning for options. Straight ahead is the grim-looking inner-city buildings bummer zone, but off to the side below I can see some kind of lit-up tour boat docked. The main structure on deck is made of observation glass and nobody appears to be home, or rather, nobody appears to be keeping an eye on what looks like a fully stocked nightclub-sized bar inside packed with liquor bottles of every make and intoxication. *It's Christmas!*

I try not to run too fast on the freshly rain-slicked pathway ramp descending to the walkway along the water's edge. From there I break into a jog and check around for signs of life in the area as I trot up to the large vacant Christmas party boat for one.

Suddenly I'm inside just like that. Wanting to restart my buzz the sensible way by not mixing my night's booze intakes up, I pull down a full bottle of Johnnie Walker Platinum from the top shelf and pour myself a large one into a beautifully crafted rocks glass. It has a classic shape textured with a stunning geometric motif. With its exceptional clarity and craftsmanship, the hand-pressed hobnail glass brilliantly showcases this fine whiskey. The eighteen-year blended scotch cascades across my palate with notes of toffee, malted milk balls, tangerines, Frosted Mini-Wheats (organic) and roasted almonds with sea salt. I proceed to drink myself down to my drunk's content and sleep soundly smiling on a large plush cushion bench the size of a sofa.

Then, just like Enrico Salvatore "Ratso" Rizzo snapping awake from one of his Florida dream-life daydreams in *Midnight Cowboy*, I hear "HEY! YOU! FREEZE!"

It's a security guard running toward me from down the walkway. I jump back and run, having never set one foot on the boat. It's still pouring rain and mostly unlit on this stretch of the riverside as I run through a treed area and around the corner of an office building. I give it a quick peek back around and either I've lost him or he just gave up pretty quick.

Now having crossed over the crummy office building-world border, I continue to wander around. I check the first door I pass. It's locked up, but then that's what I was expecting. I skip through the rain to the next one over with a sheltered entryway that reads "World Trade Center". Once out of the rain, I lean back for a minute to make sure the coast is clear, then I grab the door. It opens. An excitement rushes through me, like the kind I'd have as a kid seeing what's appeared under the tree on Christmas morning. I cautiously enter the building and stealthily make my way across the lobby, then do a reconnaissance mission of the immediate area, poking my head around in the corridors and conference rooms. No one around.

I begin another more detailed check of all the conference rooms and offices for signs of leftover Christmas party cocktail life. The only place with anything at all going is in one of the rooms where it looks like a meeting was abandoned in mid-session. A PowerPoint projector is up pointing at a pull-down screen and papers and discarded beverages are littered around a flock of single desks. The lack of humans in general tonight brings on feelings of a "last man on earth" situation. Has the world's population all disappeared except me? It's a lot harder to suss these kinds of things out at Christmas, but it would explain a lot. No one left on the planet except for me and a security guard to chase me around everywhere I go for no reason other than a continued sense of purpose. I find a tub with soda machine cans bathing in melted ice water. Well, at least this was *something* to drink.

Standing at the PowerPoint podium, I take the pointer stick and begin a demonstration by way of the hick prison warden character in *Cool Hand Luke*. "What we've got here is...failure to communicate. Some men you just can't reach. Now, I can be a good guy, or I can be one real mean sum-bitch..." I suddenly don't know what else I can tell these desks that they don't already know.

I take the elevator to the top floor. In the elevator lobby area up there the view outside the observation windows is an all-expanses-paid view of Dark Christmas. I look down at the Willamette River from this much higher vantage point and find my party boat bust.

Actually, this all doesn't seem so bad now that I've got my own private World Trade Center, and I don't have to worry about my situation while hoping they *are* worried about my situation back at Suburbia Studios. It's the best of both worlds. I go back down to the first floor and into the conference room with the beverages. I want to be in the vicinity of the front exit just in case the Benny Hill police find me, so I'll just sleep in here. I drag in two bigger chairs from the lobby and place them facing together.

I wake up the next morning in my chairs. Well, mostly in the chairs. The natural push of my night's slow motion body extending has given my hips a much larger canyon to be sag-suspended from. But, with Christmas morning's miracle now rendered, that being I didn't have to sleep out in the rain last night, I begin my trek back to Suburbia Studios, my sober and sensible mind returned.

I stroll through a small park area down to the walkway along the river's edge. It's not raining today yet and the streets are still as dead as the night before. I turn onto the cemented walkway when suddenly I hear a horse cop slow-trotting. Damn. I quickly scan my immediate surroundings. Huh. No horse, cop or otherwise. Weird. I start walking again, and the hooves return. Wait. Is the horse-clomping below me? I lift a leg up and sure enough, the rubber heel sole on my boot is gone, exposing a three-inch hollow hole that now makes the exact same sound as a shoed horse's hoof. I take two steps forward and yes, it's both boots. They must have come off while running around in all that rain last night. How did one boot know the other had given up in that same way? Is it like some cobblery telepathy similar to what twins experience? They fell apart together in the same fashion at the same time. I think back and realize that a boot behavioral pattern has been forming for a few years now. I make a mental note to continue my leather zipper boot research by acquiring a new pair of boots as soon as possible.

Up on the bridge my holiday walking journey back to the studio would make for a sentimental scene in the movie version where "You Can't Always Get What You Want" gently begins, but then this would be an indie film and licensing that song would cost more than the rest of the movie budget put together. As I start to make my way across I begin to hum it anyway. *"I saw her today at the reception..."*

I get back to Suburbia and, just in time for the breakdown in the song with the gospel choir part, I *knock knock knock* on the live-in rehearsal room door. Sophie opens it, smiles, and as she steps back to let me in I see Anton there too. Without need for explanations from anyone in the room all is forgiven, and *it's Christmas.*

Reel World for Real

"Top floor! Panty hose, illegal drugs and cigarettes!" I shout in my best "She's a Rainbow" English accent intro while riding up Suburbia Studio's gear conveyor belt. Ondi is stealthily tracking on the stairs alongside, keeping an eye on the viewfinder. I'm leading her to our room where Anton and Sophie are already.

As I lead the way to our punk-rock practice-space hovel-abode, I'm reaching out to the camera's rolling black gleaming eye and window portal to an audience on the other side, regardless of however far-off dreaming that all may seem like now. I will try to entertain them, the future people, and this camera will be the witness to the struggle and the righteous squalor and what *fun* there is to be had despite it all. The long black microphone attached in bayonet position is for me a jazz club mic and every time I see that little green light flashing ON, I will play it as if I'm on the discounted-ticket caboose car of the same train bringing The Beatles from New York to Washington DC while being caught on the Maysles Brothers' documentary cameras. I beckon Ondi and David further toward our proper bohemian beatnik drugger-freak den and *tap tap tap* a courtesy knock, or more specifically a two-second warning: *They're here*.

After some immediate "subjects in their natural habitat" footage is taken, cameras are momentarily paused for proper hellos so Ondi can feel out our enthusiasm levels for the filming day. She's soon to learn that this was an unnecessary step with us.

Anton is talking and Sophie is annoyed that her bag of make-up removing cotton balls is suddenly almost empty. David's video camera then follows Anton over to the mixing board while an imaginary movie camera comes into an extreme close-up on me. It pans down from my giant bug-eyed sunglasses to the uncovered half of my poker face, down my leather jacket, further down past my black jeans to the two-sizes-too-small zip boots. The camera shot then zooms in even closer on the three-inch heels and turns to X-ray vision, revealing all Sophie's cotton balls hidden in my boot heels to muffle the horse shoe sounds when I walk. The bottoms are taped off with silver duct tape. I'd learned that the tape by itself didn't quite do the trick, and now I'd additionally learned that Sophie was in fact going to use all those cotton balls for something.

Anton and Sophie say they are passing on tonight's Dandy Warhols New Year's Eve party show at La Luna, which could be considered non-interest due to having received the brush-off after moving up here, but its more likely Anton sees the greater benefit in showing the camera how he makes a new song.

Last week Courtney had paid us his one and only courtesy visit to "see it for himself". Anton excitedly showed him a sound collage he'd put together by recording dozens and dozens of different things off the radio, long and far beyond being able to discern any single track. Every kind of music, radio talk and various sound effects including static all crammed together and squeezed through two speakers trying to talk or play or exist in some way over each other all at once. We were all visibly and rightly impressed. So much so that one of us takes this new idea and makes his own sound collage as a last-minute addition to open his band's first major-label album releasing on Capitol Records. His record will be out long before Anton has a chance to implement it himself and thus garnish "the win". Tonight's plan becomes David hanging back to get a song recording from scratch demonstration from Anton, while I temporarily cross over with Ondi into Dandy-land.

Backstage at La Luna there's all kinds of intoxicating options and after doing some rounds of the marketplace I pass on the coke, weed, ecstasy, acid and do a take-up on my old spirit chemical, speed.

The first time I ever saw Anton while I was coming off of a speed bender was alone at his then current girlfriend's apartment, and while it was his morning coffee time, my brain was still whirring in fine-tuned maximum alertness from the night before. His unspoken response to this obvious personality enhancement and new swagger was to put on "I'm Looking Through You" by The Beatles, and then adjourn to the upstairs loft leaving me in my speed-soaked psyche to take in his observation via the song lyrics. *"You don't look different but you have changed..."*

OK, fine, but even if I was a phony, which I wasn't, I was a "Holly Golightly" phony. As in I was a "real" phony. "You know why?" Because exactly like the main character in the film version of Truman Capote's *Breakfast at Tiffany's*, *I actually believed all this phony junk that I believed.* Still, despite all the undeniable realizations since then, a part of me still found the growing self-induced delirium somewhat attractive, even romantic. Anyway, I had escaped, and now I feel safe to start a new beginning and without drugs, which is either because I'm smarter now, or because I'd been getting them for free and could not afford them up here.

Tonight's drug choice is a one-night-only nostalgic return and fitting end to what had been an extremely speedy year. Still, even with all the free booze, this whole being backstage thing just isn't hitting like it used to, but then again getting loaded now just reminds me of how I'd spent the entire last year with a party routine that turned any one day into a three, so technically I should be good on normal clocked-in party time for the next three years. What's really starting to kill me though is how long it's been since I'd experienced the simple joys of solitude that can only come with your own room with your own door that shuts. The idea of being alone to charge myself on 60s movies and 60s records and 60s books sounds very romantic to me at this point.

I remember back to one of the first times The Dandys came down to San Francisco to play at Tom Guido's Purple Onion and I was so hungover from a multi-day run run run that I couldn't even peel myself off of Matt's bedroom floor at 9 p.m. "OKaay Joel...I'm leaving now..." Matt said, last-call style, reluctant to leave me there missing out and waiting for me to suddenly spring up at the last second ready to be his good-times partner. It felt so weird not finally fully waking up until a few hours later during what would be their set time and too late to make it to the club before missing it all.

Although I hadn't been alone in weeks, I still felt so guilty as I just sat there on the carpet doodling on a BJM flyer. It felt like a betrayal. They were our soul partners from the northern dimension and we were going to make a whole new scene together with everything finally done right and in "the grand tradition" of outsiders reinventing insider rock 'n' roll. Over time I was learning that a lot of outsiders are really just insiders-in-waiting and it's ironic now sitting here in the New Year's Eve party backstage area that I feel like the weirdo trying to hang out with the popular campus kids like in some crappy 80s teen movie.

I'm wasted but wired sharp by the time the live music is over and the celebratory onstage New Year's Eve countdown brings us into 1997. From there things start to spiral deeper into the gushing boozefall and the white track lines that run right through it. Laughs and on-camera hamming can't hide the feelings locked behind a chemical's temporary façade. Of course we are all friends, but everything had officially gone from starting a revolution to Anton and I inadvertently finding ourselves in a popularity contest. Certain members and their huge entourage of locals layering on the airs back here implying *We're signed* now. *Weee've* moved up to a *higher level*. What was this all going to do to Anton? One thing was for sure, things were going to get ramped up pretty big time. This realization suddenly calls me to arms and I take it upon myself to enact revenge on everyone in the place for treating us like losers for living in the rehearsal space and rejecting Anton after they'd arrived in town.

I should probably be considering the fact that I don't *really* know exactly how it had all played out with the people involved here before I myself showed up on the Portland scene, but I don't and begin running around dispersing the various little social groups by purposely annoying the living hell out of everyone, which I am really good at it must be said, especially at times like this when it's all I live for. I systematically work my way down the corridor of different-sized backstage rooms like pest control, except I am the pest in control. Ecstasy chill-out room. Check. Couple making out in coat closet. Check. Small group in spacious room chopping lines. Check. Big group crammed into small room chopping lines. Check. I see Peter and his girlfriend occupying the kitchen area and leave them unfettered.

"*...and he walked on down the hall...*"

168

Eventually, with me still there and all the booze all gone, everyone has left for elsewheres to party through the remaining hours until day one of 1997 opens for business. Ondi drops me back at Suburbia where I victoriously slow-stroll from her SUV and through the rain up to the front door, head up the stairs, and pass out on my end of the king-sized bed mattress.

I don't know what happened on New Year's Day because I slept through it. In the end, Anton had a new song "The Devil May Care (Mom & Dad Don't)" and all I had was a tongue that felt as dry as The Rolling Stones' logo tongue must be feeling after being stuck out for the last twenty-five years. I sit up and look around. No one is here and all looks normal enough. Except the trail of cotton balls coming from the door to my boots at the foot of the mattress.

Part II

If You're Going to San Francisco, Be Sure to Wear Some Horseshoes

I was filled with childlike excitement sitting in the backseat of the beat-up old Honda Civic as we drove over the Hawthorne Bridge. I waved goodbye at the World Trade Center building as we passed, then settled in for the long ten-hour-plus drive back to the Bay Area. Anton had the hatchback packed Tetris-winning tight with guitars, amps and belongings, while the rental gear, mattress and everything else we weren't taking lay where it had originally fallen back at Suburbia.

The ball had rolled fast once dropped not even a week ago, with Anton returning from an hour-long payphone conversation with Greg Shaw, owner of Bomp! Records.

"You wanna get out of here? Portland, I mean. Move down to LA."

"Yes!" I fire back.

"Really? You'd want to live in LA?"

"YES."

"Well, here's the thing, then, we can't go all the way in like that if those guys are gonna be half-assed about it. If we're going to do it in 'the grand tradition' style, they can't just quit because it gets hard."

"I think they'd be ready."

"Really? Who knows where those guys' heads are at. I guess if we talk to Dave D he can talk to those guys. See what's up. I don't know, I'm just sick of depending on people who just give up."

"Things will be different if we're all living under the same roof together."

"Greg Shaw said he'd set it all up, but I also don't like giving away records just so people can party and not practice. I want this to go somewhere and have it mean something and not just be an excuse to think I'm cool. I don't care about any of that. Y'know? I just want to be in the best band we can be."

Some of this was rhetorical, but I understood he repeatedly put those cards on the table, even if he knew I knew, just in case the universe was multitasking and hadn't been paying attention up till now.

"It sounds like a great idea to me. Us all living in a house together like in *Help!*" I hear myself say, putting it all on the table.

"The Beatles? Ha! *Riight*...The Beatles played like ten shows a day in Germany until they were the best band on the planet. Are those guys prepared to do that? I wonder. I'm tired of wasting time on people who are just going to complain because it's hard."

"Well, we'll at least be as good as The Monkees at first. With us all in a house together? We can practice every day all day!

"I'm not so sure". His exaggeration detector knew my frequency well by this point in our relationship. "Greg Shaw says he'll rent something big enough for the whole band so we can practice and play shows, but he wants the next record for it. I don't know if we want to do that."

"Oh, man. Let's do it! What else are we gonna do?"

"We should think about it," he says to file this subject away for the rest of the afternoon.

My mind was spinning like a top over the whole idea of the band all living together in LA just like on *The Monkees* TV show. My childhood fantasy then cemented after discovering The Beatles through *Help!* being broadcast as the KTVU Saturday afternoon movie. By the time I was nine years old I'd be on the bus and walking around school falling in love with different girls just to be able to apply Beatles songs to my life. Michelle of course was "Michelle", Jennifer became the subject of "And I Love Her", that is until she got tired of my goofy staring and told me to drop dead. Then she was switched over to "Yesterday". Soon I was finding other ways to apply Beatles songs to my life. I'd scrunch my eyebrows and do my first-ever brooding thinking about some playground bullies while listening to "You've Got to Hide Your Love Away", which became my favorite Beatles song. In the performance of it in the film, Ringo moodily plays the tambourine, a premonition that I wouldn't recognize until many years later.

This would take our current Suburbia living model and make it the whole band, all sitting around a living room in a house with individual beds and its own plumbing, playing songs together just like in the film. I remained in this deep daydream state while practicing my moody tambourine Ringo on the king-size mattress for days on end. These spells were only broken on the occasions Anton returned from the payphone and I'd give him an expectant look, which he would ignore. This went on until the fourth day when he came back from an unusually long conversation and made an announcement:

"OK, it's happening. Warn all the Britpop girls in LA that Joel's coming to town and he's got tambourines."

Showbiz! LA was the other side of the groovy California coin. LA was cool and we wouldn't even have to try to make it a "home" within all its unconditional indifference. But first things first—time to get the band back together. Again. The plan was worked out in a series of hallway payphone conversations over the next few days. First, we'd be staying around the Bay Area for about a week with Dave D's parents' house as the main home base. The band members would assemble one by one as everyone tied off their San Francisco ends, then get in some rehearsals with a new guitar player. Dean (oh he of little faith) wasn't quite willing or able to just pack up both he and Christina's domesticated bliss to make the move back to the place they'd already successfully escaped from.

Anton, Sophie, Matt, Brad, me and Dave would all make the move down together, while Jeff would be flying over from his sabbatical in Las Vegas. All I knew about this new guitar prospect kid we were trying out was that he worked at a gas station and lived in his van. He'd come highly recommended from our most enthusiastic side-of-stage fanboy Robert, but more importantly his father Michael

Been, a BJM enthusiast himself and the onetime leader of the American Top 40-friendly pop post-punk 80s band The Call. They'd been talking him up back during the period before we knew Jeff wasn't going to be moving back to San Francisco. They warned us he wasn't on the same level as Jeff, but he was light on attachments and looking to learn "the life". They also mentioned he had a van. I think the idea was getting him a scholarship at The Brian Jonestown Massacre Rock 'n' Roll University with Professor Anton Newcombe.

We barrel down and out of the green mountains toward California and as we clear bottom, blue sky expands its presence to a sun-is-out situation with puffy cloud accompaniment. Over the state line and don't forget to give Mount Shasta another one of those mandatory moments of observational recognition as you breeze by. From there it's a long stretch of California daydreaming until we finally get Bay Area friendly where we stop off at Nancy's, an old school friend of Anton's on the Berkeley–Oakland border. Nancy is tight with Larry Thrasher, who'd loaned us his Emeryville studio to record *Take It from the Man!* They were of a tightly woven macramé network from the early days of enlightenment brought on by Alan Watts and later Ram Dass. After the colorfulness of the psychedelic 60s had officially faded to silver, Nancy spent many years living in the Zen Center located near the Lower Haight, also right across the street from Sophie's old place where most of *Thank God for Mental Illness* was four-tracked.

Hanging out with Nancy in her Berkeley spiritual case-study home gives me the feeling she meditated in all the heavyweight temples and the most far-out fields, yet in true yin and yang form she also had a great enthusiasm for recreational firearms. She shows us her rifle and machine gun which are strictly used for firing-range purposes to "blow off steam". I certainly don't want to suggest that she would ever condone violence, but I can't help but think if we'd had an army of five hundred Nancys, "the 60s" would never have had to end.

Tat-tat-tat..."Take THAT you un-zen sons of bitches!"...rata-tat-tat-tat-tat-tat-tat-tat...

She sees I've put on a little weight since last time and reminds me, "One can survive on just enough food to fill the palm of your hand a day." This reminds me that Diane has offered to buy pizza and whiskey for our friendly sleepover party tonight. I bid them all adieu and head for the Rockridge BART station to catch a train to take me under the Bay to San Francisco.

I step on the Powell Street BART station escalator and it slowly raises me up and up and drools me out into grand central San Francisco. There's already a 7 Haight MUNI bus loading a small line and I stride over and on to it. Settling in toward the back I now see the Flood Building's massive old-school Woolworths has been turned into a shitty new Gap store. Everything is always changing here except people like me always complaining about everything changing. I was trying to be better about it after realizing that in every movie filmed on location here, no matter what era, unless it's like a famous hotel or something, none of the businesses ever seem to exist anymore. Change is just what this place does, even if not always well. Sometimes it feels like a group of old seniors sitting in their wheelchairs watching their loud and obnoxious great-grand-children running around them in circles. Still, I didn't want to just harp on it to help further justify my leaving it. I can't get mad at snow for falling.

In just a few blocks we begin to cross by my old South of Market neighborhood and I suddenly remember the circumstances of my leaving this town. I push back against my seat a little to hold my coat in place while I slide down a little lower to create some coat-collar cover. If I'd had a noir-style fedora, I'd pull the brim down low but I don't so I just stealthily peer around to make sure nobody's put the make on me, as if it matters, but the one thing about paranoia is it gives life a little James Bond espionage flair, which right now is more interesting than just a boring MUNI bus ride. You just have to remember to be careful with it though because once you offer paranoia a seat, it's usually hogging the whole row in no time. As we pass, I crane my neck in the direction of what used to be my final stretch of the walk back to the warehouse. Well, all I have to do is stay out of trouble tonight and then I'm off to our manager Dave D's parents in Palo Alto and then my new home, Los Angeles.

I get off at Haight and Masonic and walk up and around the corner onto Waller where Diane's small split-unit Victorian apartment is. This brings me to the next sign of change when she informs me she's officially off the snorts and has hung up the straw for good. In fact, she's also made new plans herself to move out of San Francisco. She'd lived and breathed for the San Francisco music scene, primarily BJM, and it was now official we weren't returning and there was a general feeling that everything was going to continue on changing from the inside and the out. The rest of our local scene was splintering, while our popular music's heyday was also passing. *(What's the Story) Morning Glory, Parklife, Different Class* and all the big battle cries were now in the rearview mirror. You could feel Britpop's bubble was blown up full and starting to vibrate. Though we don't acknowledge the occasion as such, we have our final of what had been many time-out TV sleepovers and the listings gods smile upon us with the Peter O'Toole 60s classic, *The Ruling Class* via the American Movie Classics channel.

The next day around noon Dave D comes over as part of his last round of San Francisco errands, the final one being collecting me and our bass player Matt. "What's with those shoes, man? They don't look like they fit too good," he asks after giving me a once-over. Over the weeks the boots Ondi had given me had not only lost the heel soles and turned into horse hooves, but were finally visually splitting off of my feet, as if I were undergoing an Incredible Hulk transformation at the speed flowers grow. Dave (who honestly looks more like a bass player in a metal band than the manager of a band of 60s music enthusiasts in vintage shop clothing) towers above me as I give him the shoe deterioration play-by-play that had started as soon as I'd arrived in Portland as he nods along, assessing the situation and, knowing me like he did, sympathizes. "Well, we can't have the 'Spokesman of the Revolution' not wearing cool boots. It just wouldn't be right. Here, take this forty bucks. Don't worry, it's from the 'secret band funds'." I knew there was no such thing as a secret band fund, this was one of those moments when Dave absolutely came through.

Matt's not due over here at Diane's for another hour, so I leave them to go out on a mission to find new used boots. I walk the block from Waller toward Haight Street and as I get closer I start half tippy-toeing to avoid full on horse-clomping, but there's no way to fully stop the clomps without doing an Elvis Presley "Jailhouse Rock" collector's plate pose-walking stance on my toes, and I'm not doing that down Haight Street. My best shot for vintage boots these days is a few blocks away at Wasteland, which is by far the largest house of vintagery on Haight Street. I round the corner off Masonic and on to Haight right-passed my old dream job, Reckless Records. My previous workmates can probably hear me from inside the store clomping by and are now looking out the windows at me while judgingly shaking their heads in "what a loser" fashion, each holding a cool new record nobody else in the world has ever heard.

As I walk further down to the next block and pass Cybelle's Pizza, where I'd picked us up dinner last night, I now inadvertently pick up some Haight Street gutter punks sitting on the sidewalk out front who start following me while marveling at the perfectly replicated horseshoe-clonking sound my shoes make. "Duude...you sound like a horse!" one says just in case I haven't noticed it yet over these past weeks. I make it inside Wasteland and once within a respectable fashion dispensary with gorgeous employees decked to the nines, I go into the Elvis Presley tippy-toes "Jailhouse Rock" collector's plate pose-walking stance, which I decide after the punk rockers experience is better than sounding like a horse doing a walking handstand through the store. I even put my arms up in the air, because that's a part of the pose which is now oddly less embarrassing than echoing horse noises off the cement floor and throughout the huge store while everyone stops to stare as I clomp my way all the way to the back where the shoe section is.

Then, I see a beam of light coming from a skylight that's shining down like a spotlight on a pair of black leather Beatle boots. Size ten. Finding actual Beatle boots on Haight Street was extremely rare ever since NaNa had closed its doors a couple years ago. Proper heels were hard to come by unless it was your cowboy-style ankle boots, which are fine, but also are a little too much exactly like what they sound like. One usually had to make do with the various lesser versions of 60s boots in varying combinations of square, round, sometimes pointed toes coupled with either zipper or elastic ankle, but never real-deal Chelsea boots of the Cuban heel persuasion. These were center-stitched, elastic slip-on ankle with pull-up straps and full-on Beatle boots. Take me to The Cavern Club and drop me right there on the brick floor. They looked barely used and for a lousy $34.99 + tax. My toes dance their way in and snug-slide into the pointed shoe tips with just enough room to half snap like fingers with "cool, baby" confirmation. I'm back.

Not to say Beatle boots are the most comfortable shoe out there, because they certainly aren't. But then they're not supposed to be; neither is life. Everyone is starting to mass-adopt the comfortable shoe stance, and it's in fact getting a little out of hand. Even the Hare Krishnas and Catholic nuns are starting to wear sneakers. To which I would say, keep the faith, babies.

As I exit Wasteland all the punk rocks guys are sitting against the storefront waiting but they don't even see me, or rather, hear me and as I stroll out they simply continue searching through the pavement cracks for something. Maybe an *Alice in Wonderland*-style shrunken horse.

I stride back up to Diane's apartment feeling ten feet tall. Matt shows up a few minutes later with a raggedy old suitcase with what looks to be a dirty sock half poking out the side or who knows maybe it's a partial sleeve to a cool Spacemen 3 shirt or something. "Heyy Joel," he says with a scrunched smile. "Finally had to get away from Portland, huh? What happened, was Zia obsessing on you too hard?"

"Yeah," I joke back, "I had to tell her I'm the type of tambourine that needs to roll and she's crescent shaped. You all moved out?"

He nods as he lights a cigarette, causing him to slightly chase his own flame. He pushes his glasses back up. "All moved out."

Despite all his comings and goings, Matt was by this point the only current member from the first BJM lineup. He was originally recruited by a curious Anton, who'd heard his Stone Roses-esque bass playing coming out of his sidewalk-side basement-level bedroom in the Haight, although Anton liked to describe it as if he'd heard Chapterhouse coming from out of a window, looked in and saw a guy passed out on a huge pile of empty potato chip bags. I guess they both sound kinda plausible.

The three of us get in Dave D's van and begin the forty-five-minute drive south to suburban Palo Alto. "Anton's already down there taking over the computer at my parents' and Brad's coming tomorrow. Then we practice with the new guy," Dave says with business-stoner articulation. It's rapid fire, yet with one word somewhere in the middle and the last of each sentence stretched out long like a California beach.

"Where's Sophie?" I ask.

"Sophie's staying here and driving down with Anton when we leave for LA. My guess would be, she probably doesn't want to start her new life living with a bunch of dudes until she absolutely has to."

"I hear that." It has just dawned on me, knowing what I know, The Beatles or The Monkees would probably be much cleaner roommates than these guys were going to be.

Dog Day at the Salvation Army

Anton, Sophie and I pull onto Larga Avenue in the Atwater Village section of Los Angeles. The neighborhood is very suburban and lined with every architectural make of single family homes: craftsman's, Spanish style, English Tudor and other ranch, cottage and bungalow variations.

"3261 Larga right there—we're here." Anton pulls sharply into the driveway of a white job with aqua-blue accompaniment.

I walk up the three small steps to the main side entrance of the house and open the flimsy screen door.

The shades are closed and the room is dark where Bomp! Records owner Greg Shaw is standing with hands folded in front of him. His manner and current pose give him the air of an elder thinker sage-wizard dude with his long blond hair, sharp-chop bangs and T-shirt with comfy jeans combo. His eyelashes flutter a flurry of rapid blinks as his mind's start/stop system kicks back in from seemingly being in "sleep" mode where he's been standing still like that for who knows how long. He then acknowledges me. "Where's Anton?"

"Oh, hi! He's right behind m—"

"Hi Greg!" Anton says from behind and I side-step out of the way.

"Hello there," he says with a calm yet genuine-looking smile. "C'mon, I'm saving you the big room in the back."

They leave me standing there and then Sophie comes in. "They went thattaway..." I say, hitching my thumb toward the hall.

I scan around the immediate area consisting of living room, attached bedroom and joined kitchen and it's like a weird suburban flashback to my childhood neighborhood in San Jose. Like a lot of the different styles of architecture around here, its early-century but this one had a redo probably in the 70s so whatever old-Hollywood charming ways it originally had are now just old-fashioned family-friendly boring. Perhaps there is a skeleton of an old supper club performing mentalist buried in the backyard or an escape artist who'd suddenly lost his touch one day and is still buried inside one of the walls. If that is the case perhaps there will soon be back there with him between one and seven musicians and/or an extremely tall manager.

I do a round of the five-bedroom house and settle on the one back in the front connected to the living room. I double-check the door to make sure it, first, shuts, then that it locks properly. I'll take it.

Just then Dave D's van pulls into the driveway with Matt riding shotgun. They come inside and do their own rounds of the house. Matt's done some math and reports back his findings. "There's only five bedrooms, so some of us are going to have to share. Can I be in a room with you?" Despite having been dreaming of my own door that shuts for so long, how could I stay no after all the times I'd crashed at his apartment in San Francisco? Besides, now in some weird way I was doing him a favor just by not being a jerk.

Next Ondi and David show up with cameras and start filming us in the new house. These invited home invasions will become a regular part of the daily ritual for some time to come. Soon David invites me to come along with him to pick up Jeff at LAX while Ondi and Anton go off to do something else, which would later be revealed as going to the same place to pick up Courtney, which then makes David, Jeff and me second unit in real-life importance.

I'd thought Jeff was arriving from Las Vegas, but when we get there I'm told he's coming in from Ohio for some reason. Here he comes now exiting the gates and my first thought is that he's looking strangely buff. Not that he's packin' a six'r or even has acquired normal body mass, but definitely beefier than his usual emaciated wooden cross-pumping-Jesus-as-personal-trainer look.

An hour and a half of traffic later we pull up to the new BJM house and the gang's all here, signified by the additions of Brad's Thunderbird and Peter Hayes's van, confirming he'd gone through with turning in his shammy towel, or "chamois" as they prefer in the gas pumping biz.

I follow David who's filming Jeff as he goes room by room looking for a personal space to claim home. He's on a somewhat frantic search in that way you do when you're the last to show up to something and you know all the best bits are already gone but maybe there's somehow a chance so even if you haven't seen all these people for a long time you still don't waste one more second shooting the shit than you have to along the way while acting like it's just a casual browse and nothing's going on but inside your personal agenda has got you going a mile a minute. He finally makes it all the way back to Anton and Sophie's suite where he then runs out of option road. The last unoccupied room is a cross-through room designed for a pre-privacy aged child that can be entered from both sides, and which is in fact necessary to get from one end of the house to the other. He decides his need for personal business space is so great that he will take the nearby closet instead. A little advice to anyone out there who might be looking to rent a house for a bunch of band guys: despite what the term "band" implies, they are all going to want their own privacy just as much as a bunch of solo artists that have all decided to move in together would.

And so the BJM "map of the stars" house tour reads like this: Joel and Matt off the main living room; through the kitchen and first door on the right is Brad; on the opposite left from him is Peter, who is also solo but with a spare bottom bunk because nobody else wants bunk beds or to room with a new guy we don't yet know for sure isn't "weird"; then down at the end of the hall is a medium-sized room to rehearse in (which also includes the closet that Jeff lives in, so it's also by comparison his extra-large receiving room); then the walk-through baby's room which is now gear storage plus party pen, and finally Anton and Sophie's suite featuring its own bathroom, kitchen, laundry and private backyard. Dave has prearranged to take a tiny guest house attached to the garage, which will be kept locked up so tight I would never even see inside it once. Not once. I swear.

Greg Shaw's wallet wasn't going to go as far as furniture, so we did a lot of standing around the house on that first day. Then, a couple days later, Anton, Matt, Jeff and I were cruising some errands in the little beat-up white Subaru...

"Holy shit yew guuys, lookit all that stuuff just sitting there!" Jeff exclaim-drawls out long and lispy while rubbernecking from the backseat. We'd just passed a particularly over-the-top Salvation Army on Hollywood Boulevard, it's church-like storefront facade replete with a protruding skyward holy cross and a big "A Center for Worship & Service" sign over the doors.

What had generated so much interest from Jeff was about ten industrial-sized black garbage bags filled with mystery donation treasure, some random small furniture and even an easy chair. Better still, the charity shop wasn't open today so the rest of us enthusiastically joined in on the fantasy that we would now decorate our empty house with all of what surely must be ultra-cool vintage retro furnishings.

Anton quickly spins the car around and in the flash of an eye is pulling the e-brake in front of the store as Jeff, Matt and myself simultaneously fling open our doors all at once. First bag: crap. Second bag: crap. Third bag: crap. This was taking too long. "Just grab the easy chair," Anton instructs in a voice echoing all of our frustration. Matt leans over while Jeff bends down with his knees to each grab an end of the chair when suddenly—

"HOLD IT!"

We all look up. There's a chubby twenty-something sweaty-faced security guard holding a walkie-talkie to his ear and in the other hand pointing what looks to be a taser at us. Brow furrowed and squinting in the hot sun he is outwardly shaking and clearly must be new to the job or maybe to him we look like crazed Manson weirdos pillaging a La-Z-Boy recliner chair.

Anton, taking a hostage negotiator tone, tries to help him. "It's OK, don't freak out. You are not in danger. Take a deep breath and just try to relax."

"O-OK. But you guys gotta go right NOW," he pleads "I've already notified the police!"

"OK, we're leaving. C'mon, you guys, let's go," Anton instructs us calmly but with enough outward direction to show the security guard we are acting the rest of the scene out as promised. On our way to the car we see some cops pulling up. Anton brushes up to me and whispers, "You're driving. You're the only one here with a driver's license and the cops are here."

"But I can't drive a stick," I inform him from the corner of my mouth, thinking surely he'll just have to get us away from here quickly. He ignores this and I watch as he gets in on the passenger side. The LA Police cruiser pulls right up behind us and I also get in. "Fuuck man..." Matt mutters as I begin to mentally prepare for the big house. The security kid goes up to the cop car window and they start talking. The two cops remain inside listening and after what seems like a very long brief exchange they all turn their heads toward us in unison. They're just watching like they're waiting on us. Anton suddenly brings me into the reality of the situation. "Start the car, they're letting us go."

Like I already told Anton, I've never driven a stick shift in my life, but if I can't drive us away from here right now the police will proceed with the pending bummer scenario on hand. I start the engine and then begin to herky-jerk the shifter stick in a few different directions while also pumping the clutch up and down with my foot like I'm starting up a time machine from a 1940s film. For some reason this hasn't caused the car to stall so I gently begin to push down on the gas pedal and somehow it slowly moves forward, but then begins to jerk and rumble some and then jerks and stops. I grab the shifter again and start playing it like a video game while giving the clutch pedal another pump routine, which gets the car to start vibrating and lurching sporadically like an automotive free-jazz sax solo and by no skill of my own the car does manage to crawl further away and in what actually does take forever I eventually get us car-seizured down the street and around the next corner and out of view of the cops. I throw my door open and Anton and I switch seats before instantly blazing away from our botched heist job.

"Maan, that was a nice chaair," Jeff laments from his rear seat.

We get home later that day to find a large television in the corner of the front living room and an arrangement of some milk crates positioned in front of it. The milk crate furniture staging job implies someone thought we might all like to sit around the TV like a kind of miniaturized milk crate drive-in movie theater. The sight of this gets us into some conversational commotion-causing and suddenly Brad and Peter appear from the hallway.

"Hey you guys!" Brad says, looking excited to see us. Brad is not the greatest drummer but because his hair is exactly like Brian Jones's I'd been able to convince Anton to take him on, and despite our rocky beginning he turns out to be a pretty nice guy.

"What's going on?" Perma-spaced Peter now transmits. We are learning that the signal has a customary three-second delay.

"Running from the cops," Matt says half joking.

"Look! A friend of Dave's brought us a TV," Brad announces.

"Great, now all we need is a cement truck," Anton sighs.

"Now you can watch *Seinfeld*, Joel." Brad jokingly adds, referring to a comment I'd made in an interview recently about people becoming brainwashed and just wanting to stay home to watch *Seinfeld* instead of going out to shows.

We have come here to LA to do or die, and this is our life now. Here in LA we had band friends, connections and hookups. We had fans. We had people who recognized what we had going on and wanted to be a part of it. I'd get along just fine until we got some label suit's ink on paper. Then I'd have my own money. I'll probably even have to get a bank account. I haven't had a bank account in five years.

Manic Digression

This morning Jeff's mighty hair-pinned pompadour is coming down for the first time in like, forever. Anton wants to wield the electric hair clippers because he knows like I know and like Matt knows that this thing's pinned-together back door hasn't been opened in nearly five years, and when all the pins in the back are pulled and the hair is opened like hair French doors, like a gory samurai exploitation film when a head is sliced down the middle into two watermelon halves and peeled apart, who knows what's lurking beneath? His hair has literally been pinned tightly together in the back like this for so long now and it could all go very *Alien* stomach scene pretty quick, and we are in fact all huddled around waiting for it, most of all Jeff himself.

Anton methodically pulls the pins one by one, almost like he's defusing a bomb, and drops them to the floor. I hear the buzzing click on and sneak a peek from in between my fingers as Anton surveys for the best point of entry, but all that lurks beneath the deep is one massive dread the shape and size of a ping-pong paddle. It flops out like a beaver tail in a box and Anton's going in for the kill, but now Jeff, seeing in the hand mirror he's holding that it's nothing too gross, I guess, quickly changes his mind and begs for its life.

Anton pulls the clippers back and Jeff disappears into the bathroom by himself where he spends what turns into a great while combing at it until it returns to hair again. As for the rest of us, a single beaver tail dread is a pretty good payoff and nestles nicely between something gross but not something so horrible that we can never unsee it again.

188

Eventually Jeff comes out and is looking better than I'd ever seen him. His long dark hair is now naturally tousled up and doing what bands like The New York Dolls would have spent lots of time to achieve, while Jeff can only get his un-dreaded hair to go this flat, a rock reversal of hair-lift fortunes, seemingly. A fresh make-up job including red lipstick, a childlike hair beret added to each temple and voilà! An electric viola player.

When life gives you hairy lemons, make some lemonade, put some vodka in it and throw a cocktail party. Blow-out parties are usually furniture-less due to the customary fact that the tenants are moving out and hence the state of the place no longer matters. Then, like an action movie star slowly walking away from the building, all casual-like, it explodes into a million pieces along with whatever was left of the security deposit. With our party we went the opposite way with the concept which was to have a huge blow-out party *before* any furniture arrives. We were going to wear the place in, and anyway most of us were more familiar with the end scenario of tiptoeing away rather than alerting everyone you owe something to that you're leaving.

I slide the glass door back into open position coming in from the backyard. Anton is playing sitar, with Sophie accompanying on tambura while Greg Shaw and other representatives of the local intelligentsia watch. I continue on through the baby-turned-gear room while squeezing between a couple pairs of randos, then into the rehearsal room where Jeff is displaying his harmonica skills. Matt accompanies on guitar while Brad and some girls watch. I stop and join them for a couple rows of squonk and strum, then move on down the hall to where Peter is showing his room to a girl as the door shuts. Now I've made it through to the crowded kitchen where David is filming Dave D bartending for a couple of girls. I get a vodka with lemon off him and head into the living room and that's where I see my first celebrity since arriving in LA. Harry Dean Stanton is in tow with Robert Been's dad, Michael. In addition to leading his band The Call, Michael had appeared as the Apostle John in Martin Scorsese's *The Last Temptation of Christ*. It was during filming for that movie that he'd met and befriended fellow cast apostle-pal, Harry Dean Stanton.

Michael is a round jovial man seemingly in a perpetually good mood, at least around us. He's proudly showing off Harry, who's actually looking a little unsure, perhaps from walking into a full-blown party where he's instantly the most famous person in the place. Despite his being technically a "B-list" Hollywood celebrity, with the kind of crowd here tonight he's of AAA indie art house status with films like *Repo Man*; *Paris, Texas*; *Wild at Heart*; *Twin Peaks* and on and on. More people are staring at him now as he scopes Matt's guitar sitting against the wall in our room. He heads for it, takes the only chair and begins to tune up, alone.

It hits home now that I'm watching Harry Dean Stanton sitting in my bedroom strumming a warm-up chord or three. With my other BJM compadres holding other courts in other far-off corners, I take it alone. I sit on the floor next to him, pick up one of my tambourines and say, "I'll play with you, Harry." Without saying anything he begins to strum the 1940s Mexican classic "Besamé Mucho", which among many others was covered by The Beatles. His voice is frail but comes from a place of determination. I sit cross-legged at his feet beating away while letting my mind wander just enough to not be staring up at him weirdly. Maybe when I'm older and middle-aged I could pull a similar move, walk into a party full of young actors and suddenly...just start playing tambourine in the corner? *Hmm...*

Harry Dean goes straight into one of the rock 'n' roll revolution's first airwave strikes, Elvis Presley's "Mystery Train". By now after two songs I'm feeling settled in with Harry and I ask if he'll play "Midnight Special", the song he performs in *Cool Hand Luke*. He obliges and now it's *really* hitting me—I'm playing music with one of the citizens of the 70s American New Wave cinema world. *Pat Garrett and Billy the Kid*, *Two-Lane Blacktop*, *Cisco Pike*, *Missouri Breaks*, along with so many other films and various character actor roles on television. This town was the place where most all the television shows were made when I was a kid growing up. Back then I thought it must be something like a gigantic city-sized amusement park— *And now, live from Burbank studios*...which indeed was now actually turning out to be true, except so far there seemed to be a lot more parking lot than amusement park.

I'd grown up my whole life with that face making periodic appearances in the living room and now I'm having a hoedown with him in my bedroom. I realize what a great way this is to hang out with someone famous without all the awkward feigning and next career move inquiries. Letting a shared experience in music break the ice can mean a whole lot more in just a few songs than an entire night of cocaine babbles, which is kinda crazy when you think about it.

The room is filling up fast now and with no stopping for accolades or conversation in between songs, we continue on down the trail with "El Paso". Now, as there always is in these situations when you don't have time to lock your arsenal up in the tambourine safe, a random girl has one of my other tambourines, but more welcomely, Jeff is now sitting across from us and settling into his diamond mine before starting a run of turns across his fretboard, which is like a workout studio as his nimble fingers dance across its wooden floor like ballet slippers with ice-climber cleated soles.

By now word has grapevined around the house as to what is going on in the front bedroom, and seemingly for the first time Harry notices all the spectators crowded around the video camera lens that's aiming through the doorway like the world press piled in front of the opening door of the freshly returned Apollo 11. He then finally hands the guitar off to take a solo vocal position for an encore rendition of "Mystery Train", this time with full party attention. Now, seemingly having been the center of it all for long enough, he stands as we deafen him with our cheers and he gets up to follow Zia, the cutest of the most receptive girls in the room out to the porch, which, fair enough.

Shorty after, Harry and Michael disappear into the night. Now riding high on this experience, I proceed to hit the bottle hard *and*—
SCENE MISSING

The following dark side of the morning I wake up to hear all about how The Dandy Warhols had shown up here early to do a photo shoot home invasion while I'd been doing my *Tutankhamen Lies at Carnegie Hall* impersonation. Matt says Ondi and David caught the whole thing on film in case I really want to see it, but I don't. Not really. I mean, I would if there were just some automatic way for me to watch stuff people film, but this would require putting in a bunch of coordinated effort to make a footage screening happen. From Matt's report, apparently the Dandys had made us out to look like losers. I mean, yeah, the place was a dump, but investing time into it would signify on some level a loss in momentum. We weren't here to *live* here. Or, I might as well say, another way to look at it was that Matt, along with Jeff, god bless their groovy souls, were black-belt slobs and trying to keep up with their messy habits would be an exercise in complete futility or at best an intense course in how to go pro-housecleaner. I guess this could be a handy skill for plan B, but this is a plan B-free zone. Am I throwing them under the bus? Maybe, but we've all shown one another how the bottom of a bus is assembled at some point or other.

Take It or Give It

When I was five, my enthusiasm for my plastic Big Wheel low-rider "motorcycle" bike was so total that it inspired my mother to enter me into a Big Wheel race competition. There were at least thirty other kids participating in the race that Saturday morning, all between the ages of five to eight. We collectively represented the very first *Sesame Street* generation in a rainbow of ethnic colors spanning all along the starting line. There were a couple girls, but mostly it was boys, all adorned in the many Sears catalog uniforms of the day creating a swirling sea of corduroy shades and plaids in countless color combinations.

By the early to mid-70s, psychedelic 60s vibes had melted far enough down the age-group walls to have morphed into mainstream grooviness for children. *Yellow Submarine* was now in quarterly television rotation thanks to local Bay Area station KTVU, alongside 60s shows like *The Monkees*, *Batman* and *Star Trek*. For at least a few hours a day the far-out 60s did an encore directed straight at the kids. The giant life-sized puppets of the hallucinatory *H.R. Pufnstuf* (get it?) children's show was there to turn on, tune in while being dropped out of school for Saturday morning and going "cuckoo for Cocoa Puffs". Just a couple of flips on the dial and a young groovy-looking Morgan Freeman could be found dressed in full Jimi Hendrix regalia as "Easy Reader" on another program for toddlers, *The Electric Company*.

Being an adult track and field course, all us kids had enough room to mostly line up side by side at the start of the track. A cap gun fired "GO!" and we all began to burn plastic rubber. Peddling frantically, I was immediately among the few at the front of the pack. As we barreled toward the first turn, the others around me suddenly start to slow in order to negotiate the curve, while I on the other hand kept at full peddle speed. Now in a clear lead, I pulled hard on the Big Wheel's trademark quick-stop racing brake handle, instantly spinning me into one of the advertised selling-points and crashing over onto my side. Luckily, my protective layer of Tough Skins corduroy jeans held as true as the commercial announcer had promised, saving my knee from being scraped on the polyurethane.

I watched sideways in surprised disbelief as everyone else in the entire race proceeded to whiz past me around the corner. I couldn't believe that I was the only one who'd implemented the spin-out brake. I guess I'd just assumed that this being an official Big Wheel race, everyone would feel an obligation to navigate this feature together, with all of us spinning out in solidarity to one of its main selling-point attractions.

Now the very last kid on the track and with total disdain for the whole affair, I crossed the finish line with no discernible effort. I was then further confused upon rolling onto the other side of the finish line when they handed me a ribbon. Regardless of my being last, everyone got the exact same ribbon and weirdly the finishing order didn't even matter. Just physically cross the finish line at some point and you were a "winner". With no first, second or third place ribbons, there certainly was no special ribbon for "keeping it real" either. There never is.

Somehow it didn't take long for most of the band vehicles to disappear, starting with one of the first-ever pieces of official mail to arrive. Johnny Law and The Meter Maids had finally found the source of the trail of parking tickets that had been flying off our beat-up old Honda Civic windshield like carrier pigeons for the past year. The jig was now up and it was time for it to go back to whom from whence it came in San Francisco.

Soon after Matt and I were cruising up Glendale Boulevard with Brad in his 50s Ford Thunderbird when suddenly the engine just dropped dead and we found ourselves coasting backwards toward a blind curve because the brakes had also gone out with the engine.

By the thickness of the remaining book pages in your hands we obviously survived but unfortunately the Thunderbird did not and was taken away by tow-hearse to an auto pick 'n' pull where it was feasted upon by scavengers. Then Peter's van also died or he sold it—I, like, can't remember *everything*, maan.

So although Dave D and his van were once again our main transportation in and out of Atwater Village, during this week's studio recording sessions we were able to add Greg Shaw and Ondi and David as possible ride options to and from or hither and fro depending on what time dimension you are now reading this in or if you're some kind of Dungeons & Dragons nerd or something. You'd be surprised at how many people you know secretly are. I was.

I was also surprised to hear that Sophie had suddenly up and moved out of the Larga house. There had been no obvious build-up, at least not that I'd seen, but then I'd been very preoccupied with all the newly re-formed bandmate stimuli. It all sounds kinda detached when I lay it out in front of myself like this, but that's just how things can roll when people suddenly decide to flip the life switch to another program.

The recording sessions are scheduled for very early in the day so I've already missed this morning's band van ride. Luckily, Greg shows up at the Larga house to pick up Anton's sitar and I'm able to hitch a ride along with that to the studio. We drive deep and high into the hills of Laurel Canyon where he does a quick dump and run at the front gates of Peer studios. I approach the antique futuristic video intercom system and crouch down to its car window height. It looks like something very fancy from back when drive-thru windows were invented.

Booop!

"Hi! It's Joel."

"*Hiiii...*"

"Hi."

"*Hiiii...*"

"Yes, hello there."

"Yes, Jo-*elle* baby. *Hiii...*"

"That's right, you *m—*"

30th anniversary of the Monterey Pop Festival

Jeff Davies and Peter Hayes

I think that maybe I'm dreamin'!

BZZZZZT

The black iron ornately shaped drive-thru gate automatically draws inward. I let it open wide and proceed to walk through and up the driveway toward the large white stucco villa-style multi-structure complex. The closer I get the more the thick green vine seems to have wrapped itself around everything that was once in sight. Further up at the top of some stairs David Timoner is standing at a smaller people-sized gate.

"Hey! Sorry! We were filming you on the intercom camera and we needed to keep you on the monitor screen. The shot looks really cool!"

"Oh, cool! Kind of like how cops try to keep prime suspects on the phone line long enough to trace the call. That would also explain this déjà vu feeling."

"Really? Being under surveillance gives you déjà vu? Where did that come from?"

"Ha. Still none of your business, mister."

"Haha, OK. C'mon, I'll show you where everybody is. This place is amazing."

He leads me up some more steps and we head around the back of the main building toward the recording studio portion of the grounds. The whole complex is in a Spanish style and almost labyrinth-like, accentuated further within the lawn, pool and courtyard areas by the even thicker cover of green vine and plump trees with decades of protruding growth that have shown the entire property who's boss. It's a good fit with the overall old Hollywood vibe and the network of cool breezes that charm the sun's blaring heat away while having still convinced it to leave behind all of its brightness to refract rainbows off the shiny foliage, making for a textbook example of the best of all possible worlds. One can also feel the palpable assistance from the sonic lysergic mists Donovan had glazed the grounds with when he recorded here back in the way back.

Jeff had stayed up in San Francisco after we'd driven up to do the tragically under-promoted and failed 30th Anniversary of the Monterey Pop Festival. He hadn't been back to the Bay since the *Thank God for Mental Illness* recording period and hence felt he had lots of important rounds to make, despite all of the band's upcoming plans to record and tour.

Anton is adjusting settings on the sound board while Ondi films him. A guy who must be the studio engineer is standing back and watching, at the ready, then sees me and comes out smiling. He's all good vibes and almost Muppet-like with large bouncing glam curls and round face puffing on a cigar. He goes right into it.

"So hey, my friend, OK, this guy does the sound at The Troubadour, right? I told him I was doing a session with you guys, and he tells me that a couple weeks ago a *tambourine* of yours came down out of the rafters and *bounced OFF this guy's head*, onstage, while he was in *mid-guitar solo* mind you, OK, and he doesn't know what just happened and is looking around like *what the fuck*?! And my friend is just laughing because these guys are like hair metal dudes and very serious and my friend had seen you throw that thing in the air like *two weeks* before and it never coming down, until these guys, like, *shake it from the rafters*, and it comes down like a thunderbolt from the 60s rock gods, as if hair metal guys didn't have far enough to fall already after Nirvana hit, a tambourine of all things. Man, does it get *any better*?"

"Actually, I do have a metal Ludwig tambourine. That would have been pretty ironic."

He's really laughing now and moves in with a slap on my shoulder. "And the Viper Room? Dude, don't get me started..." His enthusiasm is delivered with a laid-back amusement that is immediately infectious. He poofs a puff off his cigar.

"You were there?" I ask.

"Dude, that was a three-ring circus."

This was a session paid for by Interscope Records to create an optional EP for release on their label. However, I don't think Anton ever had any intention of doing anything other than making an entire album on suit dime and then letting the laminates fall where they may. As far as recording experiences were to go, this was nowhere near demoing in the dingy Portland rehearsal room or the homely apartment style for *Thank God for Mental Illness,* or even the warehouse largeness of Larry Thrasher's studio for *Take It from the Man!*, but rather a proper professional studio of the caliber not used since *Their Satanic Majesties' Second Request* at The Compound. Vibes are high and Anton is in his preferred element, and like the elements, he's practically bouncing off the walls. It's a frantic race against three days of studio time to get it all down, jumping from one track to the next while the clock keeps ticking *tick tick tick tick...*

It's all possible and not only because of the beyond-normal capability work ethic and focus, but also because there were no missing song parts or anything else that needed coming up with musically. Certainly no "jamming out" for song ideas. Everything that came through the door today was already formed. That is except for one small order of last-minute business...

Matt has a song which is his first for BJM since the *Take It from the Man!* sessions, and with Anton's massive enthusiasm, we will make it the Dandys' tune that *we* wanted to hear. It's been a long time now since the groovy sounds of the *Dandys Rule OK* album and at this point we don't care so much to listen to the new stuff.

For three furious days Anton was like a one-man hurricane and we all spun within and around his vortex until he'd periodically reach out and snatch one of us, pull us in, then we'd do our part and be released back into the swirling observation circumference area.

"Is Anton growing a mustache?" Matt observes. There is definitely some allotted stubbling-up going on in the upper lip region, while the rest of his face is smooth. It hits me full on—the righteous Ringo mustache is finally coming after all! It was back just before things *really* started to go south at the warehouse, when I was bored one afternoon trying to find something to zone out to on my little white TV...

"...own two episodes of The X-Files *on each tape..."*
CLICK—CLICK—CLICK
"Bill Nye the Science Gu—"
CLICK—CLICK
"...elp McGruff take a bite out of crime..."
CLICK—CLICK—CLICK—CLICK

"Rapper Tupac Shakur is dead at age twenty-five just about a week after sustaining four bullet wounds last Saturday in Las Vegas. Shakur spent the weekend in the hospital on a resper—"

DING-DONG! went the faux-doorbell buzzer. I trampled down and swung the door open.

"Hey!" I said in high-register surprise seeing an unexpected Anton.

"Hey. I really need to shave."

"Whoa, check that three-day stubble! C'mon, Moses." I turn around and lead the way up to the hairless face lab. As we get to the top of the stairs, I offer, "Go for it, man, right over there," though these directions aren't needed. Then I remember the results of my last mission a few days ago. "So, I tried to talk to Brad bu—"

"Yeah, we talked. He can sorta play drums so I guess we'll see what happens. You guys sure like his hair."

I'm not so sure that I do now but I don't say anything. I guess we're going to see what happens.

I go into my adjacent room and turn the TV off. The sound of the bathroom sink running takes over as soundtrack now and the scene in general is awash in stillness with direct sunshine filling most all of this antique San Francisco living space in that way top floors afford. Our conversation continues from across the small hall.

"Soo...I also found a guitar player."

"Really?"

"Yeah...he was like a mod guy or something back in the day... you'll meet him at practice tonight...it's all set up because we've got to get it into shape so we can do this big show in LA."

The sink shuts off and then three beats later Anton appears in my doorway with a stubbly short but full mustache.

"Whoa!"

"I'm just joking," he smiles with face still wet and razor in hand. He turns back to the bathroom.

"Ah man! You gotta leave it! It's like *Sgt. Pepper* Ringo!"

Anton comes back. "Really?"

"YES!"

"I should leave it?"

"YESS!"

"No way, man. You're crazy."

He goes back to the bathroom and turns the sink back on.

I lament, "Maan...I wish I looked that good with a mustache."

His voice takes on an animated tone, "Man, I've seen you passed out wasted with hairy caterpillars crawling across your lip, and it wasn't a good look, it's true."

"I know..."

"Hey Joel!" Matt yells, snapping me back to today's recording reality. It's my turn to track on the record and my first experience in an isolation booth and that weird glassed-off stillness within it. In there I get fully immersed in everyone's playing through the headphones as different layers of tape cross over each other like butterfly junctions intersecting from different parts of different days. The count-ins could have random events layered from multiple people's last-second performance preparations, like a cough from Thursday coupled with a throat clearing from Tuesday interrupted by a joke cut off halfway through from Wednesday. I didn't have Anton's hand to watch on the downstrokes like I preferred when it was an important performance, but I'd long since not technically needed that anymore. I just liked it. I was surprised but not at all surprised when I got all of my takes done in one pass.

If Miranda Lee Richards had been our Marianne Faithfull up in San Francisco, down here in LA today she is our Nancy Sinatra duetting with Anton on the never-before heard by any of us, "(You Better Love Me) Before I Am Gone", another one of those songs Anton just seemed to pull out of the air fully formed.

Miranda was a model. She was young, blonde, yet still oddly enough, beautiful. She'd even done milk commercials as a teen. Miranda was also a genuinely talented singer with a voice like an angel's angel, and despite coming from the Hope Sandoval school of "this is how you want to do it", she was well on track to filing that in the "ya gotta start somewhere" drawer of experiences.

Electric Kool-Aid Puke Fest

Dave D is driving me up into the hip hills of the Silver Lake neighborhood where Greg Shaw's new place is. It's pretty around here even with only nighttime street lamps lighting the colorful houses, condos and apartments of decades-spanning casual styles stuffed within healthy clustering bushels of greenery and topped with palms that are spaced out like lingering lollipops in a candy shop jar. Like I said, it's dark out so the shop must be closed.

"Weeeeeeeeeeeird," Dave unrolls like a long strip of artificial grass. "There are no lights on in any of these houses whatsoever. Where is everybody?"

I get dropped off at the house with lights on at the top of the hills with the numbers that coincide with the scribble.

Knock knock knock...

Anton answers the door. "Hey," he says matter-of-factly while immediately leaning a cigarette into lighter flame. Then he smiles with a burst of energy.

"I'm making the cover for the 'Last Dandy' record on Greg's computer right now. You're gonna laugh, man," he chuckles.

I light up while keeping conversation-going eye contact.

"I have so much shit to do before we can leave for tour. It's crazy, man," he sighs while simultaneously blowing out the smoke signal for sigh.

"What's the cover?"

"You'll see in a minute. I just want to stand the test of time with our music. Ya' know? Be weird."

"Hit them back with their own sound that they themselves discarded."

"It isn't about that. But sometimes you have to remind people why they are great. And that it's not about being on magazine covers and that shit. It doesn't mean anything. We are going to defeat these record label motherfuckers at their own game. Get everybody to rethink it because it doesn't have to be this way."

"Do your own thing no matter what and fuck everybody."

"I just do what I do. We need to just go for it and not give a good goddam." He drags a long drag like you do when the cigarette is over before it's over and tosses the butt onto the ground next to all the others scattered around the doorway. I go to drop mine, then hesitate, not wanting to yet again incur the wrath of any angry cigarette butt fairies that Greg might have kept on staff from his old place. I give it a good flick fast and far that lands it out into the street gutter, just to be safe.

As the neighbor's stilts would indicate, Greg's place overlooks Hollywood at night and all of the twinkling dreams and fiery nightmares lighting up the darkness below. The master of the house is not home and has left Anton the run of the place, or more specifically, his computer. We take the two chairs in Greg's office corner space that is part of the large low-lit living room. He shows me the cover artwork he's just designed for the "Not If You Were the Last Dandy on Earth" 12-inch single. The front design is a portion of an ad from a 60s magazine which shows a close-up of a surprised-looking woman clutching on to her purse; on the back is a "suit" shouting into a phone with the caption "I want those bastards dead! They're jeopardizing the Dandys' career!" It looks really slick in its vintage *Esquire*-esque magazine imagery. Unfortunately, the album cover printers will botch the image specs and every copy will be pressed with only blown-out blown-up portions of their original design. The woman's purse gets cut off as well as the telephone, taking the whole concept out of the thing.

"Have you ever smoked DMT before?" Anton asks.

"*Noo...*"

"Here. I've been smoking this all day. There should still be some in there."

I take a hit. It kinda tastes like a tire. As I exhale the smoke away from me, a computer grid-like psychedelic world is released that comes toward me and surrounds the smoke from every direction, seemingly a melding of another dimension which I am now also surrounded by. The dimmed room lighting makes it all that much more luminous as I bear witness in wonder. With a small boom box in his lap, Anton decrees, "OK, here we go." And presses record. I want to take another hit, but he's recording something now and it's too late for lighter noise.

He's telling the story of how we first met The Dandy Warhols while periodically playing some of his favorite 60s songs on Greg's stereo system. It's like he's performing it to me, talking to me and smiling as he recalls. My visible body being like a memento from that first day, now years away. I'm not sure if I should join in the conversation or take more hits, then I realize the only thing required of me is to just remain present and be his audience of one. I put the pipe down.

After about thirty minutes he clicks stop on the boom box and I click the lighter over the pipe. Now the focus turns to my taking the full DMT trip, which suddenly has me flat on my back while Anton repeatedly pushes my knees up to my chest like I'm a drowning victim. "*Out* with the bad...*in* with the good...*out* with the bad..."

I have a feeling this is not the ceremonial way of doing this. Above us two cigarette butt fairies are sitting on ceiling fan blades, slowly going in circles while giving me dirty looks.

The next day Matt and I were broke, bored and abandoned at the Larga house. After tearing apart the kitchen on a booze hunt we finally found Dave D's cheap "Czar"-brand vodka hidden in a cabinet over the refrigerator. This 1.75 liter handle bottle was basically lighter fluid that would magically appear every time Dave wanted to control specifically Matt and me or tilt popular majority band opinion in his favor. It rarely failed in getting us to see things "his way" after a few swigs and especially if followed by the promise of more of the stuff.

We quickly assemble two large glasses side by side on the counter. Unfortunately, all we can find that will mix are packets of tropical fruit powder Kool-Aid mix. Part of Dave's current mission is to replace the depleted refrigerator.

Matt commences with pouring us each a tall drink filled to the brim. The heavy lean of his pour makes for drinks consisting almost entirely of the bottom-shelf vodka, leaving only enough of the bright red dusted tap water to barely blow the vodka a sloppy, hairy-lipped trailer-park kiss.

We adjourn to the living room for ghetto cocktail time when suddenly what do we see but Dave and the rest of the guys already slow-pulling up to the house in his van. Matt and I look at each other in shock as if a SWAT team were just swinging through the windows, then forgoing words we go full-tilt on our glasses in a one-go chug attempt. Before I even feel the liquid the foul smell of the cheap vodka is like pneumonia swishing under my nose. I hold my breath as to not break up the gross-guzzle and go for it. I can feel its physical presence invading my head as my inner flesh begins to quiver and retreat further back within my face. Fumes like gasoline exhaust are now engulfing my entire head and it's just as I'm beginning to see the glass reveal clear bottom that my dam suddenly breaks. All this slamming of the cheap badness has pummeled not only all of my senses but one or two new ones I didn't know about. I choke and gag hard, then puke all of it right back into the glass, filling it all the way back up to the brim.

The sight of this makes Matt crack up laughing, which is then quickly followed by his own gagging due to the smell of my now full glass of vomit. With his fresh pudding-bowl haircut jiggling, he quickly cups his hand over his now gagging mouth. His glasses vibrate down to the tip of his nose as a tiny stream as if from a water balloon poked with a sewing pin begins to squirt through his two bottom fingers. It was a thin but long healthy squirt fountain of fire-engine-red Kool-Aid barf. The sight of this gets me going again and I start convulsing like a cat with a hairball. We quickly exchange knowing glances and scramble through the living room toward the bathroom, accompanied by his thin-puke fountain-geyser spraying and my violent hacking. Matt makes it in there first and takes the toilet while I throw my head into the sink and we both unload, red faced and laughing uncontrollably all the while.

"What the fuck are you guys doing?!" we suddenly hear Dave ask from the doorway behind us, plastic shopping bag handles crinkling in his hands.

In the absence of Jeff, Dean Taylor is back again and here at the Larga house rehearsing with us as we prepare for our first ever complete US tour in the summer of '97. Dean and I had a special insider's bond. We looked for each other to share a headshake while sitting in the back of the van late to a gig, waiting for the photographer to figure out what's wrong, enduring club staff with bad attitudes, loud intoxicated people in small spaces, Matt complaining about things that couldn't be helped, waiting in a liquor store parking lot for Jeff to decide if he wants an It's-It ice-cream cookie sandwich or a piece of beef jerky that looks like a bat wing, Anton shouting at our bandmates, anything Dave D said—we traversed our band inner sanctum shaking our heads with Marlon Brando "Whatta ya got?" *Wild One* abandon. We didn't spare ourselves either—calling each other out in the throes of demoralizing moments inadvertently made us feel better. It made it part of "the game" rather than drinking embarrassments straight up.

On a recent visit to San Francisco I'd been able to pique Dean's band interest again by playing him recordings from the new album and details of BJM's first-ever full tour of America having been freshly booked. This posed the question for him: it had happened for the Dandys, could BJM be the next in line? We'd towed the line toe to toe so far, so now it was starting to seem more plausible than ever. Especially as we had for the first time a proper booking agent and a finished, professionally recorded record on the way.

Today's rehearsal is over now but Brad and Peter are going to go over the "Whoever You Are" recurring drum fill break a few more times together while Anton heads back to his band leader's suite. Dean, Matt and I head the other way toward the rest of the house.

Dean looks at me and shakes his head. "Man, what's wrong with the new guy? He's so spaced out. He's like Jim from *Taxi*."

"Yeah, I hear what you're saying but he's only like twenty-one or twenty-two or some shit. He's just now figuring it all out upstairs."

One thing that Peter for sure figured out was the girls really liked him. Today there are a pair of gals who are just kind of hanging around the living room waiting for Peter to come out. They seem like old-guard groupie types, or "cougars", who liked our young Peter, the youngest and maybe even the best looking of the bunch which I'm sure could start an argument or two around here, and harder to call now that Dean is back with his 70s Robert Redford blond tousled locks competing with Peter's dark Syd Barrett-y shade of brooding ways...Wait, where was I?

Peter is most definitely the most innocent of us all and this attracts a particular sect of the Los Angeles ladies singles scene. These two had been showing up a few times a week now in various "Momma's here, baby" gear, like for example today's see-through wide-stitched macramé mini dress with no upper-body underthings. Lately they'd been coming around and seemed to be alternating going into Peter's room, but technically we had no way of knowing what went on in there because it was always just one or the other alone with him with the door shut. Peter appears and one goes in while the other, who on this particular day is wearing a leopard-print zip-jumpsuit, looks over at me and growls a tiger-like *"r-r-r-aar"* while scratching at the air in my direction. She's rolled enough r's my way to form an "r" bridge, from which her gin mouthwash breath travels on all the way across the room to the tip of my nose. There is a hint of Marlboro miner's lung around the edges. I *"r-r-r-raar"* back, which is just good tiger etiquette, but that was it.

I exchange some covert facial signals with Dean, and we head out onto the front porch. Matt's radar picks this up and with his own lame detector readings deduces we must be making a permanent move. We find a stretch of railing to lean on.

"Man, these chicks are weird," Dean laments. "Is there anything we can go do around here?"

I'm thinking. "Not around here, but I saw a billboard advertising a new Mike Myers movie. It looks like it's trying to be all '60s', you guys wanna go see it?"

"Let me go find the paper to see where it's playing," Matt offers.

"He's funny on *SNL*," Dean says.

"The 'Sprockets' skits are definitely funny," I agree.

Matt comes back with the paper folded out in front of him. "It's only playing at big cineplexes in the malls."

"No single-screen theaters?"

"Doesn't look like it."

"Ugh."

We all break for ten minutes to do our going-out-for-an-afternoon-movie preparations. I change into a new op-art red, white and blue print top the booker at The Silverlake Lounge gave me and some indigo Levi's with matching Lee Rider jacket. My newish Beatle boots round out the ensemble. Dean's got on black stove-pipe trousers and a silver paisley round-collar button-down with lace-up winklepickers. Matt's in a black, silver-pearl embroidered Western shirt with white, gold and green plaid pants that I personally would call slightly questionable in their flirtations with "Mr. Furley"-ness. Brown leather single-buckle boots complete the look.

Two hours later we approach a bustling entrance to the mall.

"*Yeah, baby!*" A young guy catcalls.

It always makes me feel good to know I can be attractive to members of both sexes. I take the compliment with a shy nod and since I've gotten to the doors first, I hold one open for the guys. Dean quips "Thanks, chief," and nods a wink as he enters like I'm the building doorman. A family is coming out the other way so I hold position.

"*Yeah, baby!*" one of the kids says.

"*Yeeah, baby!*" the other parrots enthusiastically. I stride back up to the guys as Matt turns around. "Look Joel, the Orange Julius stand," he offers jokingly about the retro 60s concession stand somehow still being a shopping mall staple.

"Do they have one with vodka yet?" I wonder in seriousness.

"I want a hot dog on a stick." Dean says sarcastically.

"I've always wanted to date a hot—"

"*Yeah, baby!*" says some middle-aged guy walking past us.

"...dog on a stick girl. Such groovy outfits," I say, now partially distracted.

Then suddenly, "Oh my *god*," a teenage girl exclaims to her teenage girl companion *"Yeeeah, baaby.* Haha!"

"What the hell's wrong with these people?" Dean says now, annoyed.

We continue toward the escalator and by the time we get to the top three more people have *Yeah, baby*'d at us. In fact, this *"Yeah, baby"* jazz continues picking up the deeper we enter the mall.

"Yeahhh, baby!"

"Yah, baby."

It's coming faster and quicker now, almost like the *Jaws* theme.

"Yeah, baby!"

"Yeah, baby!" "Yeah, baby!"

"Yeah, baby!" "Yeah, baby!" "Yeah, baby!"

We quicken our pace.

"Yeah, baby!"

"Yeah, baby!"

"Yeah, baby!"

"Yeah, baby!"

By the time we finally make it to the multiplex cinema line it's full on.

"...Yeahbaby!Yeahbaby!Yeahbaby!Yeahbaby!Yeahbaby!Yeahbaby!Yeahbaby!Yeahbaby!..."

We get our tickets and stride into our theater room making sure no *yeah babys* are following us in. Safe under the cover of theater darkness, we find some seats as the last trailer is ending. Then the movie starts.

"YEAH, BABY!"

Oh shit.

After the movie, we are able to get out of the mall relatively un-*yeah, baby*'d while I mostly complain about all the classic movies they'd made fun of.

As my fellow SF ex-pat Randy who'd already been down here some years had put it to me recently, "Man, nobody down here had been doing the 60s thing for a *long* time, man, until you cats came down and reminded everybody." To the straight world, we were suddenly reminding everyone of Austin Powers. This "yeah, baby" nonsense continued for a few more months until everyone forgot and moved on to something else that didn't include noticing people dressing in vintage clothes. That is until the two sequels when the whole process would be repeated for each.

Outside and a few blocks away, a school bus full of kids is waiting at the stoplight just ahead. As we get closer, I can see every single kid is turned around and watching us. They all look with anticipation and are waiting for something from us. Realizing that Matt, despite being the most obvious-looking one of us, isn't going to bite, I roll my eyes and shrug, then point my fingers at them and shout "Yeah, baby!" The entire bus bursts into cheering, jumping and waving as every kid on there goes completely bonkers. No matter what, it's always all about the kids, man.

The Marlboro Man vs the Man

After the big party our address became of note to various people including yet another pair of girls who showed up every few days, always wearing workout gym clothes, who just wanted to hang out in the living room and snort cocaine. Matt and I would usually serve as hosts for these drop-ins, and I'd learn through repeated nose reps that I don't really like coke all that much. This is a key factor in why my brain still functions enough to even be writing all of this today. What was funny about these two is they really were coming directly from the gym, still in their tight nylon tanks and Capris like this was a part of the training routine. It all stays pretty innocent and that's OK 'cause I like it when random weirdness remains faithful to its original state and we also get lots of drugs that I keep hoping I will suddenly like because, well, I'm supposed to. We were waiting for the day when the cougar alchy ladies and the workout cokehead girls would randomly meet, but unfortunately this head-to-head match-up never occurred.

For some reason Ondi was periodically working for Camel cigarettes on promotional events. Feeling sorry for our regular regiment of have-maybes, she'd pulled some strings and rigged us winners' tickets to a big Camel cigarettes "random drawing" contest for a trip to Las Vegas. It included transportation and a free room at The Hard Rock Hotel and Casino with booze and buffets. Brad, Dean, Matt and I became miraculous random contest winners despite not having entered or even smoked a Camel cigarette in many latelys, while Anton, who smoked enough Camel non-filters for all four of us, wanted nothing to do with this trip to Vegas. Peter also passed in favor of something he just kind of mumbled.

We meet up in an unused parking lot off of Hollywood Boulevard with all the other contest winners. There is lots of smoking going on as you might imagine and this line is more or less a no no-smoking zone. The bus itself is actually a no-smoking zone so as each person gets on they display all the smoker styles of taking the quick last-second drags as one foot levitates in hesitation above the first step. There's the hot toots jazz solo, the firing squad three-count, the all-in-one grim reaper ash finger and of course the ground score Good Samaritan. By the time we inch our way through the line and get close to the bus door there are enough butts under our feet that it kind of simulates a sort of cigarette-filter rough-road red carpet.

The four of us take over the row of backseats on the large tour bus. Every seat holds a winner and we are ready with just enough money for beer and tequila to get us to Vegas, plus we've got some of the workout routine cocaine. Once the bus is loaded we can begin to do the same, but first I head up to the driver and ask him to play my cassette copy of the Stones' *Exile on Main Street*. I've also brought my umbrella, and just to show how little I care for conventional practices in general, I'm using my rain umbrella *for the sun*. When I think about it, I still just, wow. Not only will it help me to beat the desert heat, but at the same time provide a party partition between us and the driver's passenger observation mirror.

By the end of the double album we are feeling pretty pretty and when the bus doors open in the Hard Rock parking lot we each come off with a skip and a finger snap ready to dance into some action, tough-guy Jets-dancer style from *West Side Story*.

Unfortunately, the reality is revealed while checking in that the free booze part of the story was misinformation and it's in fact only all about a hotel room and buffets. We get to our room and waste no haste in master-planning our way into socking it to the sober conspiracy. We have to act fast because our bodies are processing all the alcohol we have within us and transforming it into sobriety juice by the second.

We collect all of our pocket change and head down to the hotel casino to hit the nickel slot machines. Like the Rat Pack in *Ocean's Eleven*, all four of us would simultaneously implement the same job on the house by pretending to be big-time nickel slot machine tycoons and get a free drink.

Our crew finds a crowded section and pretend we don't know each other, despite how out of place we look in the casino yet how in place we look ourselves if one were to imagine us all sitting close together. This move to the busiest section will in fact speed along the serving process. We see our drinks being tray-loaded and exchange covert, knowing glances, like you do during undercover heist jobs.

Our plan isn't financially backed with enough for tips so we take our single drink takes and head toward the free rock concert being put on for the Camel contest winners. The band playing is The Smithereens, and although they had an affinity with British Invasion mod groups, they were kind of like the Bruce Springsteen, blue-collar worker-friendly version and we didn't care about this band.

Despite the Camel schedules given to everyone on the buses, there's almost nobody here. There is a small group of seemingly hired "fans" dancing in a tight cluster for the cameras to keep zooming in on over and over again. On the large stage screens you can see the various camera angles quickly cut from the band to fans in a way that makes it look like something is happening here that really isn't; it's creating a reality more suitable to broadcast to the people watching at home on MTV. Suddenly everyone is simply on the clock in a fantasy scenario as the camera acrobatics paint large and broad strokes of a different picture over the failed one with each quick fly-by of the camera crane. Meanwhile, the band onstage look uneasy with all of this, like they'd just been called into the boss's office during a series of layoffs.

Ondi suddenly appears and then we all see what she looks like without her camera on. She has swung some drink tickets for us and we refortify with doubles down on each dude.

With nothing much more to see here except more of nothing much, we venture out of this lame rock casino on a search for the old "Rat Pack" Vegas. Unfortunately, the amount of classic mid-century architecture that has been demolished only to be replaced with tacky garbage of the times is astounding. We thought that we'd at least be able to visit small areas of their ancient ruins like in Rome, a special site where we could camp up, but the legacy of what made this place cool and swinging in the first place is nowhere to be found. Even the 70s lime-green polyester world of the Hunter S. Thompson book is gone. It's more like a sprawling city constructed by set designers of an 80s hair metal video, like the Hard Rock was a disease that has now spread and multiplied over the entire town.

On the other hump of the camel ride is BJM performing a tour kick-off show of sorts at a Camel-sponsored night for a new line of cigarettes at Moguls off Hollywood Boulevard. The evening is billed as "Desert Chic" and the white people-sheiks are in the house watching lounge-area belly dancers, huffing at hookah stations by the bar while we hit the stage where usually the next wanna-be Third Eye Blind, Matchbox 20, Creed, Garbage, Blink-182, Sugar Ray, Big Head Todd and The Monsters, 3-11, Dave Matthews Band, Smash Mouth, Counting Crows, Sublime or Everclear would go. Sorry, that was cruel to keep going like that, but that's what they call reality these days.

"Feel It" is the last song and that's exactly what we are doing while ceremonially evoking our war dance against all the evil spirits listed above. The song has eaten many planets by clock read 11:23 and counting as ground zero of the tension site is building and building and then Anton begins to ad-lib the opening lines to "L.A. Woman", which he loudly warbles in a wordless scat version of baritone god-like belligerence through a violent incantation where the rubber is shredded to ribbons by the road. Drums coming apart at the seams, the hiss of an eight maraca-headed snake and three amped-up hollow-bodies and a bass guitar reverbed and overdriven to the gills sonically splatter-bomb the room with a three-chord mantra set to cranium control.

…wowawow wowawow wowawow wowawow wowawow wowawow wowawow wowawow wowawow…

I light one of the new Camel-brand menthols from our giveaway stash and ping it through the air in disgust. I was prone to do this act, but I was not expecting to hit a guy square in the forehead and explode the cigarette cherry off it sending a New Year fireworks display cascading down over his entire body.

I must commit to retiring this practice now before bringing it on the road as we embark on our first-ever mighty rock 'n' roll zigzag over the whole U. S. of A. With tonight, the tour has officially begun.

BANG!

Hahaha most of the mostly hip audience laughs at Anton's in-between song banter. It was our New York City debut playing to a sold-out crowd at Brownie's. The show is going rock solid and for me this is one of those unusual moments in life where all high expectations are fulfilled. We're halfway through the tour with Ondi and David following close behind, cameras rolling constantly.

The next night the backstage area and toilets at CBGB are living up to their legend and then some, so after a few minutes of "living the dream" we can't hold our breath anymore and go do most of our pre-show hanging in the van right outside the venue doors. During the show the vibes begin to match the house stench special and things start going wrong. Anton and I are doing the solo folk-duo portion of the set when suddenly an obviously wasted dancing guy starts throwing shapes right in front of our half-nerd looking, half-cool guy Matt, who is attempting to ignore him while sitting peacefully at the front of the stage.

The vogueing dancer's shape throwing eventually incites Matt to mirror one back so as to hopefully just get rid of him, but this apparently implements the evil plan of the shape-throwing man and now having been upgraded to mutual ritual, a portal opens up where a confusion demon is allowed to escape that wastes no haste in filling up the entire room with its poison-like gas. I suck on my cocktail straw extra long while everyone else inhales the confusion gas as it swallows every space in the place, right down to the tiniest scum-covered crevasse.

Anton then begins criticizing our manager Dave D on the mic for offering no stage security assistance that might have prevented whatever is now going on, meanwhile right next to him the confusion demon has tricked Matt into flipping sides and he's suddenly defending the drunk shape-throwing guy.

BANG!

Sometimes, everyone in the room is immaculately right while simultaneously pharmaceutical-grade wrong all at the same time, and often times when this happens, much like a lab experiment gone horribly awry, there is an explosion so immense that it just blows the entire whatever it is to dust. The smoke clears and Anton has fired our manager Dave D while still onstage and before the show is even over.

In a flash of a second individual hopes and dreams and wants and obligations and loyalty and guilt trips collide in a multicolor splatter of rights and wrongs and this Jackson Pollock of takeaway variants is splattered all over the 1970s New York punk rock scene splatters already there and for all to witness.

Oftentimes it's best to bury the remains of whatever it was once supposed to be and come back down the road to see what kind of flowers grew over the plot. But, more than likely, people want to immediately comb the debris and as a result tonight is still somehow crawling around on the floor. Matt, Dean and I call a cab to take us over to a new site to spread around our own personal takeaway wreckage.

Taxi!

The next day Anton, Matt, Peter and I bust out the busking around Manhattan while "bringing it all back home again" to Broadway, Times Square, Radio City, Rockefeller Plaza and Central Park. I feel safe making such a public display with Anton in charge, knowing that there's no way his harmonica can be taken over by New York saxophone spirits that would start in on some kind of *Saturday Night Live*-style solo, which because I've never actually been here seems like something that happens a lot. We take our jamboree onto the subway and over to the East Village and St. Marks Place, where tonight's show is at Coney Island High.

Eighth Street on St. Mark's Place has a flush feel with breezy trees and neighborhood stoops with networks of fire escapes above beautifully natural hip people of every stripe striding the streets. It feels like *Sesame Street* got an expensive new outdoor set upgrade filmed in widescreen Technicolor. I love it and I feel the hit on my internal reset button after finding some proper bug-eye sunglasses and record-bin diving in slightly subterranean shops. It's a sister street to our own Haight and we are feeling at home and secure here as I spiritually feel our car on the ups-and-downs rollercoaster begin to climb steadily.

We meet back up the next morning from our various crash sites and soon everything we own—amps, guitars, and luggage—is all strewn haphazardly along the sidewalk in front of Coney Island High. Matt's suitcase even has different-colored socks unintentionally sticking out of its seams. Conversation is light on "how's it goin's" and heavy on loading gear out of the venue.

It all feels a little odd and then suddenly I get a weird suspicion sensation toward Anton's new mustache. It's almost like it's getting too comfortable with itself, not bothered with getting a little too out-there in length. The mustache that I'd originally begged him to let grow so many months ago after he'd momentarily left it on as a joke while shaving. "But it makes you look just like *Sgt. Pepper* Ringo!" I had pleaded. After much begging I eventually gave up, then months later he decided to grow the mustache for this tour. I'd loved that mustache at first, but now I think I just like it. It's mixing up my radar and as a result I'm receiving an odd read on Anton's moodiness meter, which has a gauge reading that starts at brooding and tops out on total meltdown. There's an interference which is almost as if the mustache itself is the source of a new lack of concern for others and the consequences of what I'm now beginning to suspect is its own hairy decision making. Maybe it's all in my hungover head. I don't share my concerns with any of the others because at the end of the day it's a mustache and I would probably just sound crazy to them. I take a pull of my beer instead.

Some of the guys are still inside the club grabbing the last of our gear while Dean and I watch all the stuff already outside.

As we sit crouched down leaning against the wall we are understandably a little down in the dumps. Then I look up just in time to see Joey Ramone walking by and in mid-survey of us. Now looking away again, he simply shakes his head in what looks to be very much like amused disgust as he continues on his way in his "The Who: Maximum R&B" T-shirt. Dean and I are both in mutual awe of his masterful headshake display in both style and execution, *clearly* confirming him as one of the world's undisputed masters of disgusted headshaking.

With Anton apparently unsuccessful in his last-minute endeavors to secure the required quick cash needed to rent a van for the remainder of the tour dates, Dave D has offered to rent out his van to us, with the one extremely questionable condition that he can ride along. Whether he is wanting to be there to save the day or to laugh when the final pieces fall off the plane is unclear because his permanent poker face has grown to poker full body overnight, and I should remind you he's also really tall. Though it is reluctantly agreed to by Anton, this did not sit well with the mustache who had very much wanted to be done with Dave D right here in New York. A new plan would have to be made.

Right on continued tragedy cue, Dave's van breaks down on our way from New York to the next show in North Carolina, and as a result we arrive too late to be able to play. It didn't make any sense to be skipping shorter drives to bigger cities like Philadelphia and Washington DC, but as our new booking manager explained it, we had a fair amount of shows in the South to make up for it. Unless you lose a few hours on a van repair and miss them because they are so far away that there is no time for any of the curveballs that touring will always throw your way.

With no badly needed night's pay and nowhere for the six pieces of band to stay, some sympathetic music fans offer us individual lots of wood planks around their well-weathered front porch. This works out fine because it's hotter than blazes and too humid to sleep stuck onto something inside anyway, but then when Dave takes the mustache's reserved porch bench it goes into a rage. This was the kind of argument that didn't come with a reverse option and as it escalates, it eventually gets so heated that Anton goes ahead and pours a bunch of beer he'd already drunk on Dave's prized leather jacket, which if you know Dave you know is the biggest staple in his everyday stapler. As you can imagine, it would have to have been a pretty heated argument but by now I was avoiding any kind of heat which absolutely included the argument kind so I didn't know about the repurposed beer going onto his jacket until the next morning when Dave and his van were already gone.

We are still there and so our continued presence becomes an excuse for a weekend-long party at one of the kid's parents' houses while they are out of town. It's a large house with a large swimming pool and a full bar of large bottles, and after full-time full-tilt-boogie on my part, I discovered that once the booze got in there it went on a memory-bank robbing spree so there's not much to take away even though it lasted many days.

Now our gallery of characters are all in rotating motion, floating in and out of view like in a dream sequence. The fearless leader, the idyllic dreamers, the investors, the witnesses, the poet, the physician, the farmer, the scientist, the magician and the other so-called gods of our legen— wait, sorry, somehow along the way here I traded in the blazing heat of the Deep South for going to the lost fabled utopia Atlantis with Donovan.

In reality, we were off to Florida...

Go Directly to Jail Do Not Pass Go Do Not Collect $200

Down in the jungles of the Southern states the tour just seemed to be going on and on at the speed of stubble as the mustache's consciousness grew in both length and power. Suddenly the rest of us were dropping invisible balls at any given moment. There always seemed to be something missing that was supposed to have been there. Still, I wasn't ready yet to tell the other guys or call out the mustache and expose it in front of everyone in a dramatic scene. My inner voice constantly wanted me to yell "fuck this" and leave, but then Anton would smile one of those ol' smiles and I'd realize "fuck! he's still in there!" Then five minutes later he's yelling at someone again. Those two internal forces were now constantly at war within him.

Anton had made some phone calls and convinced a business friend to rent us a van to get to the next show. Then, on our way while passing through the green wilds of Georgia he sees a van for sale on the side of the road, and so on the way back up he makes some other bigger deal with someone to get a loan to buy the van.

Meanwhile, back in LA, the booking agency is adding on last-minute shows and as a result we're starting to go into figure eights of the South, bringing on a type of road vertigo that adds to the light-headed swirl of the off-balancing act. We are also the kind of band the local party people want to do that with and a daily revolving menu of random party favors puts us each, in different ways, well over the allotted limit to be properly navigating our brains around the vertigo tracks of individual consciousnesses and all are at serious risk of common sense DUIs from the regrets police.

Speaking of DUIs, here comes the official tour face-plant. Ondi, who is catching back up with us after breaking off in New York, takes Anton in her SUV and we split off into two groups. The rest of the BJM boys and her brother David are in the new van while Anton does interviews along the drive. With both vehicles now on their own, we don't expect to see those two again until soundcheck at the venue.

"Whoa, did you see that, Peter?" Dean asks from the front passenger seat. "That electric sign just said 'Drug checkpoint in one mile'."

"Noo, huh. Should I pull over?"

"Hey guys, drug checkpoint one mile, are any of you jerks hiding anything from the rest of us?"

Nobody is but we all agree it's probably best to get off at the next exit just to check the van over for any potential lost roaches or bindles.

There's just one exit before the drug checkpoint and so we pull off onto it only to discover that the electric road sign is a lie to lure any guilty parties onto this exit which is the real drug checkpoint made up of about twenty police vehicles that we are now driving straight into. While this is all still off in the distance, it's a one-way ramp and we have no choice but to continue toward the cluster of police cars, cage vans and various officers with drug dogs that line each side of the road. This highway exit is a long wide curve and the van windshield becomes like a drive-in movie theater screen playing in a Sergio Leone-style shot as we pan around the wide expanse populated from end to end with the anti-drug police army. Slowly, reluctantly, we continue further on toward our eventual extreme close-up. Apparently this is a slow part of the day and they are eagerly waiting for the next meth'd up trailer trash or DUI teens, but we were of a much more delectable, rare and exotic breed—that of the California weirdo hippie variety, rarely seen anymore around these parts. Excited arms all come out at once in competition for first-dib rights in directing us to pull over. For a split second it kinda feels like being the belles of the South'en ball, but then I realize this is Delusion again, who by this point in the tour is like the fifth Beatle.

Now fully ensnared in the Man's all-too-real faked drug trap, I have to give it to them. No matter what you want to say about Southern derp law enforcement agents, they are black belts in being a bummer.

"Y'all steyp outtathe vayn, puhleese," the classic stereotype Southern cop instructs. He looks just like you'd think, replete with a "Yosemite Sam" mustache.

Shit

I slide the side door open and there is a dog right there who excitedly bounces up and yowlps to greet me. Narcotics dogs are usually the only outwardly excited ones in these scenarios. Another cop of the "big guy" persuasion pulls the leash back and the dog makes way for us all to exit the vehicle one by one like fashion-show models in all of our Manson hippie *Scooby-Doo*-ness glory.

I'm not so worried about us having forgotten about drugs, but I am definitely worried about joint roaches or worse still mashed into the carpet or inside one of the anonymous loose articles of clothing, boots, guitar cases, luggage, seats, cigarette butt-filled empty cups, or maybe even one of the ashtrays.

Somehow there are no drugs in the van and by this point I can't believe that there are no drugs in the van even more so than the Yosemite Sam mustache man who is really looking like he can't believe there are no drugs in the van. In fact, when he informs us with great disappointment that there were no drugs in the van, my honest response was *"Really?!"*

We get back on the road having no idea that Ondi and Anton had already been busted right here by these very two and taken to jail. Apparently Ondi had a single joint packed away in her luggage, but the good news is, it seems the mustache is apparently an incognito Freemason and after giving the proper signals to the cop's Yosemite Sam mustache they were able to get out of jail sooner than normal mustaches would have.

The rest of us try to go ahead and play the show without Anton by doing a shorter set of all Matt's songs, but the club's booker won't go for it. We're not so big down in Atlanta and he is more than happy to get out of having to pay us our performance guarantee. However, we are still allowed to order food from the kitchen and beers from the bar so when Anton finally arrives hours later to learn we're now even more broke, he just blows up. First he flips out in the parking lot, then later just after we are finally settled into the cheap motel and punched out for the day. Him and our drummer Brad, who's not that good but has Brian Jones hair, get into it next level and we were already at nosebleed-high levels as it was. I jump in between them and stop the fight by human barrier and mutual history-earned trust. Anton storms out in frustration.

Although I know it's the mustache, I'm too tired and over this night to even try to bring everyone in on what's really going on. This decision turns out to be my mistake and as I pass out within one of the human-body chalk outlines on the carpet, apparently Dean and Brad decide this was the last straw and that they would be flying back to California.

The next morning I wake up to find Anton by looking out the window all the way across to the other side of the long desolate parking lot playing guitar and singing songs by himself. As I ponder the various angles of this whole situation, despite the wrongs, I ultimately recognize this moment as the time that officially puts it into the too-many times-to-count zone that he is in many ways one of the last of the real deals, regardless. It's suddenly odd to me that no one else seems to grasp that in order for the genuine article to exist in the first place, the flaws are just as important a part of the equation as the benefits. Despite this knowledge, I'm very weary from this first-ever tour wear-down and I'm feeling way too tired and hungover to start ranting and raving about evil facial hair possession. I wonder if this whole mustache thing is just me losing my marbles and I decide to continue to just keep it to myself from here on out.

The single marijuana joint bust had temporarily also taken the thrill away for Ondi and she and David were going home early. They see the look on my face and offer to take me along in the SUV documentary machine all the way back to California. I instantly agree. Escapism surrounds me in thoughts of kicking back in comfort from both backseats while we make whatever stops that might strike our fancies all along the way. It was settled, then. As for the rest of the tour, Anton, Matt and Peter would soldier on like The Kingston Trio or something.

One last group vehicle stop at a gas station for mutual fill-ups and final farewells. As both vehicles pump gas side by side, James Brown's version of "Georgia on My Mind" plays through the outdoor area speakers. Anton is weirdly quiet while just hovering around the various conversations. Just as Dean and Brad's cab to the airport pulls out, Matt comes up alongside me, pushes his glasses up and lays it all out in a whisper. "You know, I totally understand you wanting to split, but right now you're the only one of us that has a driver's license. If we get pulled over for anything, that's it, we're getting totally busted."

"*Fuuck*...Just like in *The Godfather III*, man, 'Just when I thought I was out, they pull me back in!'"

Five minutes later I'm back in the band again and in the van with the guys. Despite me being the only one with a driver's license, Anton is driving, but we arranged so we can quickly switch spots in case the Man pulls us over for any reason. This current seating configuration also serves to keep him in a separate occupied driver space, so on another level we can all drive away from the events of last night individually together. He is still, quiet and smiling, which I read as gratefulness.

After a few minutes of driving along the winding country roads I'm beginning to settle back into my optimism armor when right on cue the van's engine "throws a rod", which is something that means it has just broken in a way that renders it beyond repair. Suddenly we are now coasting off of the deceptively peaceful leafy green-lined road and onto the upcoming turnoff exit with a signpost that reads "Welcome to Butts County". I wish that this was just me being goofy right now, but that's actually what the sign says.

We've got just enough natural momentum going that we are able to coast through the small exit curve and then off to the side of the road where we are clear from blocking any of the people of Butts path, which is definitely the place to be. Luckily, about thirty-something trees away there is a small gas station.

We all jump out and start pushing the van toward the gas station. *How did this happen?* I was so close—I was going home! Now it's too late—I know for a fact there is nothing like a payphone inside of Ondi and David's car.

We push the dead van behind a garbage dumpster on the far side of the parking lot to avoid the attention of police or anyone else that can see. For the next three days we are a bunch of Californian hippie rock weirdos hiding in a van behind a garbage dumpster at a gas station in Butts County, Georgia.

Butts County to the Bottom of the Hill

So, weirdly enough, it turns out that the gates of hell are just the side door of a Chevrolet van in Georgia. It's the middle of summer here in all its bright, humid, hot Hades. I open my eyes and the first sensation is wet. Sticky wet. Hot wet coming from my insides out. I lift off of the rear van bench in sweaty misery and try to better breathe what little of the heavy damp humid air makes it within the hot box that is the van.

Each of us has our own personal group of about five or seven flies keeping busy with some invisible purpose that requires constant readjustment. The garbage dumpster the van is hidden behind is a hive of them. I can see broken-down boxes resting on top indicating a full load and the stink of it is full on.

I'd sign a peace contract right now promising the flies could just chill rather than this current style of constant launch-and-land psych-out that repeats over and over. I'm not used to all of this fly attention. The only thing positive I will say for them is that they are all loyal.

I sit all the way up and survey the options of other people's lives off in the distance that I don't have. Walking out the gas station door with a candy bar, smokes, a six-pack of cold beer, but the biggest one is getting to leave. Back inside the van I look at the driver's area and try to wish it into movement. A fly is perched atop Peter's big toe like a pigeon on a park statue of some jerk as his bare foot rests against the steering wheel. His untamed black hair makes a bohemian halo around the headrest and his body is in pretzel position. Behind him on the first bench is Matt in full-fetal.

I stare in shell-shock at Matt. I'm actually not exactly sure if I'm staring at Matt the person or just attempting to stare through him while still stealing obsessive flashes of refocus on his personal fly crew. They are pulling the exact same shit that mine are, and at least with getting distracted by his flies in some weird way I'm looking at somebody else's problem. I judge his dilemma and it takes my mind off of my own despite it being identical.

It was day two of our "Dirty Third-Dozen" dumpster division hiding deep behind enemy redneck lines under the cover of the giant garbage container. There wasn't anything else anywhere near this gas station let alone a place to receive another money transfer. Anton had made some calls and now we were just hiding out in the van, knowing that at some unknown point a garbage truck will come along and empty the thing and expose us all. "LOOK—WEIRDOS!" they will surely scream, and then out come the rifles.

I look out the back window where I can see the men's room attached to the side of the typical gas station of white and red. I step through hell's gate and there is Anton, passed flat out on the grass in the shade of the van. There are flies orbiting above him like they're still trying to figure him out or maybe rethinking the plan after some unseen previous event. I want to ask him if he will scoot over and let me sleep with him on the left side of the mattress-sized van shadow outline, but I desperately need to go tinkle. Tinkle is not what I want to be calling it out loud around here though and I puff out my chest and stiffen my stance as I take large steps over to the men's room.

I do my thang and start to spit-bath wash up my three kinds of stinks at one of the two sinks. My current everyday look is bed head of Princess and the Pea proportions, so no maintenance needed other than dipping my fingertips in water to arrange a few of the aqua-netted stalks the way I like them. It's more like arranging dead flowers than styling. I go down to meet face with soapy praying hands and when I come back up, a dead ringer for Harry Dean Stanton comes out of a bathroom stall. He's an older version of the one I jammed at a party with a couple of months ago, this one with a stiff mesh tractor advertisement cap that seems to be resting on the very top of his head, looking the same as it would placed on a table. His reminiscing presence brings me back to happier times. The Harry Dean Stanton of this alternate evil universe begins to slowly wash his hands, then in that uneventful period of hand-soaping, glances up at me in the shared sink mirror and suddenly gets a lot more interested in finishing his hand-washing job.

Later in the day, life's next direction once again comes via pay-phone and a plan has been pieced together. Our opening band back from the middle section of the tour has relations in Athens, Georgia, about an hour and a half away, and they arrange for us to be picked up and taken to civilization.

The following morning some nervous old people come and fetch us while the van is towed away to the scrap heap which I can only assume becomes the relocated gate to hell. The parents are uneasy with our grateful yet odd presence as Anton takes a cue from the country music playing on the radio to thoughtfully explain the history of the banjo to them along the drive.

When we get to Athens we discover that weirdly Gwar, the monster cartoon heavy metal band, who are not so weirdly friends of Dave D's, are playing at the 40 Watt tonight so through them we have somewhere to be all day. For those of you not familiar with monster costume metal, there are people walking around the club in rubber barbarian fantasy creature body suits with swords on their hips. None of us mention what Dave is up to these days.

Then Anton makes some kind of other deal with one of the previous deal-making people and we are rented a small ten-foot U-Haul truck to accommodate us plus all the gear. What we get is a small U-Haul truck cab with only two seats and a giant metal box attached. The good news is another person can fit up front by sitting in between the seats on a milk crate, but the bad news is Matt, Peter and Joel all need to take rotating turns traveling in the windowless, air-vent-less metal storage area with all the piled-up loose gear. Nobody seems to care about my driver's license anymore, the reason

I'm even still a part of this situation, which only serves to add on to the almighty whatever this is.

In the case of an accident, or even an unexpected hard-braking situation, all that gear would crush one of us into a quick death, which would actually be better than the slow suffocation in the pitch-black unventilated metal oven that is one's recurring two-hour fate in rotating shifts during the blazing hot travels in between shows that only pay enough for food and gas to make it to the next day's same.

The mustache's overgrown extended length has by now lost all resemblance to its original Ringo-ness and looks much more like an old west sheriff's mustache. It's hard to know what to do to get Anton back. The mustache sleeps very little and after all, the thing is attached to his face! The mustache constantly wants to let you know that it is the new boss, but still, our Anton does seem to have held on to equal control. They take sporadic turns and you never knew when a switch was coming.

And so the tour wears on and further out as we resume our rounds of the South. It's not unlike a hot wet Vietnam and the intro to The Doors' "The End" is a recurring theme inside my head as reality begins to morph into something more like *Apocalypse Now* than *A Hard Day's Night* as we limp further on under the tyrannical reign of the mustache.

For the next three shows I forget where we are in the time it takes to finish reading the "Welcome to..." signs.

The new stage plot is four chairs around a table covered in beer bottles as if it's a dramatic play about three depressed drunk guys and a pissed-off one who sit around the kitchen table getting shit-faced and playing music. Tonight the marquee should read *The Death of a Desire Salesman Who's Afraid of a Streetcar Named Virginia Woolf*, but we somehow get through it. After the New York disaster, the North Carolina disaster, and both Georgia disasters, we are all committed now to the grand delusion of surviving this whole thing, and even Matt has stepped into some new enlightened spotlight of peacenik that I must say he wears rather well, as we all do when it's new.

Meanwhile, with his Rock 'n' Roll High School graduation day now in sight, Peter's presence suddenly changes from "just point me in the right direction and push". The mask is now off and the Hayes haze lifts like the fog revealing just a slightly more in-focus fog. But for him, this tour had always been the designated tour of duty and he discloses his discharge papers privately to Matt and me. This is all now simply a very long ride back to his waiting "real" band, the soon to be monikered Black Rebel Motorcycle Club.

By New Orleans the mustache had gotten long enough to completely take over every piece of upper-lip real estate and encroached into the neighbor's lower-lip yard. We have three days to kill before our show at Howlin' Wolf's so we do our now customary wandering around and wondering what the new town might have to offer people with no money. On the second day we wallowed in the continuation of the realization that nobody loves you when you're penniless, no matter what's going to happen to you just a couple of weeks later.

That night there is a rolling thunder and lightning storm. Anton and Peter both sleep upright in the front seats while Matt is lying asleep next to me on the bare metal floor. Lightning flashes come every few seconds and some are very near. Then one hits across the street and I now lie in wait for us to be zapped right out of this metal box like a pair of Pop Tarts.

On day three all of us are starving and the venue has been closed since we got here so we can't get them to advance anything so that we will still be alive when they want us to play. So it's every mustache for himself now and we all go into survival mode. Anton leaves us to go busking solo, while Matt, Peter and I form our own busking band. It takes a few hours of Matt songs for us to get about ten bucks and we split our booty up even. Then with the workday done, Matt and I can finally get back to complaining about everything in our lives. It is during this that in a rare moment Peter chimes in, "I don't care, it's not my band." This is the spark that causes me to lose it and I just unload all of my frustrations on him verbally. Peter leaves us to go busk some more by himself.

Matt and I take our few dollars and go to a bar next to the future venue. The joint is virtually empty so we take the two center stools at the bar. The Kenny G-looking bartender comes over and we ask if three dollars will get us two beers. I guess we succeed in piquing his curiosity and as he serves us two ice-cold beers he inquires, "Soo, what brings you two boys to New Orlinz?"

Two hours and about eight pity pints apiece later, we have told him our complete sob story up to this point. People, especially people of the kind you find in New Orleans, can be so good and we have finally found an oasis of humanity. Even the wannabe rock star drunk guy endlessly working on his Axl Rose dancing is endearing.

The sun is going down as the mustache, returning from a hard day's fight, sees us through the window from outside sitting there laughing and smiling in front of a huge collection of empty glasses and bottles. Without knowing that all the beers were free, the mustache tells Anton we must have been hiding money to get drunk so Anton flips out on us, then climbs in the cab of the U-Haul and locks the doors so he can sleep horizontally undisturbed. On top of everything else, now we have to make room for Peter to join our sleepover metal box party and I don't even want to be around that guy right now. Regardless of my inner appreciations for the bigger picture of art and the cause, Matt and I confide to each other that this is officially all we each can take as we stand there on the side of the road staring across a wide field of dirt.

"Heyyy, you guys. Wanna ride back to Californiahhh?"

We turn around and Dave D is slow rolling up in his van. He plays it off as some sort of business-related coincidence, but he could have been shadowing us for who knows how long. I knew he wouldn't tell us if he had been, but what I know for sure now is he had indeed wanted to see it when everything crashed into bits and here it was.

Splat.

His reasons do not matter to me at this moment and I am happy for his whatever it is if it includes getting me back to California. All three of us stealthily unload our belongings out of the U-Haul on tipsy tippy-toes so as to not disturb the mustache. We then drive away into the night leaving Anton to wake up in the morning to find that he is alone and on his own to finish the last two weeks of the tour. I tell myself I'm gone for good.

Blackballed from Berserkeley

It had been Anton's idea to shave the tour mustache off so ceremoniously onstage in San Francisco, like he knew it was the one thing that would make me come back. Under this stipulation I agreed immediately. I drove up from LA with him and the two new mystery girls he'd met along the string of remaining shows and who had apparently insisted on following him as he gigged his way back to LA and now up to San Francisco. All that was left of the tour now was tonight at Bottom of the Hill and tomorrow at The Starry Plough in Berkeley.

Anton and I had decided before the show that while playing a folksy acoustic number deceptively titled "Free and Easy", he would go into an extended one-chord drone-strum for a length to be determined by the time it took to ceremoniously shave off his tour mustache.

Anton sat on a stool while he played and sang and when the designated point in the song arrived he went into the single-chord drone while I set my tambourine down atop my own stool and collected my razor. Anton saw the razor coming and raised his chin, bringing this devil's broom even closer to being sent back to wherever it came from.

Below us two girls in flowing white gowns and floral wreath crowns gingerly washed his feet that were dangling just above an ornate white porcelain bowl. They were smiling in that way you do when you're listening to something funny on headphones while riding on a crowded bus and you almost start laughing, but stop yourself because you might look crazy or something but at the same time it's too late to not look crazy because you can see the first "haha" had somehow escaped which has since traveled about a foot in front of your face and now everyone else is also looking at the "haha" as it floats away in a word bubble with your old normal person identity while they can't even hear what was funny. So then you check your head and luckily you are indeed wearing headphones. These two girls weren't wearing headphones...

The mustache is dead but as usual the wall power outlet has nothing to say. I was done peeing five minutes ago and am now just sitting here in the private bathroom behind the bar at The Starry Plough. I am currently, as I am known to myself to do, staring at the power outlet by the door and looking for an answer. The power outlet is your standard three-pronged face that lives in every bathroom, or any other kind of room in America for that matter. Despite every one of these "faces" being the same, depending on what I'm looking for from it, with its blank two-plug eyes and "shocked" open-mouth stare, it can also look disappointed, mad, frightened or just completely bewildered, which is the state that I'm usually in when I go trying to make psychic connections with power outlets. I guess it's kinda like somewhere in between my own take on the idea lightbulb and talking to a statue in the park on acid or something. Anyway, as long as I can find a bathroom it's always there for me and, like I say, tailored with a small variety of looks for whichever of my varied concerned states. When I'm happy, winning, about to accept the gold, I rarely even notice it's there on the wall. In these times it's just a power outlet and who cares.

I've tried to connect with many over the years, asking for advice, looking for answers. Mostly when I'm as high as fuck. When I realize I absolutely *did not* need that last hit of ecstasy, saddened that the prolonged cocaine hours have temporarily turned me into the type of idiot I hate. Basically whenever whatever is happening is feeling/going wrong. A confessional in a toilet zone where one can step out of the immediate action and pause. Power outlets have seen all there is to see within for as long as there has been the power of light to see things to do in there, which is a lot when you're in a music venue that was built in the early 70s, which is where I am now. I'm willing the bottom prong slot to dispense some insight. Tonight I really need it but it has nothing to say, and this bothers me. It's showtime now so I wash up and walk out.

Since I've been gone the stage has acquired five wooden bar stools, two up front for me and Anton and three in lineup formation behind for the Colfax Abbey guys, who had been the opening band earlier on in the tour and were currently helping Anton finish it as deputized backing musicians. They are some big guys packing some muscle on them for being shoegazers, but this makes for a complementary combination with their gentle personalities. Good people that can "get it done" if the shit were to suddenly go down. Fast-forward one hour...

"Shut up and play some music!"

"Hey, dumbshit!" Anton returns, "I don't come tell you how to do your job at Burger King or wherever the fuck, let me do my job! Watch what happens wh—"

An ice cube lobs over the crowd and bounces off Anton's head.

Ah shit.

Anton continues shouting which brings on a few more ice cubes which is then returned with more shouting which is returned with a pint glass which is then returned with a barstool and suddenly the whole place erupts as the Colfax boys assemble behind Anton as all barstools are launched from the stage before they all dive off of the edge and into battle.

One last look before I leap and it's amazing just how fast this packed Irish pub has completely lit up. The scattered skirmishes have sent most of the crowded club stampeding for the doors as the chaos level just went from a lone flying ice cube to full-on "Old West" bar room brawl within seconds. I jump off and land next to Anton to show his own personal surly trio of opponents that he's not alone here while the Colfax guys are cleaning up the rest of the place. A few shoves in various clusters as the many groups of people spiral toward and out the doors like going down a music fan drain and almost as soon as it starts the whole thing is over. It turns out that over is over for life as the owner is an old-school heavy in the Berkeley live venue world and apparently the next morning he will make some calls that get us blackballed from the entire city. Ironically, The Brian Jonestown Massacre will go on to eventually outlive all of these music venues.

Tonight was actually the perfect opportunity for me to just remain here in the Bay and resume my old life, but I suddenly had no intention whatsoever of doing that. The power outlet psychiatry session's delayed diagnosis finally comes through and with it the sudden realization of what it's all about, which is funny because I'd already known it on an internal level, but it is hugely affirming to hear it articulated from somewhere else, even if it is a power outlet.
   IDEA
It seems to me that achieving common goals at next-level levels can only pass through the all-the-way goal posts when powered by extremity. Extremity requires both reward and hardship and one can't exist without the other, like positive and negative energies of all types (this was an especially good question for an electrical outlet). You can't cry because it's not fun all of the time. The big stuff doesn't work that way. The small stuff does. That's the trick and the mind switch that must be flipped if you are to "go the distance". This is my thinking and by the way, I know I've gone from a mustache with consciousness to a psychiatric wall socket and let me just say that I appreciate your patience, but honestly this is just how life rolls sometimes.

   Anyway, in those times of noir vibes, verbal volume matches and un-mellow dramas, this is all the other side of the scale that makes it possible for the positive side to weigh in with the magical musical experiences and career triumphs like achieving oneness with packed houses, the celebration of your artistic achievements and the sense of adventure that comes with living "the life". And anyway, in the times of nothing else, I have booze to keep me happy, and this arrangement seems to work quite well.

   The even bigger picture: I've now come to realize that the mustache was more like a stern teacher than evil hair jerk. Like an instructor enforcing a new strictness that doesn't tolerate mediocrity, it had grown into our lives to announce that the times of "just getting by" were over. I suddenly feel guilty for hating the mustache, but luckily it was not something that could be taken on and off his face, for it had come from roots implanted within. I sit here in the back of the van now grateful for this epiphany.

Despite all the tour chaos, what had really been happening was that everyone needed to step it up if things were going to go to the next level. We'd all been put to the test to show who would get in all the way and who would be shaken off when given a good hard shaking. Dean, Matt, Peter, Brad and Jeff were all gone now for their individual reasons. Now once again, just like the times before, it was just the two of us.

Between returning to LA and the SF show Anton had met our new manager Michael Dutcher. He's a big Allen Klein type of guy who has perhaps watched Martin Scorsese's mafia films too many times, but more importantly and unlike Dave D, has proper industry connections and is waiting and ready to get to work.

Without a proper band, life around the Larga house had gone from The Beatles film *Help!* to just regular "Help!" Luckily, last month's rent was already paid and we suddenly had some major record label meetings scheduled. First Capitol Records, the label that put out The Beatles, The Beach Boys and—*cough*—The Dandy Warhols, then a few days after Anton and Dutcher were flying to New York City to meet with TVT Records.

On the day of the Capitol Records dinner meeting, our new manager takes Anton and I shopping for record label good impression outfits. I find a women's brown crushed faux-fur coat with pea jacket-style lapels and large gold buttons which I button over my simple slim black pullover and matching jeans. On me, with its large curved lapels and fanning out at thigh level, it weirdly has a Carnaby Street vibe, but technically it's made for an old lady Zsa Zsa Gabor wannabe.

Anton picks up a 60s-style fur trapper hat, or Russian babushka, depending on how deep your hippie commie leanings go, but most people just say "David Crosby hat" to keep it simple. A white button-down shirt with matching Levi's 501s and *Easy Rider*-style yellow-lensed glasses give him that psych-business casual look that signifies preparedness for the next level.

Being that we are on Melrose Avenue, Dutcher drops me off at Ondi and David's which is just a few blocks away, and a plan is made for us all to meet up later at the restaurant. By this point Ondi and David's house has kinda become like my own *Melrose Place*, in that there are a group of young adults coming and going, each with their own dreams and drives, but more specifically to myself, outside of the fact I am not into TV shows like that, is that during this time it is where I can escape the doldrums of broke Larga living and be immersed in an outside environment of enthusiasm for The Brian Jonestown Massacre. It is strong fuel for the internal fire.

I head over to the meeting with David, which we are purposely late for as I'd been told by Anton and our manager to keep my distance. We get there and Dutcher is already leaving. He tells me that the Capitol rep left early, apparently she had just snuck out while Anton was in the bathroom. I take this to mean we are not going to be on Capitol. It's not all doom and gloom though, at least for me, as sometimes you can get more from the wanting than the having, and this style of sometimes life-long un-fulfillment can at least keep your dreams in their true original state and safe from disappointing reality.

Our manger vows to not do a repeat of whatever happened at the Capitol meeting and so three days later I'm at Ondi and David's and he's making me a fake ID so I can use the ticket already bought for Anton to New York for the meeting with TVT Records. See, TVT still thinks Anton is coming and the ticket cost $300, so the logic here is that it's a better deal financially to just have me illegally impersonate someone else rather than take the hit on a ticket change.

Dutcher takes a Polaroid of me standing up against the white stucco hallway wall, then cuts my head out with some office scissors. The cutting job is a little hasty and uneven, and the thickness of the Polaroid paper leaves a built-in 3-D frame around the photo. Then he cuts out an identity card-sized portion of computer printer paper which has also been cut a little haphazardly. He places my

Polaroid head upon that and then balances it all on his portable laminate machine. After running the old-fashioned carbon credit card receipt-like mechanism over the top, my new ID card is encased in clear lamination and ready for identifying.

Like Frankenstein rising from the lab table, my new ID card—"ANTON NEWCOMBE—ENGAGED BOOKING" is peeled up from the laminating machine. I sign Anton's name as my own signature, forgetting to put the "e" at the end and yet the transformation is complete. I am now Anton.

The fake ID proclaiming that I am "Licensed and boned". I even forgot to include the last "e" in Newcombe!

We get in his car and drive to the airport. I'm a little nervous about the ID, especially because the Polaroid paper is about fifteen times as thick as the computer printer paper. "Can I also see your driver's license?" they will surely ask. I do have my real ID on me, but it's just the tambourine player's and that will blow the whole plan.

We go to the ticket counter at LAX and they don't even bat an eye. Then we move on to the metal detectors and I show the short-sleeved uniform person the ID, they inspect it, hand it back and then confiscate my pocket change and Zippo lighter, but for only like five seconds while I pass through the metal detector. I'm half expecting some unexpected *Spinal Tap*-style mix-up to ensue, but real life is usually not as interesting as pretend rock documentaries and I pass through unfettered. Heading toward my gate now and with none of this taking much more effort than getting on a Greyhound bus. Wow, I really must be Anton.

We board the plane and just as soon as we reach the legal drinking altitude I order a double gin and tonic. It arrives and I put my João Gilberto *Greatest Hits* disc into my CD walkman. It's my first time flying now aged twenty-six and as we pass up through the tops of puffy white clouds the music starts and I take a long pull of my cocktail. It hits warm and fuzzy in my center and I fall in love with it all right here and now. It's so easy and sophisticated. As I gaze down, around and sip long and thoughtful, I vow to honor the code of the jet set and all that swings, as I will surely be doing plenty more of this from here on out. Ondi and her camera are sitting next to me and their plan is to keep me busy until we land in New York. Then we drive straight to a restaurant in SoHo so I can bedazzle the top people from the TVT Record label.

Fails of the City

It was just as my brother and I were passing through life's spaceship air dock from childhood to our teens that our house in San Jose was robbed. We had come home from our elementary school to find our kustom motorized go-kart, the one my father had welded together from scratch, had been stolen out of the garage. Afterwards, my mother had a hard time dealing with the home violation. Then in a masterstroke of bad luck, while relaying the incident to one of my father's college hot-rod buddies, my parents were sold on the idea of pulling out of regular society and moving us up to "the sticks", in the foothills of the Sierra Nevada mountains. Sadly, these were not sacred lands of the hippie escapist dream, but rather the opposite.

We sold our humble family home at the current very modest 1970s market value which in today's Silicon Valley money is worth millions and I went from taking on the suburban teen scene to living in a small redneck town that had long ago settled into uselessness after the Gold Rush boom died well over a hundred years ago.

What was far worse than the physical location was the undercurrent of racism, overt homophobia and all things intolerant that went on among the local teens and parents alike. Suddenly we were a long, long way away from *Sesame Street*. Not that everyone was bad, far from it, but still there was way too much celebrating of ignorance to not encourage a total personal rejection of the whole place. Looking back, the situation was like going from Obama to Trump, or Clinton to W. Bush, or Carter to Regan, which is something that had actually just happened.

How could we have packed up and left the only world I knew over a minor break-in? My mother had been spooked, and this new spook was guiding the family decisions now. I was so angry I'd been plucked from my pre-teen San Jose California utopia and dropped into the middle of 80s redneck hell, like a young, unknowing draftee pushed out of a helicopter into a Hieronymus Bosch-painted version of *The Dukes of Hazzard*.

At night the roads were overrun with "good ol' boys" who constantly combed the streets with nothing to do. The style of these teenage boys was frozen in time: cowboy boots and tilted back baseball caps, maybe a wispy mustache, huge belt buckle—all things mimicking the same uniforms of their father's fashion non-sense.

One very boring any-day afternoon in this new culturally medieval inquisition zone, my brother radio-antenna'd the frequency to 98.9 FM The Quake, San Francisco's first "modern rock" radio station. I immediately became enamored with the British guitar sounds of the depressed and outsider isolation that came with albums like Echo & the Bunnymen's *Heaven Up Here*, The Smiths' *Hatful of Hollow* and Joy Division's *Unknown Pleasures*. These and so many others were the perfect getaways to alternate and exotically grey realities where one could be glad to be sad within new worlds of electric guitar art and poetic verse, all the while with a naïveté that was blissfully unaware of the realities of shoestring budget recording sessions taking place in dingy run-down tiny rooms with stained office carpet-covered walls.

Soon after, I stumbled across a visual gateway equivalent to this new music in the moody Michael Caine 1966 espionage thriller *The Ipcress File*. With its odd camera angles, moody music and somber tone and Technicolor-esque dank, it was the perfect stepping stone from the over-the-top Bond movies into the wonderfully drab world of British New Wave cinema. To my great surprise, I could find some of these types of UK films at the lone video rental store in town. The concept of home rental movies being still in its infancy, even shops in small towns like ours had to order whatever was being manufactured in order to keep the shelves looking full. This would include a not much visited "Foreign" section that was actually stocked with British kitchen-sink dramas such as *A Taste of Honey*, *Saturday Night and Sunday Morning* and *The Loneliness of the Long Distance Runner*. England, in its interchangeably colorful and dreary 60s bleakness became relatable as I found myself stuck in my own type of dark and grey out-of-place rut glum-drum world.

Despite my brooding teen angst, or actually because of it, hitting the campus for my first year of high school dressed in all black and ratted hair got me instant popularity with the small and mostly girl goth and new-wave population. On the flip side, my brother and I's "weird" and different styles of dressing openly represented our out-and-out rejection of everything and everyone. Music had become lifestyle for life, which would eventually take me as far as quitting school as soon as I'd turned the legal adult age of eighteen, which also happened to be three weeks before graduating. I was off to San Francisco and a high school diploma was just a piece of paper that had nothing to do with being in a band.

Today I'm signing the papers that matter and I've just laid down signature number one of four that the lengthy record contract requires of me. Next to each of my JOEL GION _____ signature spaces there are two more spaces for ANTON NEWCOMBE _____ and MATT HOLLYWOOD_____, as it's been explained to me that the label feels it is we three who are the essential ingredients to what makes the BJM the BJM. We didn't mention the little detail that its third "essential" ingredient was no longer in the band.

Last night the TVT staff on hand seemed to mostly buy the story that Anton had fallen ill the day before and hence my last-minute replacing. From there I did as many *funny little dances* as I could come up with as required to woo, while with real indoor fusion restaurant grass in between my toes. We ate at low table levels populated with small but many plates passing to and fro. We drank and smoked from large hookah tobacco pipes, and by the end everyone was very pleased to find that I was indeed the real whatever they were here to confirm I was supposed to be.

It's very bright out today and especially so in the large TVT offices high up on East 4th Street in Manhattan where I'm comparing fresh record contract signatures with TVT founder and president Steve Gottlieb. He's pretty much got your standard-issue record label president thing going, with the tight ponytail and everything. I sign my second Joel Gion right on the _____ and the ballpoint pen rips through the contract page. I can't help but internally recognize this as a possible bad omen, but we all laugh it off and move on. On the next page I try not to make another sign as I sign.

In celebration of a big deal now officially sealed, TVT Steve offers to extend my stay at The Soho Grand Hotel for the rest of the week which I can only assume, because I have the inside scoop on my personal finances, is on label dime. Turns out it's future BJM dime to be charged back down the road, but that part of it is not explained, which kinda makes them more like travel agents.

That night Adam, who is as of today our official A & R rep and Nadine, our new marketing manager, take me to The Spy Bar, which is a high-end nightclub lounge which famous actors, musicians, models and other celebrity what-have-yous frequent on a regular basis. Nadine and Adam are like me, music people *totale*, and there is zero effort required for us to gel. You have to look one of the kinds of "right" if the doorman is even going to let you in and we do and so he does. Inside, the packed Spy Bar is of the red velvety type of place with crystal-looking chandeliers and lots of mirror-loaded mahogany throughout.

"See, there's Laurence Fishburne," Adam says with a lean-in, confirming "lots of famous people hang out here".

"You guys go sit down," Nadine instructs. "What are you drinking?"

"A pitcher of gin and tonic, please," I half joke. After today I am ready to rumba till I do the early-morning one-man rumble.

We find three seats together along the line that creates the inner border of the outer edge of the crammed bar area. "I'm going to go use the bathroom," Adam says and so I hold down our three-chair fort. Suddenly a blonde supermodel-type leans down. "Mind if I sit and fix my shoe?"

"Of course not," I say with casual chivalry. Then add, "My friends won't be back for a minute," just to let her know I'm not loose or anything.

She sits down and starts in on some out-of-place small talk. I imagine a mirror in front of us and it's a pretty odd pair-up for a generic pickup scene. She looks confused at my level of participation, which is polite but normal, which I guess is abnormal for this situation.

She tires quickly and leaves, so apparently I've "blown it", but then I didn't really want to talk to her all that much anyway which exposes this feeling as just a rejection-type thing. When you're talking to model types that you don't really care to talk to, you can't have it both ways.

Suddenly, another model type appears from nowhere, this time brunette. I don't mean to stereotype here, these girls could easily just be attractive white women who have designer clothes on, but my eyes still work and I'm wearing their grandmother's jacket coat and my head is a hair explosion site with indoor ginormous sunglasses, so it's still weird. Another go-nowhere exchange ensues while I'm simultaneously watching the first girl as she now begins talking to a middle-aged guy sitting at the bar. OK, despite the serious expressions on their faces, that looks more normal I guess.

Nadine hip-bumps my shoulder and unloads one of her hands on me in the form of a very tall but thin glass. "The biggest they'd give me was a triple," she smiles.

Super model #2 takes this as her cue, smiles and says goodbye, then joins the other two at the bar which officially gives it the look of a meeting.

"Did you see the Kula Shaker singer over there?" Nadine asks.

I look over my shoulder and up to the table area which she is gesturing at and there's a wispy blond bloke who I recognize from their gig at Slim's on their first time through SF.

"Oh yeah. They had such a great first album, but after the last record I think he's back to being more famous for being Haley Mills's son than a psychedelic Britpopper. Is this all they've got around here tonight? I guess it is only a Tuesday..."

I turn back around and point out the two girls to Nadine as Adam sits next to us. They are both still standing and nodding their heads along to whatever the guy is saying sitting at the bar. Then Adam tells me that the film director Harmony Korine is sitting next to him. He made *Kids* and the more recent *Gummo*, which are "difficult" and "edgy" indie movies. As if on cue, they all turn and look over at us.

Then Harmony Korine gets up, walks over and leans down into my ear and says, "Wanna do some drugs?"

"Yes."

He leads me over to the red-carpeted stairs and we head way up to the private VIP lounge area. Up here it's completely empty and in great contrast to the keep-your-cool controlled chaos downstairs. We sit down at a small glass table and I watch him pull a small plastic zip baggy from the front pocket of what looks to be by its pairing with blue jeans and Chuck Taylors, an ironic dinner jacket.

"Is that coke or speed?" I ask.

"Heroin."

"*Oh...*"

His fingers freeze in mid solo of the world's smallest violin heroin baggie twist, while his eyes move up from the glass table to meet mine.

"OK. Yeah, I'll do some," I decide out loud. He either doesn't pick up on or doesn't care that this will be my first time. On the West Coast literally all you can find is "brown tar" heroin. Brown tar heroin is pretty much what it sounds like and is one that you primarily shoot up. You *can* snort it, but you have to mix it with water, cook it in a spoon until it's hot water brown goop, then snort it. You can also smoke it, if you burn the tinfoil black enough. So, yeah, I've never done heroin. It's once you begin approaching the East Coast that it becomes a whole other kettle of OD'd floating fish by way of China white, which comes in powder form and is as easy to do as lines off a glass table in a VIP bar area.

As I go down into the second small line he's left me, he comments, "I like your coat. Do you just like to dress in women's winter wear, or are you into guys too?"

His tone is a bit condescending and as I begin snorting, the white powder going up my nose begins to double as snow in the memory globe of my mind...

After my brother and I had discovered our new San Francisco radio station, my life had been forever changed and I started dressing the part accordingly. Pointy black suede boots, tight deep-dye black denim jeans and black slim-knit pullover, ratty-tatty sprayed-in-place hair with heavy smudged black eyeliner. I looked in the mirror and thought I looked great. A little while later I went outside and was walking down the street "Fag!" Walking back out of the store with a candy bar "Fag!" The next morning waiting for the school bus "Fag!" By the fifteenth "fag" I declared a silent war on the world and vowed that I would never fit within it.

The term "fag", especially in the 80s, was an all-purpose hate term used against not only gay people, but also anything that didn't make immediate visual sense to tough guy types that confuse easy. This demographic unfortunately holds the majority at this place in this time and soon I was confronting brushes with violence on a daily basis. It was always a gang. Always someone twice as big and with an audience. An upper-class show of strength. It was bullies' rules. After my first few of now regular trips to the front office, my student counselor's advice was, "Wouldn't it be easier to just start dressing like everyone else?"

I lift my head back up from the glass table, now on heroin. The problem I'm having with it is that it feels *too* good. It feels more like *gooooooooooooood*, like, "duh" good, which in turn is making it feel alright to talk about things that I might normally not readily discuss, like what just happened with me and you in that last flashback. This I now realize must be the whole point to this current situation and it rightly prevents our "weirdo" summit from becoming a bonding experience and more like a psychoanalysis-on-heroin session, seemingly to determine my eccentricity level. Again, everyone is feeling me out, seeing if I'm "real".

After a little while I start to get the vibe we're only abusing substance with this substance abuse, which is of course always a two-way street, but for my money (which the label would have to front to be paid back through eventual album sales), the "problem" started early on after I'd divulged that I'd never bothered to see any of his films. How could any relationship possibly sprout between us in this ego-strokeless wasteland I'd presented to him? Later at the hotel I still feel doped out and the whole experience ultimately makes me further realize that I prefer the drugs that go "up". Then Ondi informs me that the middle-aged guy at the bar was a big Hollywood film producer she is in talks with about possibly producing the documentary. Now it all makes sense. I think.

The next night I was celebrating a secret. An hour before, I'd hung up my hotel room phone after successfully talking an initially reluctant Matt into rejoining the band.

"Wait, I can order *anything*?"

"Yes Joel, you can order anything," Adam returns.

I put the drink menu down. "I'll take the hundred-dollar shot of whiskey, please. Actually, make it a double."

Heaven Can Wait

I'm suddenly shaken back awake from the bump of the landing gear locking down. Turning to the window and Los Angeles flying by below I begin thinking about how to proceed. I recognize that it was in fact a little weird for me and to a lesser extent Matt, even as a songwriter, to be on the contract in the first place. However, as the label described it I was an integral part of what they wanted. Obviously, this whole situation had been mostly created by Anton's efforts, who let's face it probably isn't all that jazzed to be joined at the signature hips with Matt and me. Either way, he and management will still be in charge of it all.

While I stayed behind in New York, Dutcher flew directly home before the ballpoints were even clicked back in and immediately found and rented us a new bigger house. The gear, Anton's stuff and my meager worldlies were then moved over from the Larga House to our new BJM headquarters at 2012 Vestal Avenue in Echo Park.

I get out of the cab from the airport in a hilly residential neighborhood. A view of downtown LA is off in the distance, mostly through the bursting red maple and hodge-podge of exotic desert and general Cali-thick greenery that lines the red-clay colored steps and beyond up to the double glass-door entryway on the side of the house. I peek through the glass doors before walking inside the high-ceilinged living room to see Matt has also arrived from wherever he was. I'm grateful he's come back on my word that shit will be cool and I show him so with a big hug which he returns as if I'm a forced-upon ugly high-school dance partner.

"We'll now be living a new life on the next level, man. After everything we've been through over these last few years together! Finally, 'we made it'," I add with quotation fingers out.

Oddly, or maybe not so oddly, he doesn't seem to think so, signified by his trademark uneasy "Yeeaaahhhh...", which to me could simply signify him just being more him, but there is something in the extra-long signature of defeat that implies there is an actual situation afoot.

Then Matt deadpan-quips, "Ready to be sorry you flew home?"

The front doors double-swing open and there is Anton in the fur hat, white Levi's 501s and a white cotton embroidered kurta. At his sides are the two Mansonettes from the mustache execution gig in flowing white.

"Hey!" He yells, drill sergeant-like. "You're back. OK, *good*. Check this out. I called Adam and had TVT rip up that contract you guys signed! They made a new one and you're not on it! OK?!"

...?

Maybe I'm catching some fallout caused by Matt for having quit and then returned straight after the big payday arrived, but then Anton doesn't know how hard it was for me to convince him to rejoin, money or no money. Miscommunication strikes again and I'm robbed of my hero's welcome.

With that "little" item now out of the way, Anton suddenly lights up and begins showing me the oncoming arsenal of incoming gear. He'd had a huge new mixing board and speakers positioned in the joint dining now open-air control room with other various vintage gear randomly set up all around the living room. It's a professional-style recording studio installed in-house for roughly the same cost as an entire album's worth of high-end studio time with all the added etceteras. Now recording can happen at any time, all night long if we wanted. There would be no time schedules or restrictions. I slow-pull my finger across the twelve strings of a vintage Vox Phantom guitar resting on a stand while he begins unboxing a brand-new Neumann microphone, the same model Sinatra used for all of his Capitol Records recordings.

"Come fly with me, let's fly away..."

251

Somehow I get the feeling my dreams of joining the jet-set have just missed the plane.

It will take another day for the rest of the new studio components to be set and adjusted into place in our new home, and then recording begins with a song that will later in the day be named "I've Been Waiting". It starts with the ring of a Tibetan bell followed by a tambourine that tocks to its tick and an acoustic guitar. It's a longing plea in the key of romance that once established, signals the drums to come Ringo-rolling in, and soon after the fuzz-lead opens up The Doors and we are officially inside the sessions of our first major-label album *Strung Out in Heaven*.

The day is one of those reward-over-drama moments as Anton looks up grinning from the mixing board to Matt and I as we stand side by side returning knowing smiles. Just under the thin sonic waterine keys are added, then Anton smokes a signature wailing build-up lead guitar solo before christening the entire affair with a vocal and the song is practically there. There is an unspoken sense of relief that is palpable, like astronauts exchanging knowing glances in a spacecraft that has just successfully broken orbit still completely intact.

Around 2 a.m. that evening we all break off to go to our rooms for the night. As I lie down in my far-end corner of the house room, I can see all the other lights from down the hall switch dark. "I've Been Waiting" is given a victory performance in the dark, blasting through the overly capable home studio speakers and through not only the entire house, but also immediate neighborhood. In this theater of the dark, my imagination gathers all remaining light from the outer world and applies it to my inner.

The song starts again with its Tibetan bell tick-tock trade-off with the tambourine, acoustic guitar and key flourishes of romance. How did he come up with those lyrics so off the cuff? It certainly wasn't the first time I'd witnessed him do something like that and in fact I can't ever once remember seeing a notepad of any kind during any recording session. That guitar solo really is a barn burner though.

The song starts again with its Tibetan bell tick-tock trade-off with the tambourine, acoustic guitar and key flourishes of romance and this time I recognize that the finger move he pulls with the fuzz is like something usually reserved for a cello section. In fact, the whole thing achieves the grandiosity of an orchestrated piece with its rapturous acrobatics, yet done only with bare-bones "rock" instrumentation. It's a textbook example of the magic trick of the less spoken, the more said.

The song starts again with its Tibetan bell tick-tock trade-off with the tambourine, acoustic guitar and key flourishes of romance and it now becomes clear that he's got the track on "repeat" mode. This could be the last time, so I concentrate more on the lyrics while I still have the chance.

"I've been waiting such a long, long time..."

The song starts again with its Tibetan bell tick-tock trade-off with the tambourine, acoustic guitar and key flourishes of romance and now I begin to wonder how long this will be playing for. I mean, it's great, but I'd also like to get some sleep at some point here so I can enjoy listening to it a bunch more tomorrow with fresh ears. Maybe he'll realize it's still playing and turn it off. It's about that time. I lie in expectant wait as the music continues to play.

The song starts again with its Tibetan bell tick-tock trade-off with the tambourine, acoustic guitar and key flourishes of romance and I feel like I know when everything is coming at this point. It's kind of turning into a connect-the-dots thing where I'm waiting for each next part to happen before it happens. I'd never even heard this song mixed together until a couple hours ago and now I feel like I know it inside and out!

The song starts again with its Tibetan bell tick-tock trade-off with the tambourine, acoustic guitar and key flourishes of romance and I hate to say it but now I'm officially waiting for the song to stop repeating. One reason *Their Satanic Majesties' Second Request* became my favorite BJM album is because it was recorded during my one big spin-out and as a result I'd missed the whole thing while staging a back-with-the-parents comeback into adulthood. I'd never heard a minute of it until after I returned to San Francisco and by then the whole album was completed. That one I can listen to like a fan, rather than say *Take it from the Man!*, where we'd listen to the evolving mixes so much that even though it was exciting, by the release I knew the songs so inside that I couldn't get out.

The song starts again with its Tibetan bell tick-tock trade-off with the tambourine, acoustic guitar and key flourishes of romance and no matter how hard I push my two pillows against my head, it does nothing.

The song starts again with its Tibetan bell tick-tock trade-off with the tambourine, acoustic guitar and key flourishes of romance and I get up and walk down the dark hall. As I approach the kitchen, strands of purple Christmas lights are strung along the white cabinets and matching wall corners creating a grid-like DMT alternate dimension hallucination. I look at the large mixing board in the connected dining area and with moonlight assistance I can see the music by its visually bouncing out of the speakers. It's blasting so loud now that I'm here standing directly in the ear of the hurricane. I scan the scarcely decorated dimly lit whites and Anton is lying in a semi-sitting position against a pile of ornate pillows just a few feet beyond. His eyes are closed and he looks to be asleep. I creep closer, wanting to confirm that I can't just say, "Hey, can I turn this masterpiece off for now?" He is definitely asleep but at the same time I get a vibe that he's invisibly connected to the blasting audio. Not knowing what kind of invisible wiring connection system is in place, or how to mess with it, I decide, rather than just start rearranging the wires like I'd done to Greg Shaw's TV entertainment system so I could watch his rare Rolling Stones VCR tapes, a situation that didn't go well for me, it's probably best not to incur a mystery-wrath of levels unknown in case I just mess it all up. I retreat, half-step, half-sock-sliding back over the tiles until the hallway carpet where I pick up to straight ahead walking back to my room and lie back down.

The song starts again with its Tibetan bell tick-tock trade-off with the tambourine, acoustic guitar and key flourishes of romance as I'm now settling back down into my new option-less situation. Man, I wish I had some earplugs right now. I'd always thought they were kinda square and whenever the subject's ever come up I always make fun of the Todd Rundgren earplugs TV commercial—"Your ears are your most important instrument", I usually mimic-mock—but now

I suddenly get it. I don't think I even know what earplugs look like, so even if some were lying around for some reason I would probably just think they were AA rehab-issue nose plugs or something. I lie there and think about sober people going to parties with earplugs in their noses. "No, thanks"—points at nose—"Trying to quit."

The song starts again with its Tibetan bell tick-tock trade-off with the tambourine, acoustic guitar and key flourishes of romance and I've been waiting such a long time for this subject to change over to whatever it is going to be in my dreams while I sleep. I begin to wonder which one of us will wait the longest.

"I've been waiting such a long, long time..."

The song starts again with its Tibetan bell tick-tock trade-off with the tambourine, acoustic guitar and key flourishes of romance and to be honest I don't even understand what can be so great about this chick. She doesn't seem very reliable in the first place and a lot of times when you lay all of your cards on the table like this you're just setting yourself up to be taken advantage of. Especially since she's already been caught blowing smoke up his ass from before! I'm hoping maybe he somehow dials his offers back a bit on the next listen, like when you're watching a movie that you love but the ending is really sad so you're secretly hoping somehow the ending is going to somehow be magically different this time. The music fades and then silence.

The song starts again with its Tibetan bell tick-tock trade-off with the tambourine, acoustic guitar and key flourishes of romance which is a very different approach to how Jim Jones did it when he blasted recordings of his sermons all night long in the jungles of Jonestown. This is the only comparison I can come up with right now.

The song starts again with its Tibetan bell tick-tock trade-off with the tambourine, acoustic guitar and key flourishes of romance and I begin to wonder, why is the other background Anton vocal track shouting? To be honest, Anton has been pretty irritable and yelling a bit lately and now it's like regular Anton and irritated Anton are having a Righteous Brothers-style duet or something. The first Anton sounded like he had this situation handled but the background yelling Anton is going to blow everything if he keeps shouting about how good-looking she is, especially if that's all he plans to contribute to the conversation. If this plays in stereo and the speaker with the sensible vocal track goes out, then it's just the wound-up one yelling the same sentence at the end of every chorus every time, and in this situation she's sure to just call the police. I close my eyes and try not to get too involved with the ins and outs of this relationship.

The song starts again with its Tibetan bell tick-tock trade-off with the tambourine, acoustic guitar and key flourishes of romance and I don't even know how many more times it has played since my last thoughts. I wish I could say it had been sleep, but in fact it was my brain rejecting any acknowledgement of hearing anything that travels through the air by any means and especially audio which at this point definitely includes the song.

The song starts again with its Tibetan bell tick-tock trade-off with the tambourine, acoustic guitar and key flourishes of romance and by this point I've got PTSD from of all things a cool song.

The song starts again with its Tibetan bell tick-tock trade-off with the tambourine, acoustic guitar and key flourishes of romance and I am in mental survival mode as the sun is now starting to slow soak the sky like liquid under dropped paper until that full hot Los Angeles sun is interrogating everyone who is not sleeping. I think I've listened to the same new song like sixty times in a row.

"I've been waiting such a long, long time..."

Sixty-one. The music finally stops, signaling it's time to get up.

No sign of Matt but Anton makes coffee and a big pan of chorizo and eggs while I heat up the tortillas, which is also kind of like our relationship outside of the kitchen.

A little sangria and I'm ready to take on the customary high temps as Anton takes a seat on the drum stool by the mixing board. The harmonica around his neck is receiving some test-toots and an acoustic guitar is strung into playing position and I'm pretty sure I'm ready to hear something new.

The Burning Bug

"Man, I'm so fuckin' sick and *tired* of people who ain't got nothing but nothing to lose!" Anton had yelled as I left the house with just enough nothing for the Billy Childish show and a beer tonight at Spaceland. Matt and I had decided it was best to just "keep the peace" by outwardly going along with the fantasy that our names had indeed been #2 pencil erased from the record contract, but now Anton is going next level with it by acting as if he's put out by our "dead weight" presence.

Later on after the show, the word is there's a party at someone from Beachwood Sparks' house, another 60s enthusiast's band but of the LA homespun variety. I'm riding solo in the backseat of Jennifer's vintage Volkswagen Bug as she winds the three of us up into the hills of Silverlake.

"Are they still behind us?" Sarah asks from the front passenger seat. She is shy until you get to know her, then she's an extrovert. It's an exclusive club and it feels good to be a member. Jennifer is her best friend and has like a similar vibe to the Free Design girls. I turn around and the small carload of vacationing Japanese 60s enthusiasts are keeping up with us as we lead our convoy of two through the progressively windier curves and increasing grades.

"Yep," I return as I turn back around.

"Good," Jennifer says. "They seem pretty exci— *Shit!*"

The car is suddenly clunking and slowing on the steep hill in that choking jerk-up way when it's old vintagey goodness makes that final step over into being broken and forever uselessness.

"Ooh, that's not good," Sarah adds with ironic deadpan finality as the car begins to roll backwards and we all turn around together to prepare to slam into the car right behind. There isn't enough time to not be able to believe something like this is happening to me yet again after Brad's car. The girl driving the other vehicle reads the universal language of helpless shocked faces as we are barreling right toward them backwards. She immediately busts into evasive action. Punching it in reverse, maneuvering back down the road and around the various corners with complete command, all the while stealing quick glances to check on our continued closeness. Jennifer is also on top of the quick thinking and seizes an opportunity to roll off onto a grassy front lawn which is luckily thick with neglect and we amazingly come to a stop on the opposite end of the yard.

I turn back toward the girls and see that the situation is actually worse rather than better as flames are now beginning to flicker and rise from out of the gearshift base.

"We gotta get out of here!" I shout. Sarah's door immediately flies open and she's out and I'm right behind as I jump off and into a double roll away along the grass. I stop, flip around and the entire interior of the car is already completely engulfed in flames. Two seconds longer inside that car and I would be on fire right now and life would be very different.

Instead of burning alive inside the car or rolling around on the grass covered in flames, I watch a confused-looking man open the front door of the house wearing a bathrobe with black socks. He scratches his head. Maybe a microscopic skin bug has just caught fire on it.

We all wait around for the fire truck and as the girls deal with the neighbor, I become transfixed staring into the flames. I'm supposed to go on tour soon, not burn up with that bug. As the flames rise higher and take full control of the bug's demise, they remind me of the last few months' recording sessions and how they had taken full control of all of our lives in much the same way.

Despite Matt, Jeff and Dean each quitting multiple times over the years, Anton eventually realized what he needed was what he'd already had in the first place. Jeff, having heard about the deal, threw his hair clip in the ring and I'd talked Dean back into the band yet *again* just last week while visiting San Francisco.

"Huh. You and Matt are also on the contract? Anton let you guys do that?" I have succeeded once again in rekindling Dean's interest in the BJM.

"I guess so, we don't talk about it, but he let it happen. TVT said that was the deal, and I was sent all the way out there to sign the thing." Keeping in the tradition of my many past campaigns to get Dean to rejoin the band, I strategically leave out any negative angles, like the part about when after I'd flown back home he was all of a sudden totally pissed off about it all and claiming he'd had a new contract written up that no longer included Matt and I. A phone call to our A & R rep Adam proved this not to be true, but we decided to just let it lie until we reached more reasonable days. "I know I've said it before, but this time it actually is all dialed in! By contract!"

"Yes, you *have* said it many times before," he groans by way of giving me a hard time for past exaggerations. "But sounds like you're finally right this time. OK, I'll come down and check it out."

I knew he'd come back. The Gold Cane dive bar on Haight Street was a regular for us, but he could be doing a whole lot better than cooking bar eats in its dingy kitchen. So the lineup is once again Anton, Matt, Jeff, Dean and Joel. We just need a drummer. Same old story. I slap my liquidless glass of lime wedge and twin cocktail straws down on the bar. "Great! That's it, then. Man, wait till you see the new house. It's big, Charlie Chaplin lived down the street back in the day. I'll save you the last room, buddy." I accompany my add-on salesmanship with an elbow, joking but not at all joking.

"Gee, *thanks*." That ol' sarcasm is back again.

I leave the bar and get a strange feeling continuing down Haight Street while no longer living here. The old bowling alley is being converted into a giant Amoeba Records, which is better than bowling I guess, but it's also sure to kill off Reckless and Rough Trade, and who knows, maybe all the rest of the small record stores around here. I continue down the hill towards the Lower Haight, walking the same route I'd done countless times with Anton and Matt, but always separately, which is weird when I think about it. Introspection abounds as I pass by Buena Vista Park, then the old house once owned by Laurel and Hardy, until passing over Divisadero when the street opens back up with the oncoming attention-grabbing cafes, bars, shops and The Peacock Lounge, where it all started with the very first BJM gigs. We were always looking for something.

Dean and Jeff would be arriving tomorrow and a drummer-for-hire friend of Muddy's is going out with us. Despite being good, he's not remotely BJM personality material, but for some reason he was also being taken along with us to the official record release promo photo session with legendary British rock photographer Mick Rock, who'd done some of the most iconic shots of David Bowie, Lou Reed, Syd Barrett, The Stooges and eternal etceteras.

Jeff, Dean, Matt, Anton and myself all get our best me's on while the drummer looks like he's the extra onstage-only keyboard player for No Doubt or Everclear or something, which is oddly a huge relief since all I've seen him wear so far are Adidas tracksuits. Jeff and I vie for pole posing position while Anton and Matt don't bother and we all readjust as needed to make sure the drummer is always on an end. This is an unspoken necessity we all recognize individually. As Mick Rock snaps away at us, he's doing the David Bailey *Blow Up* routine, or maybe it was his first, of NO! NO! NO! or YES! YES! YES! and often at the same time until it's time to stop and switch out for a new film roll and camera lens.

"OK, lets go. Wait a fheckin' minute, where's sweetie darling gone off to?"

"Jeff went to the bathroom," Dean returns.

"Ah, for fack's sake. SWEETIE DARLING?" he inquires with exasperation pushed to the forefront. "Give ass a fackin' minute, pretty fackin' please?!" Mick is all shades, denim, scarves and Bolan curls on the outside but his interior delivers an authority with gangster underworld-like foreboding. Maybe we just bring that out in him.

"Sorry," Jeff says smiling naughtily as he skips out of the closet-like studio bathroom for the second time already. He will now permanently be referred to as "Sweetie Darling" by Mick today and randomly by us for the next few years.

He starts clicking away again. "YEAH! YEAH!" he goes for a bit more and then pauses.

"Lewsee"—Lucy is his studio assistant for the day—"Lewsee, can you adjust that light please. It's a bit lively."

Lucy gets on a step ladder and adjusts the light while we all shuffle around for a couple minutes.

"Right! Let's make rock and facking roll, gentlemen! Wait, who's missing?"

"Dean went to the bathroom," Matt relays.

Before Mick can start yelling Dean comes striding out. "Sorry, sorry, sorry," he says in an animated lumber that's meant to imply jogging but isn't.

Mick Rock glares at him hard, but also with respect for Dean being a "face" and lets him slide. "Jhest get in line, my son," he grumbles with annoyed affection. Mick's obviously a good guy and a rock sensei. He's been doing this a long time now and knows the band person species better than anyone.

We move it outside to the front of the studio building to do some natural light up-against-the-wall shots. He's really liking us out here and wants to switch lenses again.

"Right, now you cunts, this is how the big boys doo—wait, who's not here?"

"Anton," Dean and Jeff say simultaneously.

"For fakssake! What tha' fhack are you pricks doin' in the bothroom ev'ry five bleedin' minates?!"

I know what they're doing but I don't want to say. Also, I'm not poking fun at Mick, he just talks in an really overtly animated way, like being over-the-top British is a part of his showbiz persona.

We are all waiting around when suddenly standing in the doorway is Anton wearing an angel's costume he'd found somewhere. Mick gets what seems to be like a photo-boner over this and begins ravenously snapping away.

We all go back inside and the rest of us spectate with smiles as Anton grins mischievously while posing in the flowing white gown and gigantic feather wings. Suddenly out of nowhere I can see a tear roll down his face. His expression suggests that he's suddenly realized that he'd just inadvertently created his own obituary photo. As a professional photographer, Mick of course loves all of this and continues to rapid-snap until Anton refuses to continue. It will indeed turn out to be the true iconic shot of the entire shoot and will go down in Mick's permanent portfolio. Meanwhile, our chosen band 8×10 is nothing beyond functional, but the Stones' *Out of Our Heads*-style close-up left no room for the drummer so it's a success all around.

The official Brian Jonestown Massacre promo shot by Mick Rock

The next day Dean and Jeff fly back to San Francisco to prepare for the long haul of dates booked for the rest of the year, and "the essential three" (label's words) do a press day from the house. Magazine journalists and photographers from *Alternative Press*, *CMJ*, *Magnet* magazine and others all have staggered appointments as we drink wine and get progressively staggered ourselves throughout the all-day affair.

The album's chosen advertising slogan is "Get Ready for the Revolution Baby", which shows TVT's total enthusiasm for the band's antiestablishment leanings when leaning into the establishment. We are due to turn in the finished product this week and then it's a short pre-release tour followed by a short break before the album's press machine fires up. When it's all sung and done we will have performed 187 shows for the *Strung Out in Heaven* tour.

Finally, the flashing lights of the fire engine, cops and tow truck arrive at the burning Bug party, which has mostly been reduced to a smoking Bug party at this point. I catch a ride the rest of the way to the party with the vacationing Japanese 60s enthusiasts, but the smoke vibe continues up there at the party which is mostly other band guys of the "serious musician" type who just ignore the fresh record-deal-signed tambourine player. I take the early opportunity to hitch a ride back down the hill and then walk the rest of the way, which in a rare LA treat actually isn't all that far. I'd tried to utilize the local bus system once before to go see The Make-Up at The Troubadour, but after the twenty-minute walk from our house to the nearest bus stop over on Sunset, the hour-and-a-half-long wait, the puddle of malt liquor I accidentally sat in, the hour and forty-five minutes it took with all of the stops to get there, I decided it wasn't worth it when if I'd had a car I could have driven to Tijuana and been three beers deep in the same amount of time.

As I approach the cruising altitude of our street, the hills are alive with the sound of music. It even sounds like our inner circle's own Julie Andrews, Miranda Lee Richards.

As if a cat burglar, I stealthily open one of the glass front doors so as to not disturb a recording take or even draw attention, but the track playback announces my arrival anyway.

"SO DAMN STUPID, GOT NOTHIN' TO LOSE..." *Click.*

"OK. Got it? Let's record!" Anton shouts enthusiastically.

Somehow I've gone from being the one to first draw blood on our band's major-label recording contract to, in just a short time, being a loser who's "got nothing to lose". Here we are with Miranda's angelic voice, which is also being backed by an additional small trio of angels, all together testifying to the fact seemingly from the heavens above.

I shrug my shoulders and go to pick out the right tambourine for the track.

Thumping Bible Thumpers Bible Thumping, or Something

"Although I'm livin' low, I like to get real hi—"

"Wait. You gotta stomp harder. Like your stomping the devil out of it," the real speaking Anton instructs, not the now stopped playback.

I eye the positioning of the Albert Pike Freemason Bible on the wooden floor below. Sinatra's signature crooner's model microphone is craning downward to about a foot off the ground ready to catch my thudding rhythm track of antiquarian hardcover stomps. This book held a lot of sway once and while I'm glad it doesn't seem to so much anymore, I have to admit I'm a little unsure about beating it into the ground. Like Pike's photo on page three would be seeing to it that revenge would be rendered upon the boho that dareth to smite him. Surely a book with seemingly magical powers could at least do that, if not just open and swallow me up. The playback starts back up in the headphones. I close my eyes, empty my mind as best I can and begin to stomp the book as hard as I can in 4/4 time.

I get into the rhythm and open an eye. Anton is nodding and smiling along. I've got it now. Oddly, this is the one and only time I can remember when there wasn't a threat in the air of "I could just do this myself". I was *needed,* except it felt more like being the person who has to put the clamps on the questionable car-battery jumping situation. This realization again brings back the thoughts of cursed revenge and they flood my mind as I stomp my way through the floor and down to hell.

At-home magazine photo session of myself, Anton and Miranda
sitting and playing tambourine, sitar and maracas

This new song's fight is indeed the good fight and fought with
methods from "The Way It Was", rootsy outlaw Americana basic
and pure and middle fingers firmly back up and locked into position
like jackknives. With the struggles of the *Strung Out in Heaven* sessions
now officially behind us, Anton was able to record in his natural
spiritual habitat again with no list of major-label expectation boxes
to be checked off, which in actual fact had never been vocalized, but
naturally, they were present. As a result, this previous obligation to
a tiny label release *Bringing It All Back Home—Again*, would become
the more "real" of the two releases, which were essentially recorded
back to back, albeit back to Anton alone (with his trusty sidekick).

Unlike most of his other songs that do not exist the day before
they become complete recordings, the next one on the list is one he's
been droning around for the last few months. "Arkansas Revisited"
has like all songs with the power of drone, a never-ending quality,
as if turning on a radio knowing that despite having just tuned in
to listen, the music has never stopped since the last time it was on.

In the Jingle Jangle Jungle

The best way to be inside the playback is to banish all other outside sensations, or in this situation, distractions, and despite the technically simple instrumentation, incantation takes much chanting and the song plays loud for long hours to provide for unhurried minor adjustments; the portal must be constructed with great precision and care in order to entice something from the other into making the journey to join the trance. It's been many hours now...

Knock knock knock...

Knock knock knock...

Someone is knocking on the front door but the music is much too loud for us to hear. It is in fact a neighbor complaining about the loud music that's been going on for months. He's come to lay down the law to the cult-looking weirdos, but the music is too loud and we've been listening to it for so long we have no idea anyone is poking their head through the door.

"Excuse me..."

"...Gonna kill my mom and my dad..."

"Excuse me..."

"...I run so fast all night and day, they haunt my soul in evil ways..."

"Excuse me..."

"I spent all my dough on a gun, liquored up to—"

"Excuse me...the music is—

Click!

...TOO LOUD!"

"Excuse me?!" Anton says with the first audible "excuse me" of the evening. He would like to know what this unwanted fool is blathering about.

The look on the neighbor's face suggests he's already lost the argument to the blasting lyrics of lawless murder and mayhem and is now caught in the headlights of the protagonist's pickup truck. "Uh, hi...I live just over there," he says, starting to point his house out until suddenly thinking better of it and redirecting his finger off toward the thick trees and brush where no houses are. He regathers his composure somewhat and continues his prepared statement. "Well, for weeks now the music has b—"

"You have to understand, I am not a loud neighbor, I am an *artist*. Do you see all of this recording gear and instruments? These are my tools which we are using to start a revolution..."

266

The intruding complainer of timid complaints rendered in the key of futility (despite coming armed with what seems like months' worth of accumulated grievances) is now and in only fifteen seconds the one doing the apologizing while slowly retreating backwards and practically bowing. I mean, it does say "Beware of Anton" on masking tape freshly stuck right on the door, along with the older and fading but still very valid "Stop! Do not knock—If you hear music please wait or go away!"

I wake up the next morning to find an empty house made even more hollow by the grey damp that surrounds it. Sitting in the large living room turned studio, I look out of the windows now realizing I haven't seen this kind of rain since those few months spent in Portland. It takes me back to Suburbia Studios and its dingy dank. Walking "home" in the rain wearing heels too large on boots too small and despite a flapping umbrella with broken kite corners, my café-racer-style leather jacket soaked like a San Francisco seal, my shoulders tucked in tight while trudging further on to hopefully better days. Ironically, these days.

All of our new magazine articles are spread out together on the floor in the living room. There we are, being it, but home life has become depressing with dark habits. Matt, Dean and Jeff are all doing things back up in San Francisco so it's just Anton and me until our tour schedule starts which includes Tokyo, London and a full US and Canadian tour.

What my one quiet night in New York during my week-long stay at The Soho Grand had shown me is that you can be just as happy in a warehouse with a random book you're half interested in on a floor mattress as a fancy hotel with boring cable TV, or at least I can. If it hadn't been for Anton I wouldn't have made it out of that warehouse in time and could literally be sitting in a prison cell reading a random book that I wasn't at all interested in (not to diss on the San Quentin library department), not sitting here now. Still, despite our current career conditions, I already feel myself tugging at the strings of longing for the struggle and those distinctly downtrodden days in San Francisco.

Pow! Wham! Zap!

It's stinking hot-ass Santa Monica Boulevard bumper-to-bumper traffic spanning as far as the eye can see. I should feel liberated—Elise had given me and Matt her old piece-of-shit car, which actually still works but only until the end of this paragraph. She's an old ally of BJM who once upon a time provided Portland punk rock rehearsal space getaways to her place in Seattle, and weirdly more recently had become one of our manager's secretaries down here. The car has been diagnosed with a terminal condition, a real goner on its last wheels. Like the sick and the dying, its interiors are covered in stains and layers of time-spanning films and glazes that behave poorly in these unbearably hot conditions.

Anyway, like I mentioned before, the car is suddenly dead despite all resuscitation attempts and so we default to our playbook and employ the classic all-purpose "fuck it" maneuver and decide to get out of this smelly barf bucket on wheels to just leave the thing here. I curb the wheel all the way and we both get out and push it into the gutter along the sidewalk. We leave it right there where it lies, half in and half out of a thick Santa Monica Boulevard traffic jam.

We walk and walk until by early evening we make it to The Silverlake Lounge without ever having seen one bus pass. This place was good to us in a way, but it had a tiny stage, small capacity and insufficient amount of drink tickets. How could two beers per member ever be enough? It makes no sense when as a promoter you could bring supermarket beer in and make everyone happy. Nobody in the small Los Angeles clubs ever tries to make anybody happy anymore, if they ever did. Every time I turn around in one, the circumstances seem to whisper softly in your ear, *fuck you.*

The clock on the wall reads that it's the time in between doors and the doorman so we have a few beers before cover charge is implemented.

We continue the death march home now under cover of the night while spending most of this final stretch complaining about life, as one does when you've had to walk across LA for hours. Finally back at home we find Anton about to pair a sizzling-hot pan of chorizo with fresh eggs. He is cracking the last egg as we enter. It's a sign so obvious, yet somehow I do not recognize it. He's not wearing a "kiss the cook" apron either.

"I don't know how you guys think the rent is going to get paid around here by just fucking off all day while I have to do everything. This is *not* going to cut it. Not by a long shot."

"Well since you're oftentimes impossible to be around these days, it makes it hard to be here sometimes," Matt retorts.

"Well, *good*, 'cause I'm sick and tired of babysitting twenty-six-year-olds."

"Well maybe I'm tired of getting shit all the time."

"Fuck *you*. Just get the fuck away from me right now."

"Where do you want me to go? I live here too, y'know."

"I don't care! I don't even want to talk to you right now! Just get the fuck away from me or I'll throw this on you!" He lifts the pan about two inches off the burner.

Instead of listening to this sound suggestion, Matt listens to his internal shrink Dr. Budweiser's advice and grabs our one shitty dull-as-fuck kitchen knife lying on the counter. He displays it to the room in his clenched fist with blade pointing south. I recognize that he's in the "Matt kill" trance. Here we go. He comes toward Anton holding the knife as Anton drops the large hot pan of chorizo flat on the stove. While thankfully a face full of sizzling grease was a bluff, he's opened himself up, but the three of us know all too well that it's a bit of a show and the knife basically has the same cutting power as a ping-pong paddle, which is probably why he picked it up in the first place.

Sizzle! Thud! Chomp!

Much like the bowling alley brawl, Anton gets on top of Matt and now holds him down by the arms. "Do *not* try to stab me!" he advises in case he still needs to, accentuating each word with a push further into the black and white checkered tiles.

With that it's all suddenly over. Matt quits the band again and leaves for O and D's house who are there to help him figure out his next move.

Give us a minute while we load the camera and then tell us all about it...

"It's not even that crazy, it's just crazy compared to other things. It's still an amazing thing to have that happen though," Anton says while on his knees, putting full weight into clicking his suitcase shut. He's displaying some various esoteric idea rope knots to our new tour manager Brad, who to me looks like a mixture of early-70s cool Clint Eastwood and early-80s goofy David Letterman.

A large white rental van is parked in the driveway full of all the band gear and luggage. The letters J.O.B. read large across my white suitcase in black gaffer tape, and it only takes a look at our "grueling" tour schedule to know this is no joke. Life around the house had been heavy on the drama side with few escape options and so I, perhaps more than anyone else in our touring group, was excited to leave.

Anton and Dean are a bit shaky having just kicked the habit, but thankfully this first tour serves the double purpose of making everyone realize it was time to step up and get clean. Sorry, I know I've danced around it some. I should have come right out and said earlier that Anton and Dean had picked up heroin habits upon receiving the record contract money, and Jeff has had one before any of us even knew him. Pretty much everyone had stopped coming around the house, and after coming by one last time to capture the "and this is the last footage of him alive" insurance shot, this also included Ondi and David. They were dark days and it's a miracle the record was ever completed.

Anton is sporting a "mod alpine" look, which with his mop top is something he wears better than anyone. White thick-knit Scandinavian pullover with blue detailing and matching 501s tucked into pull-up brown leather bohemian boots. It must be said that to all appearances our camp had been looking pretty much like a cult for a bit there, which in fact had nothing to do with Anton wanting to get anyone "under his control". Those who came "wearing white when he called" all came with pre-existing brainwash conditions and he was simply a symbol they'd found to follow through with their own fine-feathered in-house follies. In actual fact he was only ever presenting his own trip. Something I've learned in life is that someone who tries to tell you what you should think will never have more of your best interest in mind than someone who will tell you what not to think, and if anything he was the latter. I was a devout black clothes person and glad to see it all go. Still, I did just score a white fur zip-up hood coat meant for Suzy Chapstick but on me it looks more Arctic psychedelic. Acid must be extremely far-out on the Arctic plains, all that white to fill in like a blank sheet of paper while equipped with a Crayola one-hundred-and-fifty-two color crayon collection box of the mind.

As for our new rhythm section, the bass player Charles was already a friend and went further back with some of our San Francisco ex-pats who'd relocated down here a couple years before, and although he came with slightly bemused put-on airs, you could tell he was excited to be a part of this "mess" and his affable style made me feel good to be a part of his entertainment. Drummer Billy was more of a no-nonsense person, quiet and thoughtful yet with a smoldering brood just under the soul's horizon line. He was technically techno and so again we had a drummer who didn't fit in with our natural look, but by now I'd learned the more important thing was he did fit in as a person. I was growing up, seemingly, or maybe it was just the swinging 90s growing later. He's also a very good drummer and in this combination a tactical jacket with revolving corduroy colors is more than hip enough. Adam is also new, filling in on guitar because something was going on with Jeff and his girlfriend or some whatever and at the last minute he opted out of going. Adam was also a good-looking guy a few years younger than the rest of us and had one of those Ron Wood of the Stones rooster hair things going on. It perched atop a sleepy baby face with bedroom eyes like a male mod model. Although seemingly quiet, he still somehow spoke a lot, like he was naturally mellow yet needed to fill the silent holes even though they were there for a reason. Regardless of his hole science, he had a lot of heart and we all like him.

Charles, Dean and Anton in San Francisco

All in all with this new band member configuration I was able to occasionally vacation-slip into more of an observer's role; it was no longer the same group of guys with the same dysfunctions brought out by just simply being around each other. Dean and Jeff, of course, were still here, when they were, but then they were always the chief comers and goers of the group. This setup kept one foot in familiarity, while the new members brought freedom from old hang-ups and setbacks. I was now able to have a second existence to escape to within the band reality in that I was now able to traverse the newness with a sense of detachment that I could come and go from whenever I wished. It was the best of both worlds.

For the first time ever, there were "foreigners" to San Francisco in the band that actually felt like members who fit in with what it was. We'd had a few misshapen puzzle pieces over the last months and I was tired of "hired guns". Really, it was now us San Franciscans who were the foreigners and they were the Los Angeles locals. It was a crossing of realities in which each validated the other. The end of 1998 was here and we were ready to hit the road again with fresh faces and an album climbing the American indie charts—what could go wrong?

Part III

He Blew It

I wake up alongside the freeway with just a cheap drape-covered window separating me from a morning traffic jam in Nashville. It had been the latest case of "this isn't so bad" when we pulled into the parking lot here in the a.m. while under the cover of night and liquor-ups, but now it's a hot blazing cacophony of car horns, while the heat and blinding white brightness frames the drapes with all the subtlety of a foot through the door.

I roll over in some attempt to get away from it and catch my still-dressed-self from falling off my raft of uneven bedsprings. Over on the next twin bed is Dean, sitting up against a pile of extra pillows, wearing his burgundy satin smoking jacket robe. He puts his paper in his lap, tilts his glasses down and quips with slight amusement, "Rough night, huh Sparky?"

I appreciate his soft delivery but the undercurrent of delight at my self-inflicted disheveled misery grates on me like a garbage can drum set being jazzed with bent-up garden rake brushes.

"How are you not totally hungover?" I mumble-complain.

"Easy. I drink about as half a much as you do."

"Oh."

"Huh huh, *yeah*," he gloats while proudly pushing his rarely seen reading glasses back up. He then continues to read whatever band van floor ephemera score he'd had the wherewithal to bring in with him last night after the show after-partying. I pull my elbow out from under me and face-plant down into the pillow to suffocate myself but then it becomes hard to breathe so I quit and decide to take a shower. First I try to remember last night. I run back over the general gist in my head as if I were writing or reading about it. We'd done about as much of the downtown Nashville strip as we could take which didn't turn out to be very much. The current nightlife vibes here made it all seem like a Las Vegas-esque tourist-douche zone populated only with cover bands. No cowboy-picking rebel-song slingers were to be found and outlaw country felt closer to in-law country, if anything.

I crumble-stumble-mumble my way to the little smelly bathroom and turn on the wobbly electric fan beating out of time behind its jail bars. Then I look at myself in the mirror while trying not to see myself, then pledge not to do that again. Already forgetting what I just said, I peel slowly and see in the mirror that my T-shirt and Levi's are reluctant to go, as if after two days and nights of playing and partying they'd assumed they were on to stay. Ultimately, deep down they understand that times change and newer things come along that make the old obsolete. Time to give those crisp new boot-cut Lee's I'd gotten at the Western wear store on the strip last night their debut in the spotlight.

Hanging out hungover on the 1998
Strung Out in Heaven US tour

A few hours on the road and we drive past Memphis with no time to stop off and see Graceland for the second time this year. It's a total of ten hours from Nashville to Dallas with no stops, and there will certainly be long gas station stops, meaning no soundcheck. It's going to be another line-check night, as in arrive, get all the gear loaded directly onstage and play. My checking under Elvis's couch cushions for lost vintage pills will have to be put on hold.

Dallas is just Dallas again and next we are going to backtrack to New Orleans where Mardi Gras is in two days, but unfortunately for us by that time we will be waking up in Florida. No kaleidoscopic mass of explosions in colors, sound and revelry, the floats and the music coming from every direction, the costumes, the cops and the almighty happy plague of beads crisscrossing the air in all directions, but rather when we arrive it's the calm before the liter-sized hurricane cocktails hit.

Today many of the locals must be charging up their liver batteries because Bourbon Street is at a stumblestill as The Brian Jonestown Massacre members walk it as if astronauts in a lost utopian Atlantis party zone on another planet. The grey rain has washed it all down because the festivity gods are cleaning everything up for the crowds that we will narrowly be missing. One thing about hard touring is the amount of near-misses there are when you've got to be getting on to the next town every single day.

We break from taking in the Creole architecture to avoid taking on the light pitter-patter and walk into a large multilevel Virgin Megastore. (The) Verve's new video "Lucky Man" plays on all the various synced television monitors and as I make my way across the first floor and up the escalator I'm able to watch it uninterrupted by switching my view to the many screens throughout. The rest of the guys have split off in various directions which turns out to be separate paths each involving adventures filled with individual life lessons, all of which in the end lead to the magazine section on the third floor.

There is very little if any vinyl in chain stores these days and cheap plastic-encased media discs surround us in the jam-packed floor racks, walls and aisle displays. Cassettes are the other analog media on the outs due to the almighty digital scam to trick people into buying their record collections all over again. Regardless, the van only has a tape player so nobody gets any music here. Road-side gas stations are more our friend in these parts of the country with the customary spinning shelf display where we can always get trucker-friendly selections like Creedence, Steppenwolf, various "'60s Chartbuster" and Motown collections.

When I was little my dad only ever had need for two cassettes which were traded off in repeat rotation, *Gord's Gold* by Gordon Lightfoot and The Doobie Brothers' *Minute by Minute*. My mother, however, couldn't stand either of these albums so we always listened to the contemporary soul music station on our family trips. Nonetheless, errands with my dad always began with him sliding one of those two tapes into the deck where I would then enjoy his palpable unspoken victory of "dad rock" time (despite my own fledgling taste siding with my mother). Once on the way to the library I found in the Doobies' fold-out inner sleeve artwork a glorified single image of a joint or "doobie" that was burnt down to the roach. "Daad, what's thaat?" I asked. It was the first question I remember ever asking him that he outright ignored. Despite meeting over a jug of wine while both participating in an illegal backstreet drag racing competition called a "Grudge Race" with my dad in his 1966 Corvette and my mother in her '55 Chevy Bel Air, by now they had a two-drink maximum on the rare occasions they socialized. Still, they'd earned many lifetime cool points through their early dates going to see Otis Redding, Sly and the Family Stone, Lou Rawls and as I mentioned before, Ike & Tina Turner where she snuck me in inside her tummy.

The next morning we're all converging at the van down in the hotel parking lot and Charles notices Billy has busted out a wool newspaper boy cap for the first time. "Well, well, well. Look who had the guts to show back up. Flanagan." Billy keeps his end of this occasional morning-time razz tradition by not responding, and suddenly I wonder what the crickets are still doing up. Maybe they had a cocaine party because they can't seem to stop chirping from last night for some reason. I'm sure some sleepy bats or frogs will shut this party down soon enough.

Then Jeff, who has always been our biggest big-time time waster, comes trotting down from his room to our half-dozen egg carton on wheels, and with that, everything is whatever it was again.

I'd somehow sold the band on the idea of going to the *Easy Rider* cemetery last night while full of impassioned insistence and not now totally hungover again. Strangely, it's under a highway overpass and our tour manager Brad having retained all the verbal instructions given by the show promoter, we descend wrapped in truth to street level alongside the border of graves. Most of the guys are starting to scratch their heads now as I'm striding toward the stones. The graves are tombs above the ground due to this being technically below sea level, so it's more of a marble neighborhood of vaults rather than an underwater headstone convention. "Ten minutes and we're leaving you here forever!" Brad calls after me in his "not kidding but kidding but not kidding way". The bigger picture is once again that there's no way we are making it in time for sound-check, so it's a chance to let me have my weird little moment that is rendered harmless by piggybacking on a pre-existing imminent fuck-up.

It's a colder and grayer day today than yesterday and the gray-on-gray scenery is color-coordinated as successfully as partly cloudy blue skies with foaming waves on a beach, except, you know, more depressing or something. I'm looking for the Italian Benevolent Society tomb, but I don't know that's its name, I just know it's the statue Peter Fonda has his bad trip breakdown on in the movie. It's the centerpiece for the LSD scene, and the cemetery itself is the unspoken pre-crash site where Peter Fonda's character realizes "We blew it".

My *Easy Rider* fantasies had already encountered a few motorcycle accidents with reality, like a drunken first date experience at a screening which ended with me standing in front of a packed house at The Red Vic shouting at the crowd and calling them "a bunch of cows" before moo-moo-ing at them because some of them had outwardly ridiculed the film's grim death-of-ideals ending. I never got a second date. Then, two years later at an embarrassing Q & A film session with Peter Fonda himself; I think we might have a clip of that, yes. Let's roll it:

The lights went out. I couldn't believe that somewhere sitting in this movie theater sat the *Easy Rider* star and co-writer Peter Fonda. He's making an appearance here at The Roxie Theater for a screening and Q & A session for what had been his first post-*Easy Rider* project *The Hired Hand*, which he had directed, starred in, and hadn't been screened since its debut. An article in this week's *San Francisco Guardian* described how he'd checked out of society for the last few years, mostly sailing around the world in his boat. Wow man, far out, I thought—that's totally righteous and in keeping with the spirit of *Easy Rider*.

The Roxie had been my first-ever experience seeing an "art house" film in an "art House theater", when I saw Ingmar Bergman's *The Seventh Seal* shortly after moving to San Francisco.

I'm sitting alone in an aisle seat close to the front of the packed two-hundred seat cinema house feeling sure that what I'm about to see must be a lost masterpiece, but after the first twenty minutes it begins to become clear that the very slow-burn intro was just the start of a very slow-burning film. All along the way there are situations that give off feelings of intended symbolism, but I can't be totally sure. Everything is vague and this movie bears little resemblance to the kind of experience *Easy Rider* is, where the symbolism was itself a visual language. That film's documentary style made it easy to equate the character onscreen and Fonda the man as the same person. It was also a known fact that much of the script was improvised as they traveled across America filming, making it seem more "real". I'd been an *Electric Company* "Easy Reader" before I was even old enough to read and for me, the film's message was artistic folklore that went beyond mere entertainment.

The lights go up and *The Hired Hand* is finally over. An excited theater curator comes down to the front and picks up a microphone, while a not so excited younger theater employee places a chair on the small riser below the screen.

"Blah blah blah…and now, ladies and gentlemen…the 'Easy Rider' himself…Mr. Peterr Fonnda!"

This introduction suddenly blasts away all lingering boredom the room's been soaking in for the last hour and a half. I see him coming down the aisle but catch myself looking behind him for another him...well, that's OK, everybody gets older and anyway, maybe it's for an upcoming role, like a hippie Buddha dude or...hmm. He's wearing loose dad jeans and a Harley-Davidson T-shirt under a stiff leather vest. A long ponytail is pulled tight before traveling down the length of his back. Where's Captain America?

If the 60s dream died during the 70s, then the 80s completely incinerated whatever residue was left in the pipe. To be fair, there's no way it could have been an easy transition to go from being the groovy ones to navigating a new fucked-up world where yuppies are the thing to aspire to. Yet, if they'd only been willing to take a pay cut and stay true to the proven positives of the past, when that dayglo synthesizer storm blew over they wouldn't have been caught going into middle age with their sleeves pushed up in pastel blazers with sock-less ankles.

Peter Fonda plops down into the chair and gets right into *The Hired Hand* backstory. Then finally, "OK, I'd like to open it up to questions now..."

My hand has been up since the letter "q". He sees me in my aisle seat, scans around at the few other raised arms dotted around the theater, then comes back to me, seemingly dubbing me the most worthy-looking fan to get things started.

"I was wondering if you could explain what you meant when you said 'We blew it' toward the end of *Easy Rider*."

His erect sitting position deflates. Then, so as to make me vanish in whatever limited capacity science will allow him, he turns to the other side of the theater, now in profile to me and states, "I'd like to talk about the movie we've just seen, *The Hired Hand*. That's what I've come here to talk about."

Arms fly up everywhere to get the room moving past my faux pas question. He chooses someone across the theater and now with every head in the room angled the other way, I roll out of my seat feeling like a pinball coming off the entry track, then continue to roll straight down the aisle until going through the game-flipper swinging exit doors.

We blew it.

I only have a few minutes to find the cemetery statue and give it a kiss while someone takes a picture of it on my disposable camera.

The problem is that the cemetery is large enough to merit three separate large sections that span for blocks. I soon find myself breaking into a trot as if I were Eli Wallach's Tuco character running around the sprawling graveyard in *The Good, the Bad and the Ugly*.

It's not easy being hangover-green, or a rudderless easy rider, and Brad waves me down from across the marble tomb tops as I walk back to the van with head down in Charlie Brown position.

Zen Bobbyism

In 1991 Primal Scream became the world's official party rebel band in not only the grand traditions of the 60s and 70s, but had also somehow pulled off slipping the raw power of The MC5 inside the acid house. Singer Bobby Gillespie was the main man the English press went to for hedonistic headlines. He was "Higher Than the Sun" and embodied the divine rock 'n' roller concept of never being taken alive sober. He was the pharmacological guru and it was even more inspiring that he played maracas.

A few years later I was working at the record store the day Primal Scream were to play a secret show at Slim's sponsored by local radio station LIVE 105, and mid-shift I spied Bobby shopping the bins. After setting him up with a tour bus CD copy of The Rolling Stones' *Aftermath* and directions to the Church of John Coltrane down on Divisadero Street, he in return set me up with a guest list spot and a backstage pass for tonight's exclusive contest winners' gig.

After the packed and chaotic show, the backstage dressing room area is like a condensed downstairs labyrinth of rooms and corridors which are currently over-capacity with bodies in movement. Nothing seems to be stationary except back in the largest small room where most of the band are draped over couches that meet in the furthest corner.

Stopping in the doorway, I was now before the power source of all the frantic winds of hustle and waves of bustle. Around this energy center, bodies are bouncing around like condensed molecules and it's through the flashes of fast-motion ballet that Bobby sees me. I can't help but read his look as I'm just something else he feels obligated to deal with. Another duty to fulfill to get this night in the bag.

Ignoring this, I wave and walk over. "Hey man, that was great!" I shout enthusiastically, then I move in closer with the hush tone. "You won't believe the speed I've got! Top of the class, man."

"Nah, we went pretty big the last couple of nights. Thanks, but it's gonna have to be one of those battery-recharge nights, ya' know whattamean?"

I didn't. I was here, he was there, and the speed was the best anywhere.

Seemingly not wanting to disappoint a fan that's as down for the cause as I am, he invites me to join him outside in the fenced-off back alleyway parking lot behind the club. We walked the small grounds like a student and sensei philosophizing. While we talked of music and the road, I saw in him the ability to not just go completely pharma-bonkers, despite having just played a high-energy show and all the after-party chaos that was in full swing backstage. I already knew the most important part of the equation: recreational drugs are supposed to be about fun. When it's fun, you're running to something, not away. Even still, if you've gone too far out and need to come back in again, don't fight that for the sake of others. "Don't fight it, feel it" works both ways. Don't be stuck. I ask myself if I will listen to the party-person sacred knowledge when the time comes. Or did it already come and go?

I then give him a rough mixtape of most of what will be the *Take It from the Man!* album while letting him know there's also a quarter-gram baggy of the best crystal meth he's ever gonna do inside the case. The guru takes it and we part.

Four years later The Brian Jonestown Massacre are on their way to the UK for the very first time. *Spice World* is the featured film on our Virgin Atlantic flight as the world is obsessed with all things England once again. The free drinks go down me at least fifteen gin and tonics deep until landing into the most devastating first-ever jet-lagged hangover one-two punch.

This massive hangover was in fact the first feeling of my actual mortality; that I'd begun the slow decades-long process of dying. It was that bad. The hangover somehow worsens on the drive to The Columbia Hotel and London seems to have very little left swinging by way of the 60s. On the plus side, every pub on every street seems to either be blasting from its doors The Verve's *Urban Hymns* or Spiritualized's *Ladies and Gentleman We Are Floating in Space*, or that Radiohead record.

After an initial lobby call attempt to take London by storm, I realize I need to play it zen-style and self-enforce a nursing job that winds up being watching Michael Caine in the 1966 classic *Alfie* (Now *this* was England!) in my ancient tiny white room.

Later and long ago having missed the American-psych-dudes-gone-wild-in-the-streets-of-London adventure, I go out solo on a mission to buy my first pair of English boots from an actual shop on Carnaby Street. Shellys London was an especially fabled mod bootery for a Yank kid like myself and this was my planned big splurge. I wore my new brown suede Chelsea boots right out the door, while my old cracked black leather zip tatters went into the trash bin just outside the shop.

Then just two blocks away tragedy struck when from out of the grey skies a flash downpour of English rain began pounding down hard. Within seconds my new un-weather-proofed light-brown suede boots were turning dark wet as I splashed through the uneven sidewalk pools. I'm now in a residential area and off the beaten path of the retail and restaurant worlds, so I break into long strides not knowing where I'm going and praying for one of the pubs that until this scenario had seemed to be every fourth building of every block.

That's when I round the next corner and run straight into one Bobby Gillespie. Now, I don't mean I turned the corner, we see each other and say "Hello!" or that we catch ourselves just short of getting in each other's path with an "Oh, excuse me...*wait*!" but I mean we physically collided right into each other.

Both jumping jack flash back in surprise, he's the first to react as his famous grin draws double wide and he points "Crystal meth!"

I guess he must have liked that stuff I sent him off with. I then have to break it to him that I didn't attempt to smuggle any through customs, but he still invites me along to the recording studio he's currently on his way to. I want to go with, but BJM are themselves finally being let up onto the British podiums to testify, and I have a soundcheck to get to.

Riders on the Norm

It's another leg of the multi-legged US tour and today we are backtracking yet again, this time from Chicago to Grand Rapids, Michigan. It's a new city for us which theoretically should be exciting, yet still, Dean and I are consummate brothers in moaning from the back of the van, headshaking at what has become an old familiar custom of going backwards.

After the gig last night a bit of a coke party ensued as they do when someone at the gig offers to sponsor one, and so it was another one of those standing-room-only Motel 6 room parties till the front desk calls in an airstrike and drops the buzzkill-infused wet blanket all over it. On cross-country tours like this, the band shares rooms in pairs to keep costs down and everyone would gravitate toward the two or three whom they feel the most compatible with as roomies and stick to rotating those. Mine were Dean, Anton and Charles. Charles and Brad were old LA buddies so they usually teamed up until it was time for a break and then I'd be his mix-it-up guy and he'd be mine. It had been one of those mix-it-up nights but then it went double mix-up which is when you drop your bag in your room but then go party until you pass out in another, waking up hanging upside down from the closet clothes-hanger rod or mashed between a couple of mattresses, so you get up and go back to your room where your never-opened luggage is lying atop your untouched bouncy bed with nary a butt imprint atop the smooth sheets and no time left for anything other than to immediately go down and join the others already hanging around the van waiting to go.

We all strap in or go strapless, each of us holding either a coffee or a stray beer. As we exit the hotel parking lot we all carefully hold them in the air like we're in some kind of Olympic synchronized beverage-spillage-preventing routine. Lenny Kravitz's current inescapable radio hit "Get Away" begins its first of uncountable radio plays for the day and we all make "who farted?" faces. It's a hippie Halloween-store costume in sound and if anything an undercover narc jam with its excruciating rhyme schemes of fly-high-sky-dragonfly-trees-degrees-please-stars-Mars-ours-how-now-brown-cow, all meant to convey a desire to escape reality or something.

"I want to get away, I want to fly away!"

Charles quips from the middle bench, "Man, if Lenny Kravitz were sitting here right now, I'd tell him, 'Dude, you've got to get away,'" accompanied with a little hand-as-broom gesture toward the sliding door, and with that, the van band banter begins where it will continue in varying lineups of duos, trios, quartets, quintets, sextets, but mostly solos for the rest of the four-hour drive to Grand Rapids.

Tour is a fucking blast but also very disorientating in having to navigate the loss of life's daily routines and time itself. Soundcheck and stage time become the only two constants and the rest of existence is a jazz solo, wild and fast or slow and cautious as dictated by the previous evening's late-night lengths of limit-stretching by having yet again ignored high hangover-level lessons learned over and over, yet I would submit that it is still better to have learned and lost the memory than to never have learned at all, or something.

I gaze out my side of the window and think back to San Francisco when there had been a brief period where Anton, Dean and I were the sole members of BJM. Anton was living in an apartment with only one roommate, Dean was still with Christina in their pad across from The Painted Ladies and I was speeding through my drug warehouse days. Anton and I had been playing shows as a duo, and Dean had become the first one to rejoin after one of my many re-recruitments. This was the move that convinced Matt to rejoin the cast, which was then quickly followed by the assembling of the "Viper Room" lineup.

During this window in time, the biggest Bay Area music magazine *BAM* was doing a piece on us, which for me was my first-ever interview. First are the photos. Then Dean cruises Anton, me and the photographer in his black 60s Ford Fairlane over to Chinatown, where we walk Grant Street under its rows of colored paper lanterns and flags that hang from building to building over streets lined with a combination of traditional Chinese motifs and Western-friendly architecture with vintage signage exploding with everyday celebration color combinations. It's a type of preserved-in-time amusement park with the 1950s roughly being the center point and reaching out in both directions, backwards to the 1930s and forwards to the 1970s.

Chinatown photo shoot

We go for a quick drink inside the faux-cavern wall façade exterior of the Li Po Lounge where we sit at the bar under a giant decaying Chinese lantern from the 1800s that's the size of a ballroom chandelier. The photographer snaps a few before going outside to shop for exterior backdrops. From my left I can smell Dean's velvet blazer infused with the various incense and candle scents Christina burns in their goth (Victorian sect) decorated apartment. Anton says something funny and I turn to my right side and there's his rugged smile, teeth together, mouth more square than pointed, as if determination was built into an emotion that didn't even require its presence. Three albums are currently in the can and scheduled to come out on Bomp! Records this year. We've got every right to proceed with extreme confidence as we know we are then going to get signed to a bigger label and right now it's that in-between period when you know you're golden but haven't had to commit to anything yet. With a little creativity we were all just getting by without jobs and it felt like we had nothing, yet owned the world. I sat there wishing that just like Chinatown itself, I could be frozen in time at this moment right now forever.

We come off the freeway into downtown Grand Rapids as Dean chuckles, "Man, I told this dude I met at the show last night that we were going to Grand Rapids today and he told me Anthony Kiedis is from here."

Anton turns around from the front passenger seat, "Man, every time I would hear The Red Hot Chili Peppers I was like, man, somebody tell this guy to stop rapping, and then he started singing the new songs and I was like, 'OK, fuck, go back to rapping again!'"

Brad is suddenly frustrated. "Man, the promoter for tonight told me to get off here, but I don't think he knew what he was talking aboot."

"*Aboot?*" Billy repeats from the front bench. Brad has shown his Canadianism and aboots begin to flutter from all around the van. Everybody knows Canadians have copied everything from us, that we are the model which all society has aspired to. This apparently seems to be the logic, at least with people who enjoy making fun of each other in any way currently available to them. Ultimately, these inner-van hijinks wouldn't even have legs if he didn't actually pronounce it "about" almost all of the time, except on occasional slip-ups and in stressed-out moments like this. Now exposed, the least we can do is make his life harder for him.

Grand Rapids was one of those big dumb cities seemingly strictly for city's sake that had no apparent character. We are lost very deep downtown which makes eventually finding the small dingy rock venue in the middle of nowhere a huge positive.

The show that night is the most uneventful in the entire history of the band, so let's just skip it in an effort to get closer to the night's horrific end:

"Where's Dean?" Charles asks. Nobody has seen him since we got offstage twenty minutes ago, and like everyone else, he's supposed to help load out the music gear. I'm even helping because I want to get out of this nasty place so bad. We'd never been here before and we would never return again, hopefully. The vibe around the van is heavy with, "Let's get the fuck out of here before we get shanghaied or roofied or something".

"Where *is* Dean?" I ask after another fifteen minutes. Most of the gear is loaded by now and this is a desolate and dark side of town. Of all of us, Dean was the most unlikely one to just go traipsing off without notifying anyone first. That was something Jeff might have done or Matt had actually drunkenly done, imitating me from when back in my heydaze I'd done it over and over again, but never out of town where I had no idea where I was and especially not somewhere I didn't even want to be. Not Dean though. Dean was a source of stability in the band. He didn't howl at the moon or get too wild no matter how much he drank. This didn't make him a stuffed shirt in any way, it made him cool. He had mastered that sweet spot of being fun to party with, yet he could always perform in a way that allows one to wake up the next morning with a cordial stance on a big hangover that only comes with freedom from regrets. He didn't "fuck up". At least not until recently.

Where's Dean?

Christina had left him. They were the most meant-to-be couple any of us had ever seen, but she knew if she didn't make a strong stand he'd never kick. She'd moved on but first made it clear that if he got clean and quit the band that seemed to be his trigger place, she would take him back. He was struggling with those necessary moves that led the way back to her, moves he was always about to do until it went on for months and then never happened. They really were perfect together and it was one of those unnatural warps in the universe that they didn't stay together.

"Where the fuck is Dean?" Brad asks after another twenty minutes. The gear is loaded now and it is time to get the fuck out of this grim neighborhood and straight to the first hotel outside of town.

Where's Dean?

There's Dean. He appears out of nowhere, already in the middle of the darkened block heading toward us. He gets closer and something looks wrong by the way he's hunched inward, pulling his lapels tightly over his chest. He gets up close now under the streetlight and he's a huddled shivering mess. *Dean?* His face is beaten so badly it's hard to even recognize him. His body has the same clothes on as before, the hair is there although thrust and pulled in various directions, but his *face*. His face is a bulbous swelling mass of purple and blue. Someone had *destroyed* him. Brad waves a cab down and tells us to get in the van and stay put. I immediately regret not jumping in the cab as I watch them race away to the hospital.

Brad comes back about an hour later with a loose and disturbing story that Dean had mumbled to him on the way to the emergency room. Apparently, he'd thought it looked like the kind of area he could go and cop a street score. This wasn't an out of the ordinary practice these days as most rock clubs are in the iffy if not straight up IF parts of cities so, when in a pinch, the street score often wasn't hard to make happen. Dean found a guy, a real big guy, and was led down a dark street supposedly to a dealer's house when everything turned. The guy proceeded to mug him and beat the shit out of him before dragging him to a deserted ATM, made him pull up his balance on the screen first to make sure all he had was withdrawn, and then took his money and beat on him some more. Drag it out like an alley cat does a mouse. Dean tries to get away, the guy catches him and beats him some more. Told him he was going to kill him. Finally, almost an hour after it all started he finally let him stumble away.

We all stay at a nearby hotel so we can visit him in the morning at the hospital. When we get up there he's still in his black stove-pipes and silver paisley button-up, which is now torn and missing a few buttons. His swelling is down from last night, but he's going to have to stay here and get some minor surgery to get his "face" face completely back where it was the night before.

294

When he gets out of the hospital in a few days, he'll fly to his father's in south LA to heal and then go straight into rehab. He leaves the rehab clean and stays that way. I reach out to him, but he says he's not interested in rejoining BJM. This time I don't try to change his mind.

Strung Out in Sunset Ralphs

It's Elise's day off from her desk with our band management and she's offered to drive me to visit Anton at the Exodus Recovery Center, which is the rehab he'd checked himself into upon our return to Los Angeles. She picks me up with her best somber soap opera expression on, but behind the situation's called-for worried concern, underneath it all she just finds this whole thing completely *delicious*. The fact flickers between the lines like flashing subliminal messages of gnashing teeth in a film. In this business, often the ones showing the greatest concern are your biggest enemies.

After only completing the second week, Anton has been green-lit for visitors as apparently he'd already kicked the habit and was now over the hump. Once we are inside the car, this subject is to-be-continued until we get to our mission's destination. For now, Elise has all the inside gossip from the inside of my own business. She is very matter-of-fact in her ritual of drama incantation, occasionally flipping back alternating sides of her Ramones-style hair as she stirs the cauldron.

She shifts both her latest car and self into a higher gear with all the managerial things that should be getting done for us but aren't, how our lives could be so much easier if only this or that, all of which to me is just playing that same old melody on a mouthful of broken xylophone teeth to the tune of we shouldn't be living so skint. She's starting to work herself up now with the drama, and the sympathy as the hair flips and the subliminal smile show how it just *tears her up* inside. She *sees* the books. She *overhears* the telephone office conversations. Now she's really aroused with all of this rubbing it in with new extra-strength coulda-shoulda-woulda have-nots

296

polish. But that, we all know, is the point. Reading my response level and realizing that maybe she's getting carried away with it all, laying it on a little too thick, she stops, signaled with a head flutter as if turning off a stimulation device. All is calm and back to boring reality again, driving through the sun-baked two-sided strip-mall streets in silence. Strangely, part of me feels like a disappointment for not delivering a more entertaining reaction to it all. Showbiz and all that, I suppose.

The start of 1999 is already turning out to be one bitch of a century closer and for us, those old familiar winds of drama were back again, albeit blowing from a different direction than during the unsigned days. Regardless, they were shaking our tree but luckily by now we had very sharp tree-climbing spikes on our Beatle boots. The new guys didn't complain once the sweet spots like Japan and London were over and it became time for the long-haul, harder-to-sell, town-to-town grinds. At least the complaints didn't come in the old dysfunctional ways, they were more like professional complaints that were, weirdly, based on logic. There are a couple more legs of the *Strung Out in Heaven* US tour ahead and with the brown stuff totally eradicated from the lineup, now we'll just have to see what state the returning Jeff Davies will bring to this latest re-re-re-re-re-re-re-re-re-re-re-re-remix.

When we get out of the car the air is thin and hot, or I guess arid, but that isn't really a word practiced in my life beyond seeing it on the written page. In real-life situations, I would normally describe this level of heat as "hot as fuck" or "fuck this shit", so, let me take advantage of the situation and say arid. We soberly make our way over to the one-level, hospital-type complex. The woman at the front desk finds Elise's name on the visitor's appointment list and we are allowed to wander in on our own down the hall on hushed toes. We find Anton in what looks like the main gathering slash meeting slash recreational what-have-you hang room. He smiles and walks across the room toward us, but stops first at the television surrounded by haphazardly piled video cassettes. Without saying a word he picks up a *Planet of the Apes* complete collection on VCR tapes and hands it to me. "Here, you should just take this." I appreciate this offer, and he knows that I'd want to, but walking around with a five-tape VHS box set under my ragged Beatles *Revolver* T-shirt is sure to arouse suspicion. I feel slight failure at not embracing this call to rebel-rousing, but the positive takeaway from the brief exchange is that my energy detector reading comes up as clearly normal Anton, and it is a relief that blows over me like a cool breeze.

I follow the breeze as he leads us out onto the enclosed outdoor patio and lawn area, and right there on a slab of cement is the Academy Award-winning actor Robert Downey Jr, who's currently staring dejectedly at the ground, probably looking for another last straw. Or maybe just a straw. Over the years the mainstream tabloid press has been wallpapering the grocery store checkout lines with aggressively printed headlines shouting out about his in-and-out-again rehab adventures. His outfit today is a sort of white medical worker's ensemble, which nobody else is wearing, giving the rehab pedestrian the impression they are like his rehab sleepover clothes or something.

Anton sees me looking and gestures across the grass with a head motion. "There's Wayne Kramer over there too." The person he's referring to looks about as much like the legendary MC5 guitarist as the male nurse keeping an eye on things, so I just take his word for it.

It's lunchtime and what's for lunch is a huge outdoor lobster tail barbecue with all the skewered trimmings. Despite this, nobody eats, nobody talks, nobody smiles. I, on the other hand, have lately begun food medicating, which is especially worrisome because I can already feel myself developing a higher tolerance. Anton has no interest in the lobster and I'm not here to eat humongous lobster tails fresh off the grill. Instead, I flip my Levi's jacket collar up in an attempt to make it look more like a uniform and affect an English accent as if playing out a scene in a WWII movie like *The Great Escape*. "Not to worry, ol' boy, the tunnel is finished and we're getting you out of here *tonight*."

"And the air strike is ready to blow all this shit up after?" he returns smiling, but not in enough spirit to do the accent, which makes sense considering what a drag of a place this is.

"Yesh, a jolly good rogering."

"Jolly Roger, you mean," he laments, now bored with it.

Then, to himself, he grins knowingly, as if regardless of all the darkness surrounding the situation, life was still all about a four-cornered kite floating high on a psychedelic lullaby. It hasn't even been two weeks since he'd first walked in, quit cold turkey and by now thankfully was already seemingly back to his old self. What's left now is for him to get through the remaining clockwork-oranging and then onto the other side of the front checkout desk. Then the old-school regular kind of trouble could start again. Anyway, that's my take on where that grin has come in. Then again, maybe he's just amused at my wearing a gut-concealing jacket in million-degree weather. Well, everybody needs *something*, and anyway I'm going to cut back before it gets out of control.

We stroll the length of the high perimeter wall and right past the section in the concrete that Kurt Cobain had famously escaped over a few years ago now, then back across the lawn toward the cement shore to rejoin Elise at one of the patio tables. She goes into hushed tones despite discussing music industry gossip, as if we're in a prison visitors' room or something while I take another look around. There's the full grill of food that nobody is eating. There's Robert Downey Jr., still sitting there looking dejected. Then I look back over to the section of wall Kurt Cobain jumped and imagine what he'd looked like doing it. There I think is Wayne Kramer. I decide to put that *Planet of the Apes* box up my shirt on my way out and then go straight on a diet.

Canadian Club

Adam has been brought back into the band, this time replacing Dean instead of Jeff who is also back again replacing himself from before. As mentioned Dean had permanently traded in his twelve-string for the twelve steps and after the mixed-musical artist kitchen cage fight, there's no way Matt is ever coming back.

We're off again for another East Coast leg of the mighty long American tour, and our manager having sensed trouble with our ongoing moody no-money grumbles, has rented us a big limousine as transportation to the airport. The catch here is we are being picked up many hours before our flight as apparently, limos come at a huge discount when you rent them during the hours nobody wants them. So, we're driving to LAX in the pitch-black darkness in group silence. He'd mistakenly assumed that we'd even want a limo, and this forced faux-luxury in turn forced us to stay up rather than get the wimpy few hours sleep.

We land in Maine where our guitar tech Travis is waiting with a van, but when we get to the Canadian border we are refused entry.

"Well, did they at least tell you the reason why?" Charles asks Brad as we return to sender.

"It was all a little vague, to be honest, but something to do with the work permits not being enough. One thing's for sure, they were *not* very helpful. I'm going to get on the horn with the head office as soon as we get to the hotel so they can sort it all out for the Toronto show.

"They said it was because of work permits?" Anton asks just in case there are any more specifics to be had. Turns out there aren't, but I know why he's asking.

We'd come over the Canadian border once before back when the lineup was Matt, Dean, Anton, Brad and myself. We had no tour manager then as it was just a West Coaster that went Sacramento, Portland, Seattle, Vancouver, San Francisco and back to LA. We also didn't have work permits because management thought it an unnecessary expense, I guess; all I know is Dutcher instructed us carefully, like a deadbeat dad sending his kid into somewhere because he owes the place money, "Don't tell them you are performing in their country. That would just make a lot of paperwork and it's much easier for you and for them if you just say you are tourists on vacation."

We were indeed able to fake out the Canadian border officers by pretending that we were five musicians with a van full of music gear just going on a fishing trip or something. Unfortunately, when we arrived at the venue an hour later, the promoter informed us that the Canadian border fuzz had randomly seen our picture in tonight's local entertainment listings shortly after we'd passed through. Our vintage-Vox-guitars-as-fishing-rods scam was blown. They gave us two choices: head back down to the border station immediately and by our own free will, or they would be coming up here for us, which they said would make matters much worse. We all decide to have our middle names changed from Trouble to other things because there was no way we were getting kicked into the Canadian can instead of heading to San Francisco next and getting Mission-style burritos and stuff.

All this may or may not explain why all these months later we were just turned away at the border, regardless of whether we have the correct paperwork this time. God forgives, Canada doesn't.

Now we had a few of days to kill, which is a rare and welcome situation actually, as tours are in fact mostly made of repeat days— check out of the hotel, drive to the next city while eating gas station garbage, disappear while the rest of the guys load gear, soundcheck, eat dinner, get buzzed, get drunk while playing, get totally wasted, pass out, repeat.

We unfold the dirty napkin and call the number of the number one fan we have in Maine who hooks us up with somebody's Uncle

Something or somebody's small temporarily vacated extra apartment. When we get there we first suss out the individual flop options, then it's time to go explore Bah Habah, or as it is also known by its spelling, Bar Harbor. Turns out there isn't all that much going on for wild retro rockers in town other than an "old man bar" we find, which I guess technically was an old man pub, but nevertheless it was pretty old and beat down which for me rendered it technically "60s".

The next day the Canadian border crossing goes much more positively for whatever reason and we still have forty-eight hours left before the next soundcheck in Toronto. This is Brad country, and he too has some relations who own a crash pad for us in the form of a vacated summer cabin. We are all aboot it and are excited for what will officially resemble a vacation abroad, replete with lakeside seclusion. There's no better cabin than a cabin already stocked with everything you need in it when the people who put it there are a million miles away.

Canadian cabin cotton fever

Having been off the highway for a bit, we ride the rolling Canadian country roads and onto a smaller road which after a while leads to a dirt road which a few miles away babushka's further down to a bumping trail where we bounce along under the thick treed sky until finally reaching a meadow clearing. The cabin is off in the distance and beyond a glistening clear blue lake for as far as the eye can see.

I get to the door first and for my own "who knows if there's unknown old people with shotguns inside" reasons, give the door a knock-knock.

"Who's there?" Jeff jokes from behind me.

I look back over my shoulder at him and smile, refraining from making a dumb joke. Brad is here now with the lockbox key and the rest of the guys are gathering behind him with various levels of interest in whatever they're wanting from the pending situation inside. Actually, since I have you captive here, the least I can do is torture you. OK, how many BJM members does it take to screw in a lightbulb? One. Anton, duh. But if he's going to screw it in live then six to eight depending on whether or not there is a keyboardist this time or if we are in between third guitar players.

We all go inside and as I'm the person behind the person who didn't flip the light switch on, I flip it, but nothing. The ceiling bulb is burnt out. In Brad logic, my being the finger that flipped it makes me the tambourine fix-it man and he points me to the laundry (!) room where the extra lightbulbs probably are. I find one, take off the ceiling light cover and change the bulb. Solo.

It's late in the day by now so we all proceed to get pretty wild and crazy with pantry products, but before we can even get the grapes peeled suddenly a worry has spread from down the hall, then is quickly working its way around the living room and now into the kitchen. Jeff is in the bedroom having some type of seizure.

"...I-i-i-it's O-O-O-K-K-K, c-c-c-co-cot-t-t-on fe—ver", he stutter-spit-shakes out. I guess that's when you accidentally get some cotton ball in the stuff and then once in your veins, makes you shake uncontrollably and could kill you. He's in the bed holding the bottom thin sheet up to his chin. I look around the room for what to do and see everyone else looking around the room, and then we all look back to Jeff. We're in the middle of nowhere.

Through locked jaw, he's still stutter-insisting it's OK, that this has happened before. Is he working through it? I can't tell because he's not lying back or sitting up—he's in between the two in a vibrating state like he's stuck there. It looks like someone hit the pause button on the VCR and froze him in still vibration. Brad is in the kitchen flapping through the first emergency pages of the telephone phone book for the closest nowhere-near-here hospital.

Anton, Charles and I are slowly closing in on Jeff as his uncontrollable shaking, which was already like something out of *The Exorcist*, starts to ramp up even more. There is no visible self-control of the situation yet he's adamant about not wanting to go to the hospital for what must be reasons beyond what's happening to him in this room right now, like not wanting to face the lifestyle-change music, but despite whatever it is he wishes, *he is not in control of this*. We're sizing him up for physical removal and then Brad comes rushing in when suddenly Jeff just stops like somebody yanked his power cord out of the wall. Gravity takes back control and he flops down onto the bed for the first time since this whole robot-jerk seizure started.

He opens his eyes. "Fuck, yew guys, that was *weeird*," he drawls in exhaustion.

"Fuuck," somebody, or maybe it was all of us, exhale and deflate back down from puffing stress balloons.

Fuck! Dope is still a thing with one of us.

After dinner we watch *Scream*, I guess because "movie nights" are rare in the traveling drunkard trade. It's also one of the only movies here and we're already doing the remote cabin in the woods slasher bait thing, but mostly we are just needing something a bit lighthearted and stupid after what happened.

We all drape ourselves over the living room surfaces while Brad switches us from overhead light to television glow. The movie starts and the funeral plot commences as the be-robed slasher diligently performs his nightly knife errands to the tune of Nick Cave hitting the US mainstream jackpot cauldron, and it doesn't take long to realize we are temporarily slaves to the groan.

I end up inadvertently providing the most exciting part of the film when about an hour or four in, just as the killer is once again flying into the shot in close-up view to his or her signature musical shriek cue, knife held high, that glass ceiling light cover I'd screwed back on earlier suddenly comes dropping down to the center of the floor. A flash of TV light refracts off of one of its pointed corners much like a slasher's knife blade as we all, well, scream at this out-of-nowhere 3-D effect. Realizing what has just happened, we all laugh and it is a true and welcome release.

We hit Toronto and head straight to the Queen West area, which fully represents its British roots and is kinda like a genteel version of London's Camden Market goes Haight Street. We start working our way around the neighborhood while slowly losing one another until Anton, Billy and I are spotted by the 60s Canadian ambassador Davie Love, who is DJ'ing our after-party tonight. With his Oliver Reed-like barrel chest and apostle-of-Paul-Weller haircut he strides us through the streets, proud chin pointing high like a figurehead on the bow of a ship over to his bar, The Yellow Submarine, which is you guessed it, completely Beatles-themed with *Yellow Submarine* the lead motif.

John, Paul, George and Ringo are peeping through the portholes in cartoon style along the wall at the backs of Charles and Brad who are already there sitting at the bar. Charles greets me with a "Hey, nice purse" referring to the vintage 60s Canadian Airlines shoulder bag I've just scored down the street. "It's a flight bag," I correct for the first time of what will be a lifelong defense of my preferred choice of street-strutting accessory.

Sensing our immediate desire to never leave this place again, Davie soon herds us over to his nearby apartment decorated fully to 60s specs. It is in fact so thoroughly period-accurate, that without the slight diffusion of grainy 60s film stock it almost doesn't look real to me. In fact, that's the problem—it's *too* real. Too clean, too of this reality.

That night we play El Mocambo, the modest-sized club where in 1977 the Stones unforgettably performed a string of shows for the forgotten *Love You Live* album. The event is more famous nowadays for Keith Richard's big heroin bust the day after that nearly bought him seven years in a Canadian prison.

The Sunny-Side Up Eggs vs Both Kinds of Bacon

After a stop-off in Boston we continue gigging our way westward and then go *back* up into Canada where we will then continue to play our way along the snow-plowed trail to the few gig-able spots toward the West Coast, being Winnipeg, Calgary, and Vancouver, then exit stage down into Washington for the big *Price Is Right* Plinko board drop to our most historically familiar towns of Portland, Frisco and Los Angeles to conclude the 187 show-long *Strung Out in Heaven* tour.

Thankfully, we are driving past Saskatoon this time, which had been one of our stops coming from the other direction on the first round of Canadian shows we'd ever done, now some months ago. It was a big roadhouse-style rock bar in lumberjack country with a city arts funding program purchased from the ninety-nine cent store, which is even less after you convert it into Canadian cents. There were exactly four drunken brawls in the crowd during the course of our set. On the plus side, the place came with free lodging upstairs, until we saw what the free lodging upstairs entailed. Small claustrophobic rooms heavily populated with bunk beds that were originally barracks for the Paul Bunyan Brigade of the lumber trade that had over the decades morphed into a sketchy run-down Tenderloin-type of hostel hotel with a *Twin Peaks* make-under and an activities schedule right out of *The Shining*.

We were divvied up into two rooms. The one I was in had a healthy smear of human blood on the wall or else the mosquitoes here come as big as your fist. Drunk haunted groaning could be heard through one wall, while drunken yelling could be heard through the wall on the opposite side. Starting at around 3 a.m. the sound of heavy boots lumbering back and forth across the wooden hall leading to somebody or something knocking on our door every hour or so. We didn't answer. The Sonny James earworm "A Little Bit South of Saskatoon" provided me with the internal nightmare jukebox as it ran through my head over and over.

Things go this, that, and the other and soon enough we are rolling up to the Canadian Border Patrol back into the US again with nothing up our sleeves, or our rear ends for that matter, but regardless these experiences never make it any easier on the sphincter. Border patrol offices are technically just stations where you cross over borders, but they are also like police stations where everyone is a potential suspect of who knows what until you can prove otherwise. One's life could change forever in an instant. That's the vibe, and they go out of their way to make you aware of it. This is usually the case for any indoor room designed-for-waiting that has no magazines or snack machines or anything like pinball.

Slowly, we are moving our way up in one of the vehicle lines as the band banter is in full swing.

"...I would go as far as to say that you can actually hear his beard in the music." Charles is discussing the influence Paul's beard had on his songs for The Beatles *Let It Be* album. "Even without watching the studio performance from the *Let It Be* movie, whenever I hear that song or his others from that album, the beard is still there, you can *hear* his beard." I ponder bringing up my own brushes with influential facial hair in front of Anton for the first time when suddenly it's our turn at the drive-thru booth. Brad reaches out our stack of passports to the window agent, who then begins flipping through them like maybe he'll just start stamping away like we're normal folk, but he and we all know what's going to happen next. It's only a matter of how long he's going to prolong his page-flip improvising in the scene. "Pull over there, please, and unlock the trailer." Not quite a minute.

"Okey-dokey," Brad says with a pointer-finger salute in the only direction choice on the border office menu and into one in the row of inspection parking spaces. It only takes a moment for an agent to come out while strapping some rubber gloves on. We watch the fingertips jiggle like a car dealership flailing balloon man's do as he heads straight for the back while Brad opens the trailer. A few white plastic fold-out tables are scattered around and he positions one next to the trailer where we can all see him do his inspection routine from the rear-view mirrors. Brad is climbing back into the driver's seat as we all get our best angles of the reflected proceedings. The first suitcase he pulls out is my battered white hard case with "J.O.B." pieced together on the topside with black gaffer tape.

"What are they doing?" Adam now casualishly-like wonders. Apparently, Adam, who's been doing his first-ever border crossings in a band vehicle, didn't realize that we've just been "lucky" so far and there is always a high probability of being searched, especially for a band who have previously been busted and sent home before.

"Ahh, that's mine," I say by way of providing an announcer's commentary track, "Looks like they're gonna give us the full service here," I add while watching him poke through my clothes now in the backward glass view, knowing I haven't had anything on me for a while now.

Suddenly, "Oh shit...Oh shit." It's Adam sitting behind me. A realization of some sort has just settled inside him. My suitcase goes back in and out comes Brad's. I doubt he has anything on him because I heard him on his hotel room phone before the show last night asking a friend if it would be "snowing tomorrow".

"Oh shit oh shit..." is now being mantra worry-whispered from behind.

Then the border officer pulls Adam's bag out of the trailer.

"Oh no! *Oh shit oh shit oh shit..."*

We are like an audience to his breakdown, but the seats are facing the other way so without the visual, we only hear it, kinda like Charles hearing Paul's beard.

Brad finally addresses Adam's situation *"What* is your *problem,* man?"

"...I— I have something."

Charles turns around. *"Really?!* That may have been a good thing to know before we got to this border, considering what's happening right now."

So, the play-by-play of what the agent sees goes like this: it's a maroon canvas suitcase that zips from all the way around along the edge, on which the agent now begins the zipper journey. *Zzzzzzz...*

"Fuck fuck fuck fuck..."

Then he flips the hood up and the very first item in view and right on top of his clothes and everything else is a metal cigarette case. He picks it up.

"Fuck fuck fuck fuck..."

He clicks it open, using the extra focus needed due to the blue rubber gloves he's wearing.

"Fuck! Oh shit oh shit oh shit..."

When the Canadian border cop opens the cigarette case, rather than finding any cigarettes, or even a naughty but friendly doobie, there is only a white paper bindle with "1G" hand scribed on it.

Despite having only gone through three of our suitcases, they stop here as what was unfolded in the bindle (one gram of coke probably minus a couple bumps) is already more than enough to send us back to our own home-team law enforcement. We are all marched inside the office where we wait and we wait some more. Anton is strangely silent. I am not so strangely silent, as after all of my close shaves with the drug law enforcers and never getting busted despite for months risking thirty-to-life every day laying acid sheets or all the all-nighters capping hundreds of ecstasy pills, after hundreds of party baggies on my person over the years while raging a one-man never-ending spin-cycle party throughout San Francisco without ever getting caught inebriated enough to "blow it", I was now for the first time being busted and it was solely because of someone else.

Finally, after all that rebel bragging I just did, they don't bust us. But they do let us know they have notified the US border and are sending us there to be busted. We all get in the van and slowly move our way down like a pat of butter melting on the frying pan from the 80s "This is your brain on drugs" commercial.

"I *told* you we could wait," Brad berate-mutters in an animated way from the corner of his mouth." I already made the call for when we get there. But like it matters now."

"*Greaat.* Well, that was smart. I guess the tour's over," Anton sighs.

"Fuuuuuuuuuuck," Jeff drawls after finally sitting up in the small space he's taken over between the last bench seat and the rear doors. His delivery seems sleepy, yet the amount of "u"s used gives it an implied impression similar to not wanting to tell the dinner party you just burnt the dinner.

Billy doesn't add on to the choir of groans and bemoans as he usually doesn't when there's nothing to further to add to the obvious, once again exemplifying his high-level powers of traveler's zen.

Then the US border patrol drive-thru booth comes into view as we have no choice but to drive by our own free will to be busted for drugs. The situation has been called in by the angry neighbors so now they're waiting for us, already armed with all the details so there is no need for any back-and-forth, just "park there and go inside", the toll bummer booth Officer Stern instructs.

Once inside the police station-like interior of the building, we all take a high school principal's office standard-issue plastic chair lining the back wall. It's only a few beats before an agent comes out through a side door and shout-inquires, "OKaay, which wonna y'all had the coke-cane?"

All fingers go up pointing at Adam who is kinda perfectly positioned right in the middle of us, giving the proceedings a momentary gangster-themed 1940s film musical vibe. *It was him shee, meah.*

"OK, you. Come here with me." Adam disappears behind the door. *Click.* We sit in the office stillness and watch the waiting. People come in, wait, and go.

"Can I use the bathroom please, officer?" Jeff inquires with a raised hand from our Saturday school area. One of the short-sleeved blue button-ups from behind the glass motions the go ahead, and as Jeff prances into the toilets the corridor buzzer blares him inside the men's room. I'm surprised they even let him, considering.

First Brad, then Anton, Charles, Billy, me, then Jeff all take our individual turns in a back room different from wherever Adam is. We all get the same line of questioning, *Do you have any drugs? Do you use drugs? Drugs? Drugs?! Drugs.* Drugs? I can answer all of these questions feeling like I look at least half honest by phrasing it in half-truths: "Nope, Just booze."

I'm not held long and when I get let back to society, the gang's all there sitting in the plastic molded chairs except Adam and Jeff.

For whatever reason, probably because it's almost dinnertime, we are all let go. Despite this being a situation you want to end and get away from as quickly as possible, Jeff actually asks if he can go to the bathroom again, and surprisingly he is able to. The rest of us wait in the van.

We're all receiving our black-belt status in readiness to go when Jeff comes skipping out the double doors and jumps into his private rental van conversation pit in the back of the van. As we pass over and into Washington state's freedom, we all get to group-grilling Adam.

"What did they do?" Brad asks.

"He made me take off all my clothes," he says, shaking his head yet grinning with relief.

"Everything?" Charles inquires for the rest of us. We are all finding this pretty humorous, as you can imagine.

"Yeah, everything. Then I had to stand with my nose touching the wall."

"Oh shit! Then what?" Jeff shouts excitedly from the back.

"He told me to spread 'em and cough."

Dean and Charles in the van with Adam not long before losing his innocence to US border customs

We are all laughing pretty good at this and then Jeff secretly taps me on the shoulder from his hotel blanket pile behind all the seats. "Hey, look what I had." He's cupping in the palm of his hand a ball of tar heroin the size of a golf ball. Despite my negative feelings toward that stuff, I am rightly impressed. Apparently, when he'd gone to the bathroom the first time, he'd simply set it on top of the paper towel dispenser and left it there. Then, after his turn being searched and questioned, he asks permission to go back to the bathroom the second time, when we knew we were on our way out again, and grabbed it back off from top of the paper towel dispenser.

The parable of this double drug busting is to exemplify the difference between the pro and the rookie. The difference in the drive between wanting a drug and needing one and the measures of importance between "party kicks" and survival of lifestyle, and sadly dear reader, there was yet even more in this vein to come.

The Final Blow It

The *Strung Out in Heaven* tours are all finished and it's time to start album number two under the TVT contract. Jeff had gone back to San Francisco, and despite another brand-new BJM band house, this time at 2323 Merrywood Drive in rock dreams fulfilleds-ville Laurel Canyon, Anton had fallen back on the junk sword and Ondi had long given up filming us and wasn't planning on getting back to it anytime soon. She'd decided to focus on keeping herself busy with the Dandys' still growing success and other less "depressing" projects. We weren't supposed to burn out and she wasn't supposed to burn out on us and the whole thing was very different from what it had first started out to be just three short years ago now.

I'd been given the tour of the place and was included in the residency plan, but the read on what life would be like up there, even being in such an amazing house of stilted and window wonder-walled mid-century Canyon space-cruiser replete with indoor sauna stature, there's no way I can live there, no matter how much I want to. It's the same situation as Echo Park, except this time with no Matt, no Dean, no other band members to help support each other. I couldn't go through that alone again even despite Viper Room owner Johnny Depp's backyard being within maraca-loaded potato launcher distance.

I would still periodically visit, hoping the next time I could envision myself in this mix, but always went away spooked and empty handed. As it was, all of my tools to deal with this kind of thing were too worn and stripped. I would have to wait it out.

Instead, I've been hooked up with a neighbor of Charles's who's got a spare room to rent me and TVT has agreed to pay my meager rent there, but that's it. And just like that, life turns normal again. Or at least the real plot to this whole story has found a new place to hide out for a while. All the freedom-flowing momentum of the last few years suddenly stops, and now everything has flipped from living in a Monkees-style band house and touring to moving in with a stranger to a pedestrian second-story two-bedroom apartment at 1347 North McCadden Place, Hollywood. It's a sleepy little street but within walking distance of central Hollywood's tourist attraction action. LA is cool enough for not being SF, and I need somewhere to stick it out a while until the BJM curse lifts and we can get back to where we once belonged, or something.

The Cat & Fiddle Pub on Sunset Boulevard is just a ten-minute walk from where I'm renting and along with The Egyptian Theater, this place has become the other shining light that can briefly guide me out of my situational doom. Owned and operated by Kim Gardner, the bass player from top-tier 60s mod outfits The Creation and Ron Wood's first band, The Birds, it was a regular destination for UK groups on tour and permanent British expats alike.

On any given night you might see regular Dave Davies of The Kinks sitting at the small corner bar waxing poetic about the Swinging London daze with Kim from behind the bar, or Morrissey sequestered in one of the large indoor dining area corner booths. Tim Burgess from The Charlatans lives in LA now and has become a part of the local party crew. Then there were other English regular characters like Harry The Dog, and a coterie of silver rooster-haired vets from various 70s English rock star party crews that had so far refused to hang up their straws.

I'm here early enough to get a stool at the bar and Kim is down with the BJM cause so I get my first for free. By my second the place is jumping. Then Charles shows up, bestowing on me his usual greeting that goes: flash of bemusement followed by a warm-tinged inquiry as to the current goings-on. I sort my report while pints are poured, then splits to see if Randy's here or there or somewhere. It's really filling up now, which excavates the realization that this is Friday. The crowd of drinkless empty hands behind me is growing by the minute, causing the smaller more intimate private-party dining room to be opened up.

The empty hand-wave recedes a little and I order another beer, but soon enough the tide starts to come back in until it's a nonstop brush barrage of sleeves reaching over my shoulders pushing money in and pulling teetering foamy pints back out which is annoying so I duck out. I don't see any of my crew among the full tables, so I let myself blow in the breeze a little until wandering by the windows of the small packed second dining area. I'm bored now and so I peek inside for some people judg— I mean, watching. There are ten or so small tables clustered tight together, filled with mostly older members of the Comfy Jeans with Blazers Committee. Servers do interpretive bar tray dances throughout, swishing and leaning and placing, and all of this doesn't look like a very comfortable dining exp— *Whoa!* That's Peter Fonda sitting at one of the crowded tables...

Now, you've already heard plenty from me about *Easy Rider* and it being one of my favorite things ever. I've watched it dozens of times over the years, leading to some less than dignified scenarios and it's odd to me how such a cool film brings out such uncool situational behavior from me, but I can't help but...erm, "blow it" with what at the end of the day is just a movie.

I stalk-in-place for about thirty more seconds and then Charles walks up. "Look, it's Peter Fonda!" I whisper with raised-voice persona. "Huh, no way," he confirms with far less excitement. Then I see Peter Fonda catch me out of the corner of his eye. He turns his head and looks right at us. I've only got this instant so I quickly flash him the "thumbs up", a primitive salute but all the situation will afford me in this sudden chance to right my past wrongs and hopefully get a gesture of "Cool, man" recognition.

Instead, his face takes on the classic "What the fuck do you want?" annoyed expression, while adding the "Whatever" upturned palms and high-shoulder-shrug mime combo. My erect thumb slowly deflates back down as he returns his attention to his companions.

Life idles idly along until I get an offer to put on my own weekly night at a new small bar and live venue called Goldfingers. For a starting fee of a hundred bucks, I can book two bands of my choosing and DJ whatever I want in between. Not a lot of dosh considering who supposedly owns the place, but with TVT only paying for my room rent, I was now booking my own night and I had enough friends in bands who also had friends in bands and so on and so on, making for a enough so-so's to keep it going indefinitely.

They give my new night a minuscule ad in the *LA Weekly* music section and the morning it comes out I grab a copy of the paper and go out for breakfast at Highland Grounds, my neighborhood spot. I've got my *LA Weekly* and so I lay it flat and start pinching paper corners and flapping for the supposed existing print ad.

The waitress comes, I order and flip more paper. The couple next to me leaves, allowing my elbows to fan out a little to eight and four o'clock. I find the ad and pull the paper up close to my face to inspect it thoroughly for correctness. Firstly, there's my name as DJ...the bands are listed correctly...club address. Cool. I set the paper back down on the table to reveal film directors Quentin Tarantino and Peter Bogdanovich sitting next to me. I pull the paper back up.

They see my private eye-esque move and hesitantly start up some pretty stiff self-conscious small talk. I'm sure this must be a common thing for super-recognizable famous people, choosing an off-the-radar spot to hopefully hang like normal people, but then you wind up sitting crammed in with some super film nerd, or even just a guy reading the paper with the coolest-looking sideburns ever, which they probably really dig, I'm sure, but then you can't get any real conversation going because everything you say can and will be re-blabbed by the cool sideburns guy to his whole circle of cool-sideburns people, then they will tell all the mustaches and the mustaches will tell the beards and then the evil Van Dykes hiding inside of the full beards will use the information for some nefarious purposes because that's just what Van Dykes do, especially here in Hollywood. Although this is a great time to ask these guys how historically in the Hollywood movies that particular style of facial hair profiling came about, I just leave them alone because I know that's what they are after here. It's the least I can do considering how much I love *Paper Moon* and *Jackie Brown*.

So instead of talking shop, like discussing the stylistic choices Bogdanovich made while shooting *The Last Picture Show*, like replicating the film style from that same 1950s era that it takes place in, or praising what some critics are calling the lineage from Ford to Kurosawa to Leone to Tarantino, instead, it's literally like, "Boy, I'm hungry" or "Nice weather we're having" or "The traffic wasn't too bad" and "I hear this place is good". It's like they were undercover spies or something. Here I am in the cinema fantasy-ville that is Los Angeles, and every time I run into one of its architects, they're "off the clock", to which I would probably say if anyone would really like to know, fair enough. I guess.

Meanwhile, as far as my own architectural project goes, word comes from on high that Anton has it not only bad again, but worse than the unbearable *Strung Out in Heaven* recording days, which you don't even know how bad that was, because at this pre-published time he is still my close friend. I know in a weird way he *knows* what he is doing, that he could quit but doesn't want to, but would rather burn it all down.

Gordon's Heavy Foot

I get back to "The Compound", which was the name given to our small cluster of neighbors consisting of Charles, SF music scene expats Randy and Christof, Helmut, and my new roommate. I creak open the tall wooden medieval-ish gate door and head into the fence-enclosed yard, hidden from outside view. Then up the painted green cement steps to the second level, down the outdoor vine-lined walkway and through the living room. I close the door of my little drywall cell behind me.

My room's view is of Charles's tree-covered small house and large open backyard of patchy green grass and growths. I gaze down and try to imagine Miranda's pup tent lifestyle down in the yard, as she'd apparently been camping there while in between apartments recently.

Bang bang bang! on the door. It's my new roommate who it's turned out is a raging depressive alchy and he's spouting some fucking surly drunken nonsense so I decide it's better to just leave again. I get back down the steps and then stop to decide where to go, which is in itself a risky move, attempting two trips through these yard grounds so close in time together. I'll have to proceed with great stealth if I'm not going to be spotted by the senior-citizen-complex landlord Gordon and have my ear talked off for a minimum of twenty minutes. He's the "sweet little old man" type, but that's just the problem: it's impossible to cut him off and he is a master of conversation pause destruction. You could be standing there with the same mouthful of "OK, well I gotta go..." until almost passing out. Does he know this is the deal and is doing it on purpose? Definitely probably, but that's the mind smoke-and-mirror game earned rightfully by many an elderly. He's also the owner of the building, so there's that.

Inside this fenced perimeter, it's one of those LA mini jungles with trees and bushes that have been overgrowing for years into all shapes and sizes until nearly concealing his ground-level house. The second-level stairs are along the side of it and once up them you were pretty much safe because he didn't make it up those more than once a week to water.

The ground floor, on the other hand, he watered constantly, always seeming to be lurking in and out of the foliage with his garden hose. His one good giveaway was that he talked to either himself or the plants constantly, so before rounding a corner or committing to the front or back ways out, you could stop and listen for which direction the mutters were coming from, which usually worked most of the time. Although, even if you didn't hear anything, you still had to creep like a soldier way behind enemy lines, yet with striding intent as suddenly at any moment from behind the bushes he's there. "OH!" Gordon exclaims. He's caught me. Twenty minutes.

His white, short-on-the-sides with shock-topped hair wisps straight up, which complements his "resting face" of the same nature, his jeepers-peepers perma-peeled all the way back, grey-green and foggy adding to the eternal look of disbelief in whatever he's maybe seeing and probably hearing. His height comes up to about my chest, age-rounded in that circular way almost a century of gravity will do you, as if he'd been tall and skinny once, but over time had been smooshed into curved carnival funhouse-mirror reflection size.

He goes into all of the things he's now talking about until he suddenly kicks it up with an overacting animated tone. Maybe it's just normal tone in his mind-world. "Saaay, you look like a big *strong* man, can I get you to help me bring back my new toaster oven? It's right over there down at the mall on Beverly. Will you come with me? I can't carry it back with me, you see?"

I did see, but "right over there" is actually still a ten-minute drive away and I'd already lost over an hour of my life in episodic politeness and who knows how many days the other guys had spent incrementally so far over the years, so one could rightfully worry that by going off-site you might get sucked into a bottomless chatterbox and never get out again. I also can't help but feel he's profiled me as the least busy one around here, which is in fact a correct deduction, and yet even though I do in fact have nothing to do, I don't really want to deal with this.

Meanwhile the truth is, his problem is actually more genuine than almost all of my neighbor friend's usual self-imposed dramas. Still, he's right and just looking at him, it's easy to see how impossible it would be for him to even get his arms around a toaster oven box, let alone carry it around with a toaster oven in it. It's nobody's fault we all slowly fall apart.

"We can just go straight there and come straight back?"

"Ah yah, *shuuuuuure...*" he says with chin in chest like it's a long celebratory tuba note.

"OK."

We climb into his little beat-up green Karmann Ghia and he revs up the internal orchestra of factory-made and wobbly worn-out-sounding mechanics blasting throughout its rattling dinged and rusting shell.

As he gets this classic-sports-car-gone-jalopy up onto Sunset, we commence with the peas in an escape-pod existence that is our customary situational driving small talk.

"*Soo*, now, what is it *you* do?" he asks me for the fourth time since I'd moved in.

"I'm a musician."

"Ohhhhh, a muusiciann! Y'know, I used to play tennis with Gary Puckett of Gary Puckett & The Union Gap! For years!" he tells me for the fourth time since I'd moved in. Apparently, it's his one musician-related story and despite my never getting into those records, it's the kind of personal trivia I have no problem hearing about multiple times.

"What instrument do *you* play?"

"Percussion," I answer, trying to beef it up a bit for some reason.

"Ohhh, I love the drums!" He starts playing pretend drums on the wheel which looks more like bongo playing but the actual sounds that are coming out of his mouth sound like Godzilla stomps which abruptly end when he accidentally hits the car horn. Luckily, this serves to snap him back into the non-drum-playing driving reality where he's been slowly veering us into oncoming traffic. He now quickly corrects our lane disposition while I slide my seatbelt on. "Well, it's more like hand percussion. Like tambourines and stuff," I say, trying to move us past almost just dying.

"*Tambouriine?* Ohh!" he exclaims, now turning his face in my direction to accentuate his being impressed by all this while I guess I take over watching the road ahead for us. "Well, you'll have to come over and play your tambourine for me sometime. Must be awwfully good!" He's about to rear-end somebody so I "Hey!' loudly and he hits the brakes.

After an "Ohh jeeez" we are able to accelerate again while I'm grappling with the mental image of me doing a solo tambourine performance for Gordon in his living room. Now I'm really on the lookout and up ahead I can see the traffic light turn yellow in the still very far-off next intersection. Gordon stays true to his current senior cruising speed while the light has turned comfortably red way before we even have a chance to blow the first crosswalk a kiss.

Facing toward us in the opposite lane is a car that's been waiting to make the yielding crossover left turn, which they can finally do, but it's now so late in the game its right of way has turned wrong with the bygone light change, which they point out angrily to the tune of a extended single-note honk with released finger bird out the window accompaniment.

This all turns Gordon's face red, as he then rumbles with chin in chest about that son-of-a-so-and-so being *just crazy* or something. I guess LA-style "road rage" is for life around here.

Then just a few blocks later it's Gordon's turn to make the same style left turn but the car going the opposite way mimics the exact situation in reverse that had just played out with the finger bird handler from before, except this time everybody in the whole intersection abruptly stops and a heated car-horn argument ensues right there, translating inner aggressions which also allows the other cars to chime in some horny commentary on how they all think this is going so far. Soon everyone has honked out their opinions on the situation, which then green-lights us all to proceed at once to never again remembering what has just happened here, regardless of direction. Gordon's face has turned red again, revealing that this red face changing color thing works on both sides of the same situation.

The Beverly Center is a gigantic shopping mall and cineplex that I haven't been back to since Matt, Dean and I saw *Austin Powers* here and met face to face with its mainstream false-grooviness that came in the form of being "Yeah, baby" cat-called by normos of all ages all the way out the doors. So, it's back into the belly of the *Yeah, baby* beast I go, but luckily that movie is old now and the sequel has yet to be released, plus I'm only wearing a black pullover with matching jeans and Gordon isn't wearing any of his old 70s swinger garb meant to impress Gary Puckett, of Gary Puckett & The Union Gap, so we just pick up the pre-paid toaster oven from Macy's and get out of there yeah-baby free.

It was on the way back when it all hit me. No, not a convoy of semi-truck drivers all high on cocaine, but a life revelation. Here I was with Gordon, who'd lived a very long life and was now just passing what little time he had left before it was all over, and here I was in the car with him passing what few minutes I had left before he killed us both, and all that I had been doing with my time for the last few months was mostly just sitting around waiting for the band situation to miraculously return back to "normal", but the only thing I knew for sure was that "normal" was nowhere in sight. I had to make a change. A big one. The last move I have available with any chance of having an effect on this dire situation would be to pull my *Five Easy Pieces*-style ending for real this time. My second "big disappearance".

"That's *it*," I say out loud to my empty room, the same way I'd done in my little black box inside the warehouse three years ago, except that time it was me who needed help. While all I can think of to do now is just blow this blow town, I still owe it to myself to go over to Anton's house and finally speak my piece. It's about an hour-and-a-half walk from where I am, but unlike here, walking isn't such a big deal if you're from San Francisco.

After many long blocks of mostly strip malls I make it to the mouth of Laurel Canyon Boulevard and up the winding forested canyon road up into the hills of the original 60s rock dream. Not too far up the winding stretch is the Laurel Canyon Country Market, where the Canyon's 60s celebrity counterculture characters would make their neighborhood beer runs. The sun begins to set once past the market, the sidewalk tails off into a dirt trail and not much further evaporates away and all that's left is the road shoulder divide-bump, that is if one wants to balance on it as they continue forward while traffic roars by in the dark just inches away. The road is all upward curves and any one of the whizzing cars flying past could easily take me out with just the right circumstance of lax negotiation of turns into the succession of swerves. I continue forward in a state of total numbness, and rather than care, I imagine the spirits of Laurel Canyon past like Gene Clark, Mama Cass, Frank Zappa or Jim Morrison roaring past in ghost sports cars. Despite this, I don't put my thumb out.

I walk about the same distance it took from the mouth to the market and make it up to Merrywood Drive, a small and precarious bumpy dirt road carved out on the side of a large hill that leads to just a handful of houses. I'd always hated being a passenger in a car while driving on this, with zero room for steering error and usually with someone driving while turned around talking with joint hanging out of their mouth wanting the liquor bottle back. Despite the circumstances, this leg of the visitation is oddly the most comfortable yet by having both feet on the ground this time.

The old Harry Houdini Estate is down below, but the connection doesn't dawn on me that I'm about to be reprising my own disappearing act. Again. I walk around the now darkened bend to the very expensive single-story on stilts and the door is wide open so I walk in. It's easy to see the house is covered in chaos despite all the lights being off except for a few strands of purple and blue Christmas lights.

Every week at my Goldfingers night successive rounds of friendly well-wishers would stop by the DJ booth excited for my new night, but also just as many musical peer "friends" that seemingly wanted me to know from behind the bush they were gleefully beating around, that word on the LA avenues and boulevards was BJM appeared to be the next band to go up in junkie flames. Implying that we were just the next in line of Los Angeles's too many to count almost-was's's's's's's's's's's —sorry, I just need to relax in a calming drone just a sec—'s's's's's's's's's's to explode at the finish line.

Accounts full of shocking sights and sounds were piling up from visitors coming back down from the Canyon top. All the faker friends, counterfeit colleagues with their "support" and "enthusi-asms", all coming to light as having just been some sort of disguise that can now be revealed. Their smiles are still there, but they have switched directions. Now they take in rather than give out. So much relish stuck in their teeth. Musicians, especially LA musician types, tend to make a big competition out of everything because we're all after the same things, and there are *so* many bands and yet only so many resources. Only so many dates on the venues' calendars, only so many pages in the magazines, only so many groups a record label can sign. Yet, regardless of BJM's success level at any of the stages along the way, from busking for cigarette money to belting down one-hundred dollar shots, it was always the current stage that made me whole, simply because I was doing what I wanted to be doing and that made every step a good one. Any-which-whatever way, I had my I-me-mine, or at least I thought I did. I wasn't even thinking about all this shit, but they wanted me to. Fuckers.

Anton is in the kitchen just past the entryway. Upon seeing me he goes directly into talking about how great everything currently is for the band, but three sarcastic responses later he exclaims in hazed surprise with pointed finger, "You just came up here to be mad at me!" I've cancelled my "big speech" because I've been here before and I know it makes no difference. The jig is double-down-up and in less than five minutes after I'd arrived I leave to walk all the way back. What I don't fully realize is that I've just quit BJM. The Big Something in the Sky or Whatever It Is had just swiped the board clean, and now I was to be cast adrift within the belly of a Greyhound bus on the concrete seas leading me to all things I'd always wanted to avoid.

Beach Town Massacre

The Greyhound I'm riding pulls into the San Luis Obispo station. It's of the Spanish Revival architectural style and as we move in, I'm almost eye level with its red tile roof. With its exposed rafters and colorful decorative tiles it's much easier on the eye than all the other stations so far. The air here is arch-enemy arid and so I simply take a smoke out under the shady side of the bus and then just reboard, despite this being a thirty-minute stop.

Once back in my seat, I put my headphones back on and skip through the tracks of the Stones' album *Aftermath* to where I was before, which had been the last audible seconds of the fade-out to "Paint It Black". While I'm at it, I just skip over "Stupid Girl", because that song can be kind of annoying, honestly, and I will suggest to you now that it is the unconscious prototype for the much later semi-slapstick delivery narratives of songs like "She's So Cold", "Start Me Up" and many others, which is weird considering this is from the stone-cold cool period and many years before they had to regularly fumble to find something. I skip to the next and very righteous track, "Lady Jane".

Keith's gentle fingerpicking begins and I return to my window-gaze position, when suddenly I'm back on that same old mattress in that Upper Haight apartment watching *The Complete Rolling Stones on Ed Sullivan* VHS cassette like it's Saturday-morning cartoons, because, well, it is.

It's weird how awkward Mick could be on some of these mid-60s performances. Here, the overly acted royal bowing gestures on "Lady Jane" are borderline goofy. It would still be a few years before they would invite Ike & Tina Turner to open up for them, which so happened to be as soon as they'd been legally allowed to tour America again after having to sacrifice Brian to Satan to do so. It was on tour that Tina had inadvertently given Jagger the stage moves template he would be emulating for the rest of his days, which I get, as I was taken to see Ike & Tina a year later inside my mother's stomach and I too was inspired to pull similar moves from within her tummy dance chamber.

For now, on the TV screen there is to me what looks like a competition going on between frontman Mick and original band conceptualizer and leader Brian. Visually, the higher confidence lies with Brian, with his customary to this period nod and a wink at Mick as the girls scream equally for the two of them. Brian is clearly the master of ceremonies, having just personally elevated them from a blues cover band with a psychedelicized makeover introducing sitars, marimbas, flutes, harpsichord, Eastern bells, maracas, piano, and for this tune, "Lady Jane", the dulcimer. Brian's hand is bandaged and broken, which adds to the rebel menace and he plays it with aggression despite the injury.

Musical lore and narcotics legend has it that the lyrical subject of our romantically exasperated protagonist, Mick, is proclaiming that he must leave his "Lady Ann" for "Lady Jane", which any head will tell you is code slang for amphetamines and Mary Jane, as in, like, weed, man. Still, shortly after the release of this song, Mick, Keith, Marianne Faithful and others would be involved in the famous Redlands bust, which resulted in Mick having to go to court over a few speed pills, meaning the lyric is either a false anecdotal antidote, or he's two-timing his drugs. The British chapter of the Man was after all the Stones by now, and Brian was the next to be busted. This is all the reason why they couldn't get visas to tour America, specifically Brian, who was busted twice.

Back during these last of the simpler times on this *Ed Sullivan* appearance, Brian's wearing the same pinstripe suit he'd wear to his first court date, except in this performance the suit doesn't know it's going to be going to court soon and should probably get rid of that hash in the front right pocket.

The bus pulls off the freeway and into San Jose, the place of my birth and childhood days, but this isn't the last stop for my next whatever-will-be-will-be future. Greyhound doesn't have a direct route from LA to where I'm going, so I'll have to switch to a shuttle commuter bus for the final stretch of my spontaneous life reshuffle. We swing into a little loading roundabout, stop, and the door swings open in front of the large red-brick building that is Diridon station.

It's now sunny but not hot as I deboard and walk over to my new bus stop island area. Stepping up on its curb, I then survey all the nothing of interest. I look away before it causes boredom to take rule of this space I have to wait in for the next half an hour, and ask myself to remind me again of how I got to be standing here right now.

Yesterday I was sitting on another curb, that one next to a pay-phone on Highland and Fountain in Hollywood, flipping through my a-little-bit-bigger-than-a-little-black-book for a name. Any name that I could call up right then and head for the next day. The editor of *High Times* magazine in New York? Sounds nice, but I was already dreaming. Mod DJ Davie Love up in Toronto? I called him up but he couldn't help me out. I kept flipping, but then it was hard not to apply the reasons Davie had just given me to all of the other maybe possible names.

While it was fun to fantasize about a complete and total change, I realized that what I really wanted was to go home to San Francisco, but the last way I want to return there was by showing up with nothing but my couch-surfing board. Besides, who was even left there? All of my old party stations were gone, and even if they were still there, I'm not looking to party. At least not that way. I'm looking for a clean start. Then I realized I have a cousin in Santa Cruz, a beach town about an hour and a half south of San Francisco. I don't have much bread, so maybe I could crash there while working on a plan to get myself back in San Francisco, despite its currently quadrupled dot-com inflated rents. I dropped a quarter in the slot and got the go-ahead.

I told Charles the news and he put together a little thing for me in his backyard that night. Ondi showed up, without the camera, like capturing this didn't matter anymore. Maybe it didn't, but she did bring me a vintage suitcase for my "happy trails". Anton even came down from the Canyon for a first-time visit, but there was no dramatic scene, no big ending (the footage of me quitting BJM in the doc was actually from the first US tour, just so you know I haven't gone crazy), and in fact we barely even spoke. For the first time ever since knowing him, he didn't seem to know what to say.

It's dusk now as I get off the bus at the Santa Cruz Metro Center station on the edge of "downtown" and walk onto Pacific Avenue, which is like if Haight Street went Main Street Mayberry, where right across the street, lights turn on in Streetlight Records, which serves as a group idea lightbulb reminder that I'm going to have to find work. Reality now abounds in the winds of what-am-I-doing-here wonderings, when suddenly I follow my ears into a turnaround where two guys that look a little like they could be my younger brothers begin blasting what sounds like Acid Mothers Temple at their most blistering from inside a small bus-station pizza booth.

They are both wearing mirrored aviators and are completely covered in white flour, smiling large while they work with looks of self-satisfaction that somehow resemble an un-hippiefied cocaine-covered version of members from Electric Mayhem, *The Muppets'* rock band. This welcome straight-off-the-bus visual analogy will turn out to be the last time I think about powdered drugs for a long time, which is good.

I hook up with my cousin, and for the next couple of days explore the area while also fine-tuning the résumé Elise had suggested I start back in LA, when she'd like to have seen nothing more than watch me get some horrible day job. This was also around the time she and I visited Anton in the Kurt Cobain rehab, and these two things together would have really brought her entertainment center together.

My "plan B" had always and only been going back to working at a record store, which leaves no other reason to make copies of the résumé. Anything less than working with music, I told myself, would not do, and in that unfortunate scenario, I would go the simpler wayward traveling-stranger route of dishwasher at one of the many restaurants around here. Showing up at the back door, Levi's trucker jacket slung over my shoulder, one of the workers hadn't shown up that day and so I start immediately, wearing the clothes I have on. I get by for a while, renting a little hotel room where I write songs on an acoustic guitar about loving and drinking and life's hard road. Then I get discovered while playing at one of the little dive bars around here, and funnily enough, record a huge hit record and make my fortune.

Almost walking smack into a no-parking sign, I snap back into reality. I then head through the back entrance of Streetlight Records with my one résumé. It's a really big store, but this is around opening time so there's only a couple people sprinkled around. I ask the uninterested Asian guy sitting on a stool at the counter if a manager is here. He's got sort of a goth-rockabilly thing going, which is a good sign. Begrudgingly, he stops reading the CD liner notes to what looks like a Nick Cave album to get the store manager.

"There he is," he half-points, half-waves me away to the only person standing in the general area. The manager looks kind of rockabilly too, but not in the Elvis way, more like a blond hot-rod gearhead type. He's a bit older than me, with lots of tattoos coming out of his three-quarter sleeve shirt that's buttoned to the top. He seems pretty chill as we exchange standard inquiries and he proceeds to peruse my résumé.

"Gion? Are you Paul's brother?'

"Yeah, he's my older brother."

"Huh, I used to rent a shared garage space with him a little while back. Cool guy."

"Yeah," I agree while straightening my stance in that way you do when you suddenly realize you have an unexpected in.

"OK, wanna start tomorrow?"

Santa Cruz is a sleepy yet with one-eye-open beach town heavily populated with college students and elderly hippies of the baby boomer generation, and in general the type of place where armchair activists go to continue the fight by complaining about the state of the world to each other before and after meditation class.

Record store life here not only became about learning how to cope with unhip hippies and goofy college kids that as a species all loved Weezer, but also the glazed-over eyes and serene Manson Family-like demeanor of the California New Agers, the amount of white people with white dreads versus the almost complete absence of black people, but maybe the weirdest of all, considering, was the lack of old-school real-deal *Endless Summer*-style surfer bums. Where were all the AWOL kahunas that had made this place what it is in the first place? Were they still here among these people, just stylistically morphed into the incoming whatever this was? Or had they for some reason felt the need to flee the copious amount of tasty sacred waves? I can only suppose that they must have internally gone where everyone goes when they allow themselves to become something else.

As I've already bitched, the majority of the population here had either come to retire or attend college before leaving for somewhere else, which made it seem like there was almost no one in between, as in my age. Regardless, I'd landed cool and all this felt like some kind of rehab retreat where the daily program was working in a record store, but then I still got to drink every night.

As an undisputed renegade tambourine master, the odds were stacked against me. Maybe I didn't know how long I was supposed to hang on to my ATM receipts, but what I did know for sure was that on this version of *Planet of the Apes*, I wasn't going to trust anyone who was *under* thirty.

This place did have a small music scene, mostly folky groaners and awkward art rock, but Santa Cruz was also growing some good stuff, like Ben Chasny's Six Organs of Admittance, and Comets on Fire, a band who were started by the two bus station pizza Muppets. Along with prime movers Joanna Newsom and Devendra Banhart, these would be choice acts in the soon-to-be, ill-defined neo-hippie "freak folk" movement.

One of my co-workers and new addition to "Comets", was Noel, a handsome, smart, blond-bowled retro-fashionable twenty-something who was sort of the head honcho of a shared "head" house near the Boardwalk. He offers an empty room up and I take it, which seems like the obvious move, as it's a living space where musicians all lived together and put on parties and shows. Turns out the uninterested Asian guy also lives here, who's actually nice but had been flying the unspoken "record store guy" snob flag when I'd first encountered him.

For better or for worse, once in there the seemingly never-ending parade of amplified agony that regularly plays at what is the town's party-all-the-time house that I now live in is revealed. For any DIY band on the road, it's a convenient add-on house party show, either coming up from Southern California or down from Frisco, mostly via Portland and Olympia, where everyone here would rather live for some reason.

I was now living in a West Coast version of *Animal House*, albeit more artistic minded. Not wanting to fit in *too* much around here, like becoming the elder past-it party-loser figure, I stay out of the house as much as possible.

After seeing a new movie, *The Limey*, at the Nickelodeon art house theater, which centered around a comeback role for 60s "Swinging London"-era legend Terence Stamp, I then tap into the ever-growing dregs at the bottom of my unseen list and do *American Pie* at the big Del Mar cineplex along the main drag, literally. It really does sound like an incredibly stupid kind of movie, but so's my life right now, and anyway, it's a huge hit that's been playing for months so I go inside thinking that there must be *something* to it.

There is. Not the movie itself, which is dumber than shit, but hearing "Going to Hell" in total bewilderment during one of the very first scenes. The right side of my body wanted to stand up in the dark and shout "That's me on tambourine!" to all the college kids and solo oldster moviegoers, as if I was still "somebody", still a "contender", while the left half rightly sank lower in my chair in ironic depression. I may have been out of the loop for a while, but I can't believe I didn't know about this before, but then by now I'd have no way of knowing TVT Records were pulling back from the three-album deal I'd signed and were finding other ways to fully recoup on their investment.

On my way home afterwards and still eight houses away I can hear live "hip hop" loudly coming from what to be sure is my new place, and sure enough the house is packed tight as an all-blonde white-girl trio are laying down some for-real whatever-this-must-be to someone in their first year of art school. I know that people are just trying to have a good time, and it was, I guess, somewhat "artsy", in its way, as well as a good example of girls flexing female representation, but it was mainly just white college girls rapping horrible raps.

"Yeah, 'cause you know that I'm down, and I jam on it. I'm like a pizza with ham on it."

I walk in the door, hear this faulty French-language class rap and immediately prepare to declare tambourine law, when suddenly for the first time in my life, I realize that I am indeed now the older person, which is weird because I'd been one of the younger ones in the scene I'd just left in LA, so apparently I have brought this new-old status upon myself much earlier than necessary and decide to drink myself into oblivion.

By early a.m. the cops have arrived and busted it all up and everyone is gone or passed out. I wake up, go to the closest bathroom and uncharacteristically pee while standing up, finish, then promptly black out. Falling straight down, I slam my forehead on the edge of the open toilet seat which splits a gash on my head, then continue down to the inner edge of the dirty bowl where I almost dislocate my jaw, followed by a curtain-call finale where I flop myself the opposite way and into the towel rack loaded with wet bath towels that had been used to mop up the toilet after it had overflowed earlier in the party.

I wake back up at first daylight, on the floor next to the toilet covered in pee towels. I climb up to my feet and see in the mirror that there is dried, cracked blood all down my face. With this ritualistic ceremonial blood sacrifice to the party gods, I was now officially a broken tambourine man.

Hey Joel, Where You Gonna Go?

Listening to things like Nico's first album *Chelsea Girls* while depressed can lead to some obvious outcomes. It's glum in that good way, but that gentle melancholy also comes with a volatile concoction within the delicate melodies and detached deliveries that can knock you on your ass if you aren't careful with how you use it. I was taking the full gut punch from "These Days" while coming out of the park, over the river and to the backside doors of the largest independent bookshop in Santa Cruz, Bookshop Santa Cruz. Before entering, I take a moment to join the regular world around me again by hitting the pause button on my CD Walkman, which has a double-pause function, as in pausing my actual reality momentarily while I go on a space walk among the whatever.

I head straight to the magazine section where I'm secretly, as always, wondering if I'll run into something Brian Jonestown Massacre within one of the music rags. I have yet to these last months, and this is what adds to my surprise when I see a puff piece on "rock 'n' roll sideburns" in the new issue of *CMJ New Music Monthly*. Along with a mock-up pair of cut-out carpet samples in the shape of mutton chops, there's a small photo gallery collage which includes Derek Smalls, the bass player from the fake rock doc *Spinal Tap*, Greg Allman, Sly Stone, and Cornelius from *Planet of the Apes*, along with a few others to pad out the concept while at the top and in the largest frame is me, as photographed by Mick Rock.

I buy it, go back to the party house somewhat cheered up, but in that same slightly frustrated way I felt hearing my tambourine in a dumb blockbuster movie I didn't know about, and sit in the living room looking it back over with nobody around to show. The article concludes with my grooming tip, "Just let 'em ride." *Wow, that cool guy must be having a great time.*

I pull my Creedence *Green River* record out and drop the needle on "Lodi", which had been an especially favored tune of late, as well as from back in the *Strung Out...*tour gas-station cassette-collecting days. I sit here alone looking out the window with the wrong outside world on the other side of the glass. Thanks to TVT's album-recouping press machine, my old life was still walking around like a zombie that didn't realize it was dead. Maybe this was a sign that it wasn't just yet...

Almost a year had passed before I broke my vow of disappearance and called my old Compound compatriot Randy to get an update on the situation in Los Angeles. Anton had gotten clean, but was hitting the bottle pretty hard in its place. Regardless of how hard *hard* is, it was still incredible news and he would go on to stay off the junk permanently. Additionally, apparently my depressed alchy ex-roommate had also cleaned up his act, started a new career as a studio photographer and had just acquired a new house with someone he was in a serious relationship with. *Great!* Nice of everyone to wait until I'd completely screwed myself to suddenly see the light. I'd like to think my second "disappearance" had something to do with these wake-up-call call-backs, but who knows. Regardless, the BJM revolution had restarted.

After the phone call word made the rounds down in sunny Psychtown that I was holed up in Santa Cruz, and lo and behold Anton tracked me down. He asked me to join them on a full US tour of small- to medium-sized venues, many of which were the same from the *Strung Out...*tours.

I went, and while in the end the tour turned out to be, I guess, what I could call mostly drama-free, considering, I was somehow still spooked after experiencing a year-long-and-counting trauma of feeling that I'd had to walk away from everything my entire life had been building toward up until that point. Still, I made it understood that I was always available for any future Bay Area shows. It seemed so strange, after all my dozens of one-night quits over the years displaying the emotional level of importance it all held for me, living and breathing the cause for so long, that it now bizarrely felt like it made more sense to be out than in. I was getting closer to breaking back into San Francisco, despite the recent skyrocketed rents, and resuming a life in Los Angeles was not on my menu.

Some months later the band came up to play San Francisco again and as agreed I hit the Greyhound. I got very drunk and I suspect maybe some other things that added to the begging of the morning-time question: *What the hell happened last night?* Some sort of ceremonial sacrificial hoodoo *fer sher*, and I was exorcizing something. The Great American Music Hall had always been one of the more prestigious San Francisco stages to aspire to, and we'd only ever played it one time, which had been enough to get us banned from it. Now here we were, allowed back up on the grandstand, with only two from that old gang left. In actuality, those "gang" days were done, as well as any future situation that cultivated other "indispensable" members. From here on, The Brian Jonestown Massacre would be an entity of one, which now that Anton was the sole songwriter, fair enough. Still, I do recall the extra-long impromptu boozy monologues signifying the new way taking some getting used to; just standing there and waiting after every song, which I guess is what resulted in my harder-than-needed tambourine beating and self-inflicted bloodbath from the opening prologue of this book. Would my story have been any more believable if I'd just told the police the truth? "This blood? The human blood completely covering the front of my jacket? I did that with my tambourine. See, last night I broke it during our show at The Great American Music Hall and it cut my palm pretty good, and well, I guess I'd had so much to drink that I just got carried away. The more it broke apart the harder I hit it and the harder I hit it the more blood sprayed on myself. You know how it is."

Night of the Bloody Tambourine

I managed to make it back to Santa Cruz unmolested by the Man, and then things really began moving into place for me to move back to San Francisco. By now I had a 1967 Dodge Dart and enough money saved to move into a modest apartment near Hayes Valley with my workmate and fellow escapee, Tim. Alice, another Street-light Records friend who'd already defected to San Francisco, set me up with a job at Amoeba Music on Haight Street, and from there I was absorbed into "record store guy" life.

The next time BJM advertised a San Francisco show, I didn't hear anything from Anton. Over the coming weeks I accepted this as final closure, and by the day of the show had actually built up an excitement. I could now enjoy watching the band as just a fan.

My BJM life-trip had involved some pretty serious rough patches, and while working at a record store was technically still not a "real job", it came with a paycheck and the sense of security that all was in place. Yet, I still had an uneasy feeling about it all. Had my return to "normal" society changed who I was? Had I traded in the reality of my own creation for the one society had constructed, or was I just trying it on for the time being? Like an undercover agent sent to infiltrate the ranks of an enemy organization only to be won over by them, the lines had blurred.

Cafe Du Nord is an old speakeasy bar that has retained nearly all of its Prohibition-era splendor. The classic vintage neon sign beckons one down the plush carpeted stairs to the subterranean supper club-turned music venue, and when I reach the bottom and enter the bar area, I purposely slide along the back wall and into the crowd, careful not to be spotted by BJMrs, fans or otherwise. I want to have this experience on my own and I've planned it out perfectly, arriving at showtime, knowing that they will be on the stage tuning and starting a little late. Once settled in, I notice the bar actually looks pretty clear despite the place being close to packed, maybe I can grab a quick pint and then return to my cover of people that are still filling up the smallish club.

I slide up to the bar, order a pint of Anchor Steam, then peer across the bar area and through the show room to the stage where I can see Anton and co. are indeed tuning and banging out test chords. I take stock once again, glad that I'm still eager to watch the band without me and for the very first time since those first revolving lineup days in 93, now almost ten years ago.

Then I see Anton set his guitar on its stand, take a quick glance out at the audience, see me from all the way across the venue at the furthest possible place I could be and still be in the building, and lock eyes. He's seen me. He's not only seen me, he's hopping off the stage now, eyes still locked on mine. He's moving through the crowd, cutting a straight line, all the while his eyes are locked on mine with that invisible tractor beam. His head remains perfectly level with eyes wide and fixated as he continues moving through the club uninterrupted by all the zigging and zagging fans and tech implant curiosity-seekers who seem to just naturally move out of his path like a slo-mo ballet. Part of me wants to leave right then but I'm caught in the trance. "Hey Joel," he says and without further word he has a hold of my wrist and we're heading back toward the stage. There was no conversation, no question, no excuses. When we get to the stage he let's go of my wrist and I step up.

Anton walks around to the side-stage entrance and when he comes up the small steps, he's extending a tambourine out to me. Then he straps his guitar on and I step into position and it's show-time. "OK, so check this out..." Or at least Anton is going to talk for a while and then the musical portion of tonight's performance will begin at some point.

We play "Whoever You Are" and then Anton grabs the mic again and apologizes if the band went on late, which was because the Oakland glam-garage opening band had played well over their set time. Now, he's not going on about it more than anything else and it's all pretty normal-to-us grievance levels, but not to the uninitiated and soon out from backstage comes the token fat-guy keyboard player holding a chair which he throws at Anton and here we go again...

Rather than letting the show deteriorate into a brawl, Anton schools the new kids from the mic and now I've got something to sit on while he does so, giving me the time to step out of the onstage head space and realize how grateful I am that he'd brought me up here. Regardless of my own current place in the mix, it was good to see Anton being kickin'-ass Anton again and it was also undeniable that the new music was flush with the sounds of revamped artistic explorations. After this Cafe Du Nord appearance I would continue to join the band on subsequent Bay Area appearances, no longer willing to fully let go, or just not noticing that The Universe wasn't really giving me a choice in the matter.

Meanwhile, The Dandy Warhols had been living the signed life to the fullest. They had just released what would become their signature album *Thirteen Tales from Urban Bohemia,* were doing massive world tours, television, the lot. The Dandys were advertised as decadent yet harmless bohemians for the masses, and while they were playing this image up to the English press as a big part of their deal, the truth was now that the last residues of the 90s philosophies had completely melted away and we were firmly in the 2000s. Heavy drugs for both bands had made way for the days of wine and roses and the times of keeping up with the Brian Joneses was over. Or so it seemed...

Digging to the Roots

"The goin' up was worth the comin' down..."

I look down at the snow-covered Utah mountains while listening to *The Essential Kris Kristofferson* collection in mid-descent into Salt Lake City International Airport. A few weeks ago Ondi contacted me with the news that she had not only finally completed her movie on BJM and the Dandys, but it had been accepted at this year's Sundance Film Festival. Sundance is the biggest and most prestigious film festival of its type in the US, created by actor and activist Robert Redford's Sundance Institute, which gets its name from his character in the classic 60s film *Butch Cassidy and the Sundance Kid*. She invited me to come out and do some post-screening Q & A sessions with her, to which I gave a heartfelt "Dig!" in response, which apparently also happens to be what she has named the movie. Her brother and co-filmmaker David, Dave D and Miranda were also among those going, as well as Black Rebel Motorcycle Club, who are playing a Levi's-sponsored gig after the first screening.

After landing, I catch a crowded festival shuttle van for the forty-five-minute drive to Park City, a ski resort taken over by the festival for two weeks each year. The shuttle drops me off in the central and historical part of town and I make my way through the streets of brick buildings on sidewalks flush with slush. Mountains surround on all sides and cold dampness dominates the vibe. Armed at the wrist with one of Ondi's plastic filmmaker bands and a handful of festival tickets she'd acquired for films I'd chosen from the schedule ahead of time, I have access into the Filmmakers' Lodge, which is a sort of festival hangout headquarters where I can waste some time before the festival's opening film tonight—*Riding Giants*, a surfing documentary that turns out to be *Endless Summer* meets *Dogtown and Z-Boys*. "This movie meets that movie" is a very popular way of describing things around here, and the whole festival kinda already feels like a *Best in Show* for films meets the Winter Olympics or something.

Crowded casual hangs perk into surprised attention when Robert Redford himself makes an unscheduled appearance here in the Film-makers' Lodge, which for me brings the focus of the goings-on into crystal-clear view. *Barefoot in the Park*, *Downhill Racer*, *The Candidate*, *Three Days of the Condor* and of course *Butch Cassidy and the Sundance Kid* are among his great movies from the 60s and 70s, as well his face being one from the gallery of celebrity constants since childhood. He says some stuff for a few minutes from a small stage and then splits before the crowd has too much time to block all the exits in "Excuse me, Mr. Redford" positions.

After the surfer documentary I meet up with Dave D and crew of Miranda, Rob Campanella, who is a new guy playing with Anton and has just mixed the sound for *Dig!*, and a girl Dave is going out with or is not anymore or not yet or whatever, all I know is, as I'm a last-minute add-on I have to sleep on the floor of a room at The Holiday Inn between a bed and a window for the next few nights. My film-nerd side is very excited to even be here, coupled with the unreal reality that me and my friends are now one of the more hyped stories being told this year.

The next morning, all the daily press outlets covering the festival want to know where Paris Hilton is going to be. I meet up with Ondi and the whole *Dig!* crew, which by now includes some new faces who weren't around for all those rough and tumble filming years, yet it's a big deal for all of them now and their sense of accomplishment is palpable. There was an intense group trance in the air, and with none of my old inner BJM circle around to descend into digging the hijinks with, I watch these other people's time in the sun from an invisible mobile observation box.

Ondi most of all is ready to shine in the lights, to which I would say, fair enough, but the centered down-to-earthiness I'd known her for and which had helped us all feel like friends and safe to be totally open in front of the cameras now feels to be somewhat missing. Maybe it was just a matter of Jane Goodall leaving the jungle. Maybe seven years of huffing BJM and Dandy Warhols fumes had been plenty enough...as weird as that would be...

David seems to be the same person from all the way back on that first night when we all met in front of Popscene while being refused entry into our own gig after arriving hours late. There are tons of people for them to talk to and places for them to be and the whole day feels like a series of events being ticked off a list like a wedding-day schedule that's working its way to the big event.

The big event is the world premiere of *Dig!* tonight at the Metropolitan Redstone 8 Cinemas. I wait outside in the slush and snow until the Holiday Inn gang arrives, then Ondi and I pose for press photos in the lobby standing by the official *Dig!* movie poster. We all head into the screening room and to our reserved section. It's a big theater room and, being one of the hot-ticket events of the festival, very sold out.

I'd been shown a lot of random clips over the years, mostly of myself to keep me pumped on the project, but had absolutely no idea what it had all been turned into. What I do know is that I'm about to be the first one from either band to see the finished documentary in a packed house of film industry people and tastemakers. The lights go out. From the start the crowd are openly responding to everything they are seeing, including laughing at Courtney for supposedly sneezing out hits, and then just about everyone else at times when they didn't really mean to be amusing. This all pretty quickly has me waiting for my own moment to look unintentionally silly, but it never comes, because throughout that whole experience I was trying to be funny on purpose. Every time those cameras had been pointed at me, I would immediately envision some future audience on the other side of the "forever camera", and rather than always talk to the camera about myself or to Ondi behind it, I would try to entertain them, the people, regardless of however far-off dreaming that all may have seemed while goofing on a gear escalator going up to the punk rock rehearsal space that we were financially forced to live in, or at a gas station mini-mart store mixing soda pop on an all-day drive just to play for five people in Kansas. Like The Beatles had done for me when I was younger with *A Hard Day's Night* and *Help!*, sitting here in the theater the younger me was now doing it for me, reminding me what it was all about, and I was passing the torch back to myself.

The crowd continues to react to every little thing that happens onscreen and are completely hooked. This fills me with a charge in my seat, not because the FBI had wired my theater chair in order to take me out before I could turn the world on with my indomitable antiestablishment smile, but because the all-in crowd reaction was being caused by us just being us, with no PR machine or industry money fueling anything we were doing. It was us against everything, sometimes including ourselves, and this was oddly not only enough, but was in fact much more, despite it all at its heart simply being what happens when you and your friends are trying to do things and stuff.

Doing radio interviews for *Dig!* at the Sundance Film Festival:
"I don't think you're grasping just how many drinks went
down my pants..."

Afterwards, Ondi, David and I line up in front of the screen for the Q & A session, and I see photographer David LaChapelle in the front row, who smiles and waves at me but since we've never actually met back in the day, and I've just been reminded of how lame the

"Junkie" video he'd made for the Dandys was, I slight him, but then immediately feel bad. Now I've dissed him twice, once in real life onscreen and now in real life in front of the screen.

Over the next couple of days, Ondi's crew and the Holiday Inn gang do things together like a group photo shoot in the snowy front yard of a cabin condo thing. We're all being encouraged by the photographer to act overly excited, like flail our arms and legs about as if we'd just scored the winning goal or something, but I'm already saving those types of antics for the skiing scene in *Dig! 2: Help!—Again*.

Then we all go back to the center of the festival action where the subject of conversation that has taken away the top spot of the small-talk charts from the weather is: Where is Paris Hilton going to be? None of our crew cares and we've got our own PR work to do. I start hearing things like "*Dig!* is like *Hoop Dreams* meets *Spinal Tap*."

I break from the others to go cash in my film passes for *Chisholm '72: Unbought and Unbossed*, a great documentary about the first African-American congresswoman and then the big-buzz documentary screening of the day, *Guerrilla: The Taking of Patty Hearst*, which is an especially enjoyable recounting of one of the wildest stories from the times of 60s radicals in the Bay Area.

As I leave the theater I overhear people speculating as to where Paris Hilton is going to be, which thankfully is not at the big Levi's party where Black Rebel Motorcycle Club are playing, but Ashton Kutcher is, so everyone is on their toes for possible hidden camera pranks to be perpetrated upon persons, or maybe they are not. It's the biggest club in town and Black Rebel Motorcycle Club hit the stage to a capacity crowd.

Did these guys just get back from the crossroads where you sell your you-know-what to you-know-who? Sure would explain a lot, because they suddenly seem pretty intense in that way people who wear leather pants do, but then it's like they don't even have to wear leather pants because they *are* leather pants. The pants are on the *inside*, man. So I guess Peter is being a good sport by even being here tonight and finally accepting the now unavoidable fact that the film is here and he is officially being exposed to the world as an ex-member of The Brian Jonestown Massacre. For the last few years and two high-profile albums later they had been able to—for whatever reason—completely suppress his previous involvement with BJM to the music press, despite us taking him in and showing him how you do it, which I guess must be why.

I watch them from a side balcony area above, mostly Robert as he is closest and also because I become preoccupied with this thing he does where after every single song he takes a big full-tilt chug from his Evian water bottle and then hucks it aggressively back at the foot of his giant bass amp. Next song is over and again, *glug glug glug*, "Now get out of here, water!" he seems to say by the way he throws it, his dark thirst temporarily quenched until the next song.

Afterwards the Holiday Inn gang, the BRMC gang and a smattering of who-what-wheres are after-party hanging in the back room of yet another condo pad thing. Apparently BRMC have quit drinking, which is weird to me, but I also know that's just a thing I would think is weird, and that's my problem, or not, depending on who's got a problem with what, but then word is that on BRMC tours, because now that they don't drink, bands who open for them can't even have booze in their own dressing rooms, so that's weird no matter who's got what problem. They do look pretty tough when they drink water these days though, so I guess it all evens out in the end as far as the laws of rock are concerned.

Regardless of what bag you're in, vice is still very much in the house and on a small counter near the pool table is Robert's private extra-large and full party sack of Chips Ahoy chocolate chip cookies. I rack the balls, then Robert snaps on a cookie while surveying the angles. I acknowledge this event with an animated "It's cookie time", because that's what it is and then Robert breaks the balls, which would be a good album title if they ever need to, out of career desperation, fall back on an AC/DC-style guitar-riff phase. I pull my beer, take my turn and drop a solid in the corner pocket, because I'm the hero of this story, but then I miss my next shot because life is real and I don't really ever play pool except when I'm getting drunk in a bar that happens to have a pool table. Robert chomps another cookie down while surveying his next move. I acknowledge the event with an animated "It's cookie time", because that's now my new nickname for him, and then he hits one in. It's a pretty good shot.

Then he misses. Now I make one, then miss one. Robert bites down on another cookie while surveying his next move. I acknowledge this event with an animated "It's cookie time", then quickly it is but Robert misses. I pull my beer, take my turn and miss. Robert bites another cookie in half, then pushes that half further into his mouth with the other half so the whole thing is now in there, pre-halved. He then surveys his next move and I acknowledge the event with an animated "It's cookie time", and Robert taps one in and...OK, you get the idea, it kinda just goes on like this for a while and then I call for a cookie-time time-out. Miranda takes over playing Robert while I head out the side-entrance for a menthol smoke and some alpine air, which we menthol smokers call "full immersion".

After a few drags, Peter Hayes comes out and lights up. He takes a long drag and blows out a smoldering fire and ice elemental mixture of hot smoke and cold frosty air, dangerous like black leather and gleaming silver, and says, "Sooo...'stupid fucking hippie dumbass', huh?" (I drunkenly call Peter a stupid fucking hippie dumbass in the film.)

"Well, if you think about it, Peter, what was going on at that time, you kinda *were* being a stupid fucking hippie dumbass."

He doesn't say anything and we both drag our cigarettes. Then nobody says anything after that either and I'm left with the feeling we didn't solve it.

The next afternoon there is a second Sundance screening of *Dig!* at the smaller Prospector Square Theater on the outer edge of the old-town action. I nurse my pair of last night's to-go bottles during the film, which I'd taken with me specifically for this purpose. I'm starting to feel pretty again by the time I see myself onscreen pondering as to whether life is leading me to the penthouse or the gutter, which these days feels more like it's as the building's doorman. I quickly change thought gears before this pondering moment of mine has time to transfer into somebody else's mind for the Q & A.

The first two questions are for Ondi, which is fine with me and my foggy noggin notions, and then a younger dude asks me about what I'm currently doing in music. I suddenly have to think about it. "Well, I play with BJM every once in a while...whenever they come through San Francisco...other than that, not much, really."

He nods in recognition that I have answered, but looks confused by what the answer is, or at least deflated by its lack-lustereyness. Suddenly, I realize that's exactly what it is. Then an older lady in the front row puts her hand up. "Joel, I have a question for you. What was the deal with Matt? Was there something deeper going on there, or was he just an unhappy person in general?"

It's actress Karen Black asking me this, *Five Easy Pieces* and *Easy Rider* Karen Black. Though suddenly very excited to get a question from her, I have no clear answer for that one either, at least not one I want to give right now in front of Ondi, who it turns out has recently made friends with her. After the screening, Karen Black finds me and we have a great one-on-one. She gets what was going on onscreen. She'd worked with Dennis Hopper at his most "out there" and went on to be a seminal figure in the highly artistic American New Wave cinema movement in the 1970s, which was heavily populated with extreme-personality actors, writers and directors.

My work at Sundance is now done, and as the invitation doesn't extend as far as the awards ceremony, I'm flying home to San Francisco as *Dig!* wins the Grand Jury Prize by unanimous decision. I am once again listening to *The Essential Kris Kristofferson* collection, while right now somewhere back in Park City there's another million free beers that I ain't drunk, *and lots of pretty thoughts that I ain't thunk...*

I walk into work for another Amoeba shift and on my locker some anonymous co-worker has taped a Xerox copy printed from a music website reviewing The Brian Jonestown Massacre show from the Mercury Lounge in New York last night. There was a picture of Anton talking on the mic with a quote underneath from a girl in the crowd calling out "I miss Joel!", to which he replied "Well, why don't you go to fuckin' Amoeba Records and visit him? And while you're there, buy a record so he doesn't get fired!"

Then magically about a week later I'm invited to rejoin BJM for a full-on head-to-toe hip-to-hip eight-week tour of Europe. Amoeba gives me the time off and as the tour approaches, I prepare for life back on the road. My last errand requires me to weather the big crowds of the gigantic San Francisco Virgin Megastore on a busy Saturday afternoon. I'm instantly hit with a surreal feeling as I begin the three-floor escalator journey up to the "Top floor...!", all the while switching views to the various TV monitors everywhere throughout the store watching myself sitting on an escalator while currently standing on this one.

Dig! also happens to be the showcased film currently on Virgin Airlines, but Anton's new big-time BJM management hadn't booked me on that airline and so I'm here needing some in-flight music magazines, most of which feature new reviews of the film's DVD release. It was the must-see music film of the year and there are no negative or even lukewarm reviews to be found anywhere.

Now I don't want to get all motivational speaker on you, but this is a pretty incredible moment for me, and I'd just like to offer for your consideration that no matter how bad things get, they will always eventually get good again. I know this is true because even though heroin had systematically destroyed what the band had originally built up, we'd by then already given our true nature to the documentary cameras, and that footage served as a time capsule with contents that work equally well in yesterday's, today's and tomorrow's time dimensions. Stay true to yourself, who you are at the core, your essence, and the center will hold. You will weather whatever b.s. storm the fucker gods can make. Things will come around right again, and I know all this because it just happened.

As for Anton, the music he'd been releasing since my departure had a next-levelness to it and sounded fresher and more artistically driven to me than most songs on the *Strung Out in Heaven* album. Perhaps with that same special sheen *Their Satanic Majesties' Second Request* has for me, as it was recorded during my OD (original disappearance). Traditionally Anton had always done his deepest work when life had him up against the ropes. There was still no one else I'd ever known who could evoke the best elements of the tried and true and yet dismantle and distill them down into a sound totally anew. This is what they mean by the "real deal", where there is no curtain to yank back, no mirrors to break or smoke to fan away that will reveal the "trick".

With the TVT contract mutually nullified, he'd also soon be moving on from indie labels as well and to his own music-business game, and the de facto strangest twist to my own personal plot was that this was the exact right thing to do. Whether or not he could have any idea Napster was coming within months of my departure, he'd already put all of BJM's music on the internet five years previous anyway, predating the "end of the beginning" of the music business as we knew it way before anyone else. By imploding BJM's big TVT Record deal and the whole situation that came with it, including my own part in it, he was not tied like so many others to the big-business major-record-label model and had survived to go on to do it his own way and by his own rules.

As for me, there was a whole new band lineup to befriend and share the original dream, now alive against all the odds that had befallen us oddballs. We were booked most of the year doing lengthy tours of Europe, the US and Canada, having graduated from small- to medium-sized rock clubs to large venues and concert halls.

Early on during the first tour we were in another van leaving another hotel heading to another sold-out show when Anton turned around and called "Hey Joel!", back to me from the passenger seat. He then slightly laughs to himself before down-shifting to a smile. "So, check this out, I forgot to tell you, Tara and I were in line at the Sunset Ralphs Supermarket and Peter Fonda was a few people behind us in the line. She was wearing like a flower wreath and a white flowy dress and I had on my big boots, all in white with an Indian tunic on, and he was just all smiling and nodding at us like, '*Yeaahhh*,' then puts his thumb up because he knew we knew and he was totally digging' it, ya'know?"

Suddenly I realize that I'd never told him about any of my past brush-ups and foibles with the *Easy Rider* star. "*Really?* Wow, man. That's *soo* cool!" I return, because that's exactly what it was.

And, dear readers, that final anecdote is the short version of the story of my life, but you had to read everything before that first for it to make sense. Or maybe, as sad as it is for a dreamer like me to accept, life is in fact not like a movie. Oh wait, with the release of *Dig!*, turns out it all actually *was* a movie the whole time. *POW! ZAP!*

Acknowledgements

Anton Newcombe, Lee Brackstone, Natalie Galustian and Michelle Swainson. Also, Julie Simons, Tony Rasonsky, Yvonne Josefina Hernandez, Sean Carney, Tim Daly, Charles Mehling, Jean-Paul Ligon, Lindsay Ljungkull, Desiree Pfeiffer, and, most of all, my wife Sarah.

References and Credits

Quoted Song Lyrics

p.52   "Take it from the Man" by The Brian Jonestown Massacre (A Recordings Ltd./Warp Music Limited)

p.56   "Performance" by The Happy Mondays (Universal Music Publishing Group/ Warner Chappell Music, Inc.)

p.65   "Hyperventilation" by The Brian Jonestown Massacre (A Recordings Ltd./Warp Music Limited)

p.90   "'Cause I Love Her" by The Brian Jonestown Massacre (A Recordings Ltd./Warp Music Limited)

p.92   "(Sittin' on) The Dock of the Bay" by Otis Redding (Universal Music Publishing Group)

p.156   "London Town" by Donovan (BMG Rights Management/ Songtrust Ave)

p.164   "You Can't Always Get What You Want" by The Rolling Stones (ABKCO Music & Records, Inc.)

p.167   "I'm Looking Though You" by The Beatles (Sony/ATV Music Publishing Limited)

p.168   "The End" by The Doors (Primary Wave Music)

p.197   "Monterey" by Eric Burdon & The Animals (Warner Chappell Music, Inc.)

p.251   "Come Fly with Me" by Frank Sinatra (Concord Music Publishing LLC)

p.253   "I've Been Waiting" by The Brian Jonestown Massacre (A Recordings Ltd./Reservoir Media Management, Inc.)

p.263   "Nothing to Lose" by The Brian Jonestown Massacre (A Recordings Ltd./Reservoir Media Management, Inc.)

p.264   "The Way It Was" by The Brian Jonestown Massacre (A Recordings Ltd./Warp Music Limited)

p.266   "Arkansas Revisited" by The Brian Jonestown Massacre (A Recordings Ltd./Warp Music Limited) p.290 "Get Away" by Lenny Kravitz (Universal Music Publishing Group)

p.339 "The Pilgrim Chapter 33" by Kris Kristofferson (Sony/ATV Music Publishing Limited)

p.346 "The Best of All Possible Worlds" by Kris Kristofferson (Universal Music Publishing Group)

Quoted Movies

p.77 *Pulp Fiction* (1994), Dir: Quentin Tarantino, A Band Apart/ Jersey Films; Miramax Films. Screenplay by Quentin Tarantino

p.163 *Cool Hand Luke* (1967), Dir. Stuart Rosenberg, Jamen Productions; Warner Bros Seven Arts. Screenplay by Donn Pearce and Frank R. Pierson

p.167 *Breakfast at Tiffany's* (1961), Dir. Blake Edwards, Jurow-Shepherd/Spinel Entertainment; Paramount Pictures. Screenplay by George Axelrod

p.209 *Austin Powers: International Man of Mystery* (1997), Dir. Jay Roach, New Line Cinema/New Line Productions/Capella International/Moving Pictures/Eric's Boy/KC Medien; New Line Cinema. Screenplay by Mike Myers

p.226 *The Godfather Part III* (1990), Dir: Francis Ford Coppola, Paramount Pictures/Zoetrope Studios; Paramount Pictures. Screenplay by Francis Ford Coppola and Mario Puzo

p.281 *Easy Rider* (1969), Dir. Dennis Hopper, Pando Company Inc./Raybert Productions; Columbia Pictures. Screenplay by Peter Fonda, Dennis Hopper and Terry Southern

CREDITS

White Rabbit and Joel Gion would like to thank everyone at Orion who worked on the publication of *In the Jingle Jangle Jungle*.

Agent
Natalie Galustian

Editor
Lee Brackstone

Copy-editor
Seán Costello

Proofreader
David Watkins

Editorial Management
Susie Bertinshaw
Sophie Nevrkla
Jane Hughes
Charlie Panayiotou
Lucy Bilton
Claire Boyle

Audio
Paul Stark
Jake Alderson
Georgina Cutler

Contracts
Dan Herron
Ellie Bowker
Alyx Hurst

Design
Nick Shah
Dan Jackson
Joanna Ridley
Helen Ewing

Photo Shoots & Image Research
Natalie Dawkins

Finance
Nick Gibson
Jasdip Nandra
Sue Baker
Tom Costello

Inventory
Jo Jacobs
Dan Stevens

Production
Sarah Cook
Katie Horrocks

Marketing
Tom Noble

Publicity
Leanne Oliver

Sales
Jen Wilson
Victoria Laws
Esther Waters
Tolu Ayo-Ajala
Group Sales teams across
    Digital, Field, International
    and Non-Trade

Operations
Group Sales Operations team

Rights
Rebecca Folland
Tara Hiatt
Ben Fowler
Alice Cottrell
Ruth Blakemore
Ayesha Kinley
Marie Henckel